Angular for Material Design

Leverage Angular Material and TypeScript to Build a Rich User Interface for Web Apps

Venkata Keerti Kotaru

Apress®

Angular for Material Design

Venkata Keerti Kotaru
Hyderabad, India

ISBN-13 (pbk): 978-1-4842-5433-2   ISBN-13 (electronic): 978-1-4842-5434-9
https://doi.org/10.1007/978-1-4842-5434-9

Managing Director, Apress Media LLC: Welmoed Spahr
Acquisitions Editor: Nikhil Karkal
Development Editor: Laura Berendson
Coordinating Editor: Divya Modi

Cover designed by eStudioCalamar

Cover image designed by Freepik (www.freepik.com)

Distributed to the book trade worldwide by Springer Science+Business Media New York, 233 Spring Street, 6th Floor, New York, NY 10013. Phone 1-800-SPRINGER, fax (201) 348-4505, e-mail orders-ny@springer-sbm.com, or visit www.springeronline.com. Apress Media, LLC is a California LLC and the sole member (owner) is Springer Science + Business Media Finance Inc (SSBM Finance Inc). SSBM Finance Inc is a **Delaware** corporation.

For information on translations, please e-mail rights@apress.com, or visit http://www.apress.com/rights-permissions.

Apress titles may be purchased in bulk for academic, corporate, or promotional use. eBook versions and licenses are also available for most titles. For more information, reference our Print and eBook Bulk Sales web page at http://www.apress.com/bulk-sales.

Any source code or other supplementary material referenced by the author in this book is available to readers on GitHub via the book's product page, located at www.apress.com/978-1-4842-5433-2. For more detailed information, please visit http://www.apress.com/source-code.

Printed on acid-free paper

To my parents, who inspire me.
To my wife and daughter, who let go
all those weekends.

Table of Contents

About the Author

 **Venkata Keerti Kotaru** has been in software development for more than 17 years. He is a three-time Microsoft MVP. He is the author of a book on AngularJS and several technology articles that appear on DotNetCurry.com and DNC Magazine. He holds a master's degree in software systems from the University of St. Thomas in St. Paul, Minnesota.

Keerti started a technology meetup group, AngularJS Hyderabad, for which he has been a regular speaker. He has presented multiple sessions at Google Developers Groups (GDG) and Google's annual DevFest event. He has presented technology sessions for TechGig, AngularJS Pune, and AngularJS Chicago meetup groups.

About the Technical Reviewer

Giancarlo Buomprisco is an Italian software developer specializing in building front-end applications.

Giancarlo's journey to become a software developer started at the University of Pisa, Italy, where he studied both computer science and humanities.

Soon after graduation, Giancarlo moved to London to work for King's College London as a research developer, developing applications with JavaScript and Python to help researchers with their scientific studies.

During this experience, Giancarlo developed a great passion for building rich client-side applications with a great user experience, which led him to specialize in JavaScript and various front-end technologies, such as Typescript, Angular, and RxJS using clean code and agile practices.

Having worked for large and small companies, Giancarlo is currently a front-end consultant for top-tier financial institutions in London.

Other than writing code, he is likely to be found working out at the gym, writing articles on his blog, or trying culinary specialties across London.

Introduction

This book explains building a web user interface with Angular, a powerful framework for web applications. The book describes using the Angular Material library with Material Design components. This library provides multiple, ready-made, easy-to-use components that work well with an Angular application.

This book uses Angular with TypeScript, which is a JavaScript superset. TypeScript enables you to use data types and to program constructs such as classes, interfaces, generic templates, and so forth.

This book guides you to build applications that take advantage of various Angular features, including data binding, components, and services. It describes building a single-page application and interfacing with remote services over HTTP.

This book is for beginner to intermediate-level professionals. In addition to building web applications using Angular and TypeScript, it explains Material Design—a design language by Google—constructs and components. It has been popular since its introduction into Android (version 5/Lollipop). Various Google products, including Gmail, YouTube, Google Drive, Google Plus, and Google Docs, have been built with this design language.

CHAPTER 1

Introduction

Welcome to implementing web applications using Angular, TypeScript, and Material Design. As we begin the journey of exploring features and capabilities in this introductory chapter, we look at

- Web technologies

- A brief history of Angular and its evolution

- TypeScript

- Material Design and the implementation of the Angular design language

Web Technologies

Web application development has evolved. It has become a powerful, rich, and complex. In yesteryear's web applications, the heavy lifting was done on the server side; only servers had the processing power to build rich and complex applications. Browsers presented data to the users, captured user input, and sent it back to the server for major processing. Browsers and JavaScript code on the browser performed basic validations.

Over the years, client machines became more powerful and browser technologies evolved. HTML, CSS, and JavaScript languages have transformed. ES (ECMAScript) is a language specification created to standardize JavaScript. Over time, browsers have adapted features standardized with ES.

Browsers have widely adapted ES5, a version of JavaScript specification released in 2009. It made the JavaScript language a first-class citizen in programming languages. A minor version, 5.1, was released in 2011; however, ES6, or ES2015, has provided major improvements to the language and allowed developers to take the best advantage of the platform. So far, ECMAScript updates have been made yearly. Currently (at the time of authoring this book), we are at ES9/ES2018.

1

© Venkata Keerti Kotaru 2020
V. K. Kotaru, *Angular for Material Design*, https://doi.org/10.1007/978-1-4842-5434-9_1

JavaScript continues to add new features. The ECMA TC39 committee is responsible for evolving JavaScript. They have defined a five-stage process, which takes an idea to a fully functional feature adapted by various browsers (see Table 1-1). Each JavaScript feature goes through these stages. Once a feature is standardized and implemented by browsers, it is ready for JavaScript developers.

Table 1-1. *JavaScript Stages*

Stage 0	*Strawman.* A new JavaScript feature specification.
Stage 1	*Proposal.* Demonstrates the need for the feature addition, solution, and challenges.
Stage 2	*Draft.* Provides details on syntax and semantics.
Stage 3	*Candidate.* Enables users to experiment and provide feedback. Based on feedback, the specification might evolve further.
Stage 4	*Finished.* Ready to be included in the ECMAScript standard.

As more capabilities are added to the language and to browsers, more features are moved to the client on the browser, the complexity of browser applications increases, and new-generation web applications take advantage of sophisticated HTML5, JavaScript, and CSS3 features.

Additional complexity, scope for reusability, and patterns mean there is a need for frameworks and libraries. Angular is one of the best open source frameworks available. A tremendous number of applications and developers have taken advantage of this framework.

Introduction to Angular

Angular is a framework for building front-end applications. It is an open source project driven by Google. Contributors to the framework are from around the world. Angular helps build applications that cater to multiple device form factors—desktops, tablets (e.g., iPads and Android devices), and mobile phones. This book primarily focuses on browser applications for desktop screens.

Angular's Roots in MV*

The AngularJS 1.x framework began as an MV* framework, which could be MVC or MVVM. The MVC architectural pattern—Model-View-Controller—is popular. This pattern helps build highly cohesive, loosely coupled, modular applications. It helps with the separation of concerns.

The pattern began its roots in 1970s with the Smalltalk programming language. It has since been adapted in various modern programming languages. It is a tried and tested approach, especially for front-end applications. The following are a few highlights of the framework.

- Model is the data presented to the user.

- View is the user interface.

- Controller combines both. It applies the model/data on a template/ view.

Figure 1-1 is a representation of the MVC pattern.

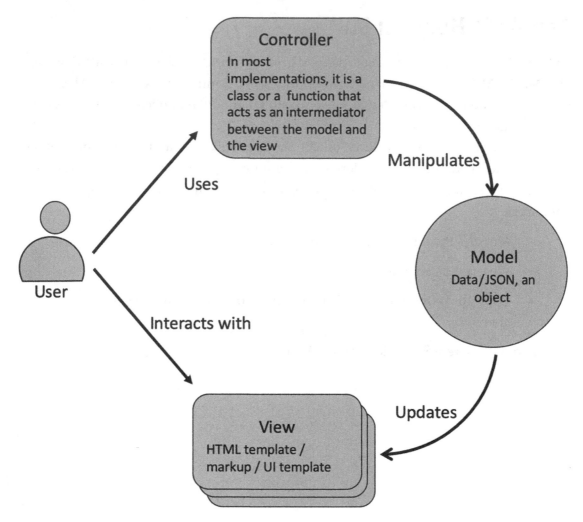

Figure 1-1. *MVC pattern*

There is a variation to the pattern called MVVM, or Model-View-ViewModel. It is suitable for an application that extensively uses data binding on the user interface.

With MVVM, a model represents a domain entity. Typically, it is used with a business logic implementation. The model object is independent of the presentation logic. The same object might be shown on different views or screens.

Hence, the model object may not be easily bindable to controls on the view. The pattern recommends creating a ViewModel, which is a separate object that is specific to each view or screen. It is easily bindable with the controls. We transform model to a view model. Figure 1-2 is a representation of the MVVM pattern.

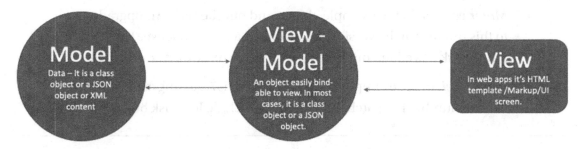

Figure 1-2. *MVVM pattern*

Angular from AngularJS

There have been advances in frameworks and technologies. Consider the following highlights.

- Web Components, a standard for building reusable HTML elements

- Frameworks like React, which allow composing a complex user interface with reusable components

Front-end web application development moved in directions that either put together reusable components or built libraries that created those building blocks/components.

Angular version 2.x and upward saw major redesign. The 1.x versions are referred to as AngularJS. Today's framework is known as Angular. The convention is to refer to the 1.x versions of the framework as AngularJS and everything beyond version 2.0 is just Angular.

Angular is a modern framework that primarily uses components to create views. Although components are the building blocks for views, during the course of the book, you also learn about modules, services, dependency injection, and so forth.

Angular has had incremental updates. The version number includes three parts; consider 8.2.7, for example.

- *Major version*. In the 8.2.7 example, the first number is 8. An upgrade to the first number of the framework version is considered a major release. It is potentially a breaking change. Developers need to be involved in the upgrade.

- *Minor version.* In the example, the second number is 2. An upgrade to this number in the version is considered a minor release. The framework has added minor features that are backward compatible.

- *Patch level.* In the example, the third number is7. An upgrade to this version number is a patch release, which include low-risk bug fixes.

Note   The Angular framework continuously evolves, with a major release every six months.

When version 2 of the framework was released, it supported the following three flavors:

- Angular with TypeScript

- Angular with JavaScript

- Angular with Dart

Angular with TypeScript had the most traction in the developer community. This book extensively uses TypeScript when developing Angular applications.

TypeScript

TypeScript is a superset of ECMAScript. It is an open source project backed by Microsoft. It supports data types. This book uses the TypeScript language for building an Angular application.

As discussed, ES6 (ECMAScript), or ES2015, was a major upgrade to JavaScript as a language. TypeScript compliments JavaScript features. TypeScript supports all JavaScript features, including data types, interfaces, generics, and enums. TypeScript compiles the code in browser-understandable JavaScript. It can be integrated with major bundling solutions like Webpack.

As you will see in this book, you can build high-quality applications that take advantage of the powerful features that TypeScript provides beyond JavaScript.

Material Design

Material Design is Google's design language, which provides a rich set of guidelines. This design language mimics real-world objects, hence the "material" metaphor. Components and controls on the user interface show depth and texture, cast shadows, and use animation in a meaningful way.

What Is a Design Language?

User interface (UI) designers help create the user experience of a company's products. A design language is developed to bring consistency in the look and feel, behavior, and experience. It describes aspects such as color schemes, patterns, and textures. Material Design is one such design language developed by Google; other examples include Flat Design, which is used extensively in iOS, Microsoft Metro Design, which is used in Windows 8 and Windows Phone, and the Fluent Design System, which is used in Windows 10.

How Does It Help Us?

When envisioning, designing, and building a system, a problem statement or requirements are defined for various features. We define a technology solution for data storage, the user interface, and so forth. In this book, we use Angular for building the UI. The missing piece is the user experience. A user needs to easily locate and navigate between features, locate all the available actions on a screen, and have the data laid out in an organized fashion. This is very important. Regardless of the system's efficiency and capabilities, the user is interfacing with the UI. Features, consistency, and organization determine the good, bad, or ugly feedback about our product.

Material Design has been popular since its introduction into Android (version 5/Lollipop). Various Google products, including Gmail, YouTube, Google Drive, Google Plus, and Google Docs, have been built with this design language. Over time, many organizations and individuals outside of Google have used it. For the application that we are building, user adaptability will be easy and fast. Importantly, Google researched and laid out the guidelines; hence, it is a great head start.

How About Brand Value?

We desire to be consistent but unique. We do not want our application to mimic an existing product.

The Angular Material library provides enough extensibility to build a unique identity. Themes play a major role in this aspect. We can choose from an existing list of themes or build our own custom theme.

Typography

Typography describes the scale of the content (headers, titles, etc.), letter spacing, and font characteristics (font face, weight, size, etc.). Angular Material stylesheets and fonts provide prebuilt typography and theming that is confined to Material Design guidelines.

Angular Material Components

The Angular Material library provides a sophisticated list of components that are used with Material Design guidelines. These components provide ready-made functionalities in data forms, navigation, layouts, and multiple other aspects.

Conclusion

Angular, TypeScript, and Material Design are a powerful combination used to build rich web UI applications.

Angular helps build browser applications with high reusability, consistency, and scalability. This framework helps build single-page applications with out-of-the-box features, like routing. It enables easy communication with RESTful HTTP services, and manages and validates user input with sophisticated features building forms.

TypeScript is a superscript of ECMAScript. It allows you to use data types. It provides great integration with code editors and IDEs (integrated development environments). It integrates well with bundling tools like Webpack.

Angular Material provides components that confine to Material Design guidelines out of the box. It eases integrating the design language with an Angular and TypeScript application.

This chapter began with the context and history of web applications, described Angular and its evolution, and introduced TypeScript. And at the end, it introduced Material Design and the value it brings to the user experience and UI development.

References

AngularJS (`https://angularjs.org`)

Angular (`https://angular.io`)

Angular Material (`http://material.angular.io`)

Material Design (`https://material.io`)

Wikipedia page on Design Language (`https://en.wikipedia.org/wiki/Design_language`)

Wikipedia page on MVC (`https://en.wikipedia.org/wiki/Model%E2%80%93view%E2%80%93controller`)

A blog on JavaScript features (`www.dotnetcurry.com/javascript/1405/es8-es2017-javascript-new-features`)

Process documentation and stage definitions for ECMAScript (`https://tc39.github.io/process-document/`)

TC39 proposals (`https://github.com/tc39/proposals`)

Angular versioning and releases (`https://angular.io/guide/releases`)

CHAPTER 2

Getting Started

This chapter is a "getting started" guide for Angular applications made with TypeScript and Material Design. By the end of the chapter, you should be able to set up a sample project—a basic "Hello World" version of an Angular application made with TypeScript and Material Design. This chapter introduces concepts that are elaborated in upcoming chapters.

This chapter begins by describing the prerequisites for starting a sample application. We run it to see the first page. The chapter also introduces basic scripts for running an application for development, and packaging, building, and generating static code analysis results.

This chapter introduces a sample application and a storyline used throughout the book. The goal is to achieve consistency in the application's requirements, which helps you better understand Angular, TypeScript, and Material Design concepts.

Prerequisites

Before we start developing the Angular application with TypeScript and Material Design, the following prerequisites need to be set up on your development machine to work with this book's examples and instructions.

Node.js

Node is a JavaScript runtime. Preferably, you should use the latest version of Node. At the time of writing this content, Angular recommends using Node version 8.x or 10.x.

To verify that you have Node installed on your machine, run the following command in the terminal (Mac) or command prompt (Windows).

```
node -v
```

© Venkata Keerti Kotaru 2020
V. K. Kotaru, *Angular for Material Design*, https://doi.org/10.1007/978-1-4842-5434-9_2

If Node is correctly installed on your machine, the command returns a version number. If it is not installed, this command shows an error. Download and install Node from `https://nodejs.org`.

Package Managers

While working with the Angular application, you will need a package manager. A JavaScript application or a library has dependencies. These dependencies have more dependencies. A package manager makes it easy to install and manage these dependencies.

npm and Yarn are two popular JavaScript package managers; both are open source. This book provides instructions for both options.

npm

npm is installed along with Node.js. It is the most popular JavaScript package manager. Millions of developers use it and download packages from its repository every day.

Yarn

While npm is reliable and has a huge developer user base, there is scope for improvement. Yarn is relatively fast. It made improvements to its security when running a package's dependencies. It is an open source project driven by Facebook, Google, Exponent, and Tilde.

To install Yarn, run the following command.

```
npm install --global yarn
```

Note   This command installs Yarn globally on the machine. You will need administrative privileges (run the command prompt as an admin) on a Windows machine, or you need super user access on a Mac (sudo npm install --global yarn).

If you are new to either of these package managers, pick one and consistently use it while performing the examples in this book.

Angular CLI

Angular CLI is a powerful tool for improving developer productivity. It helps create a new Angular project from scratch and maintains the project throughout the development life cycle.

Throughout the book, we primarily use Angular CLI for various development tasks (on the sample project); however, where necessary, I provide alternatives that don't use Angular CLI.

Angular CLI helps improve productivity a great deal, but by no means is it a mandatory tool.

Install Angular CLI

It is preferable to install Angular CLI globally on the machine.

Run the following command for npm.

```
npm install --global @angular/cli
```

Run the following command for Yarn.

```
yarn global add @angular/cli
```

Note   Angular CLI is installed globally on the machine. Use sudo on Macs and administrator privileges on Windows.

Visual Studio Code

You need an editor or an IDE to work with Angular and TypeScript code. Choosing a particular editor is a personal choice. I've seen many developers who are very good with a vi editor. They prefer doing everything with a keyboard, without switching to a mouse, for the speed. There are other choices, like Sublime, Atom, or even a simple text editor like Notepad in Windows.

My recommendation is Visual Studio Code. First, it is free, lightweight, and open source. The features set is driven by Microsoft. I've always seen monthly updates that add features and enhancements.

Visual Studio Code is great for working with TypeScript. It quickly shows warnings and errors as you type code. There are easy-to-peek-into definitions for the functions. It also has a good echo system and extensions created by developers from around the world. To install Visual Studio Code, download it from `https://code.visualstudio.com`.

Having said that, however, pick an editor that you are comfortable with.

Getting Started with a Sample Application

To start an Angular application using TypeScript and Material Design, consider the following two options.

- Use Angular CLI, which creates a new Angular application with TypeScript and Material Design. Angular CLI is a productivity tool that is helpful with creating and maintaining the sample application. Throughout the book, we add many features to the sample application using Angular CLI.

- Manually add Material Design to an existing Angular and TypeScript application.

Option 1: Getting Started Using Angular CLI

To use Angular CLI to start an Angular project, run the following command.

```
ng new superheroes --routing
```

`superheroes` is the name of the sample project. This project creates and lists superheroes and their data.

The routing option (`--routing`) includes a routing module and default configuration values. Routing is important when building a single-page application. We explore this more in upcoming chapters.

After installation, use the following command to install the Angular Material CLI schematic. It helps install the required dependencies for Material Design.

```
ng add @angular/material
```

Figure 2-1 shows the details of the command, which prompts the following.

- A Material Design theme selection.

- Optional setup of Hammer JS for gesture support. This is useful on touch screen devices like iPhones or Android phones, tablets, and multitouch-supported laptop or desktop screens. For the current project, select Yes.

- Optional setup of browser animations. Choose Yes for the sample project.

- Choose your style sheet options. For simplicity, select CSS.

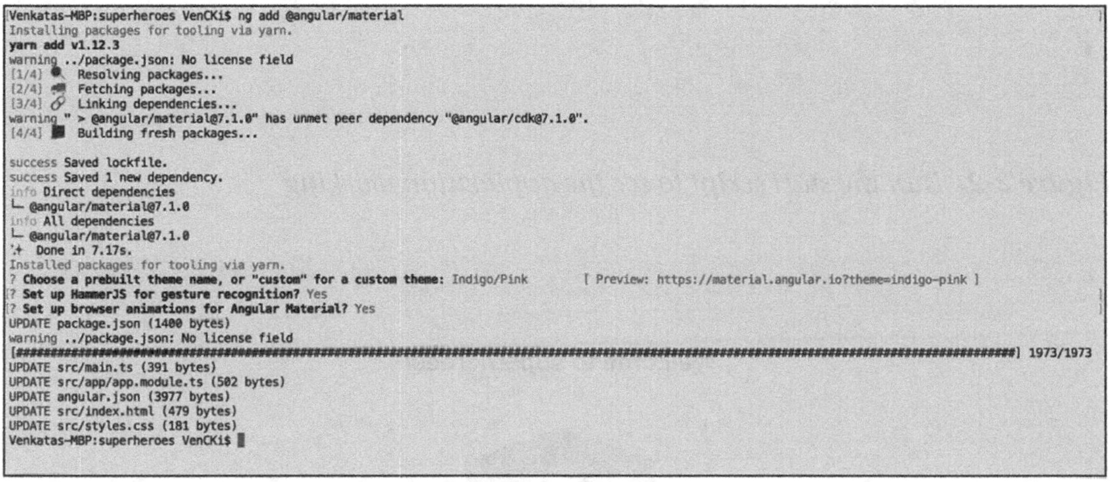

```
Venkatas-MBP:superheroes VenCKi$ ng add @angular/material
Installing packages for tooling via yarn.
yarn add v1.12.3
warning ../package.json: No license field
[1/4] 🔍  Resolving packages...
[2/4] 🚚  Fetching packages...
[3/4] 🔗  Linking dependencies...
warning " > @angular/material@7.1.0" has unmet peer dependency "@angular/cdk@7.1.0".
[4/4] 📦  Building fresh packages...

success Saved lockfile.
success Saved 1 new dependency.
info Direct dependencies
└─ @angular/material@7.1.0
info All dependencies
└─ @angular/material@7.1.0
✨  Done in 7.17s.
Installed packages for tooling via yarn.
? Choose a prebuilt theme name, or "custom" for a custom theme: Indigo/Pink          [ Preview: https://material.angular.io?theme=indigo-pink ]
? Set up HammerJS for gesture recognition? Yes
? Set up browser animations for Angular Material? Yes
UPDATE package.json (1400 bytes)
warning ../package.json: No license field
[######################################################################################################################] 1973/1973
UPDATE src/main.ts (391 bytes)
UPDATE src/app/app.module.ts (502 bytes)
UPDATE angular.json (3977 bytes)
UPDATE src/index.html (479 bytes)
UPDATE src/styles.css (181 bytes)
Venkatas-MBP:superheroes VenCKi$ ▮
```

Figure 2-1. *Add Angular Material schematic*

The application is generated, installed, and ready to use. Use the following command to see the application compiled and up and running. We can further develop and debug the application with a start script running in the background. Figure 2-2 shows the start script configuration. Figure 2-3 shows a first look at the up-and-running application.

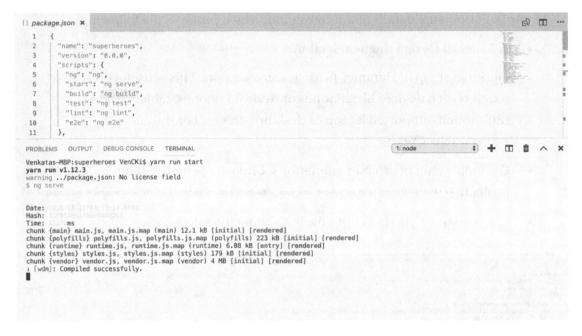

```
{} package.json  ×
 1   {
 2     "name": "superheroes",
 3     "version": "0.0.0",
 4     "scripts": {
 5       "ng": "ng",
 6       "start": "ng serve",
 7       "build": "ng build",
 8       "test": "ng test",
 9       "lint": "ng lint",
10       "e2e": "ng e2e"
11     },
```

```
PROBLEMS   OUTPUT   DEBUG CONSOLE   TERMINAL                                    1: node         +  ⊡  🗑  ∧  ✕

Venkatas-MBP:superheroes VenCKi$ yarn run start
yarn run v1.12.3
warning ../package.json: No license field
$ ng serve

Date: 2018-12-21T04:13:14.863Z
Hash: 12691866346bc9442267
Time:        ms
chunk {main} main.js, main.js.map (main) 12.1 kB [initial] [rendered]
chunk {polyfills} polyfills.js, polyfills.js.map (polyfills) 223 kB [initial] [rendered]
chunk {runtime} runtime.js, runtime.js.map (runtime) 6.08 kB [entry] [rendered]
chunk {styles} styles.js, styles.js.map (styles) 179 kB [initial] [rendered]
chunk {vendor} vendor.js, vendor.js.map (vendor) 4 MB [initial] [rendered]
ℹ ｢wdm｣: Compiled successfully.
```

Figure 2-2. *Run the start script to see the application working*

Welcome to superheroes!

Here are some links to help you start:

- **Tour of Heroes**
- **CLI Documentation**
- **Angular blog**

Figure 2-3. *First look at the generated application*

Use the following with Yarn.

```
yarn start
```

Use the following with npm.

```
npm start
```

Please note that in the sample, Material Design is installed but has not been used yet. It is a starter project with Angular and TypeScript. The next few sections add Material Design references in the code.

Note   Jump to the "Add Material Design Code References" section to continue with the newly created Angular application with CLI. Option 2 describes the changes required for an existing Angular application to include Material Design.

Option 2: Material Design for an Existing Application Without Angular CLI

If you have an existing Angular project that doesn't use Angular CLI, consider the following instructions.

Install Angular Material Packages

For npm, use the following command to install Material Design and related packages.

```
npm install --save @angular/material @angular/cdk @angular/animations
```

For Yarn, use the following command to install Material Design and related packages.

```
yarn add @angular/material @angular/cdk @angular/animations
```

Reference Style Sheet/Theme

To use an existing theme provided by Angular Material, use the following line of code you styles.css (or an equivalent global style sheet file). Notice we are using the Indigo Pink theme.

```
@import "~@angular/material/prebuilt-themes/indigo-pink.css";
```

Reference Font and Material Design Icons

Update index.html (or an HTML file loading the Angular content). Add the following references, which bring Material Design typography, fonts, and icons to the application, respectively.

```
<link href="https://fonts.googleapis.com/css?family=Roboto:300,400,500"
rel="stylesheet">
<link href="https://fonts.googleapis.com/icon?family=Material+Icons"
rel="stylesheet">
```

Follow the next few sections to add code references for Material Design, and run the project as you always do (considering that it is an existing project). Typically, npm start is used to start an Angular project (or any JavaScript project) for development and debugging purposes.

Add Material Design Code References

The required packages (Material, CDK, and Animations) for Material Design have already been installed. Now, let's add the code references. For the first example, let's add a Material Design toolbar and a card to the application.

Module Reference

The toolbar and card are packaged in their own Angular module. Refer to Listing 2-1 to import the modules to the TypeScript file and the NgModule. Open src/app.module.ts and make the changes mentioned in Listing 2-1.

An Angular module is different from a JavaScript module. It encapsulates Angular components, services, and so forth. A component in a module is scoped internally. It can only be used across modules when exported from the containing module.

I explain Angular modules in an upcoming chapter.

Listing 2-1. Module References

```
--- app.module.ts ----
// 1. Add the following line
// Import toolbar and card modules
import { MatToolbarModule, MatCardModule } from '@angular/material';
```

```
/* Considering it is a getting started sample, importing noop animation
module, disabling animations. */
import {NoopAnimationsModule} from '@angular/platform-browser/animations';

// 2. Update imports with the two additional modules
@NgModule({
// Deleted additional properties for brevity
 imports: [
   MatToolbarModule,
   MatCardModule,
   NoopAnimationsModule
 ],
})
export class AppModule { }
```

Modify Template

Update the app component template to show the Material Design toolbar and card.
Delete the code in src/app/app.component.html and replace it with the code in
Listing 2-2.

An Angular component has a template, which is HTML code that takes care of the
presentation logic. It acts as the view for the component.

Listing 2-2. Template Using Toolbar and Card

```
<mat-toolbar color="primary">Superheroes</mat-toolbar>

<mat-card> Hello Material Design World</mat-card>

<router-outlet></router-outlet>
```

As you save the two files, the application recompiles and refreshes the browser to
show the result (see Figure 2-4).

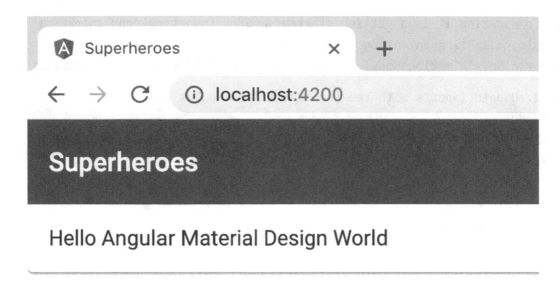

Figure 2-4. *Material Design*

Sample Application

As you embark on the journey of learning how to create Angular applications with TypeScript and Material Design, it is easier to visualize the concepts with an example. It is a sample application that we will build as you learn the concepts in the book. It helps to have a consistent story.

Storyline

We will build an application for superheroes. You might have noticed the name of the sample application generated with Angular CLI.

The application allows the superheroes' data to be added, modified, and deleted. A superhero can search for and list other superheroes, view the details, and maybe fight other superheroes. Fights might be in movies but not in our app!

Features

In the upcoming chapters, we continue to build the superheroes application. The following are the high-level requirements for the application

- Superheroes like sophistication in functionality. The application needs multiple screens. It needs to be built as an SPA (single-page application) so that there are no page reloads when transitioning between pages.

- Superheroes like consistency. The application needs a consistent look and feel. The controls on the pages— labels, buttons, drop-downs, lists of items—need to look and behave the same way across the application.

- Superheroes like to make life easier. The application needs to be intuitive; for example, the user should be able to locate the primary actions at a consistent location on the pages. The user needs to easily find the functionalities.

The following are the set of screens and low-level functionalities to build with the Angular application using TypeScript and Material Design.

- An intuitive list of superheroes with images and interactive animations

- The ability to filter

- A detailed information screen for each superhero

- A form to create a new superhero

- The ability to edit a superhero

Note   At this point, you have everything to move to the next chapter. We have a basic development environment set up, and the sample application is up and running. The remaining sections describe the files and folders generated by CLI, which is nice-to-have information (at this stage).

Files and Directories Generated by CLI

Let's review the files and directories generated with Angular CLI. This section provides a high-level overview of the files generated. At the end of this section, you will understand the purpose of each file. The sections do not detail all of the available options and configurations.

Configuration Files at the Root

At the root of the application, many configuration files have been generated. Consider the following file list. They are the primary configuration files. There could be additional configurations, depending on the IDE, the source control product, and so forth.

Package.json

Package.json is a primary configuration file for the new application package. It maintains the name of the application, the version number, and other types of metadata. npm (Node Package Manager) or Yarn maintain the application and dev dependencies here. It is the root file using the generated and installed dependency tree.

It also has configuration for scripts, which are the common tasks performed when developing, unit testing, and building the application. The scripts in a CLI-generated application depend on an Angular workspace configuration.

angular.json

angular.json is a workspace configuration file. Angular CLI creates this file when the first Angular project is generated. More projects can be added to the workspace, including libraries, end-to-end test projects, and so forth. Angular commands and configurations are in this file. Some of the configurations include the following.

- Serve, a configuration for running the application for development purposes

- Build, a configuration for compiling and bundling the Angular application.

- Production optimization options

- Unit test and end-to-end test configurations

tsconfig.json

tsconfig.json is a TypeScript configuration file. It has TypeScript compiler options, module system–related configurations, a directory location for type definitions, and so on.

It is the root configuration. For each project in the workspace, there is a specific TypeScript configuration, which extends the configuration from this file at the root directory. Remember, we are in the context of a workspace when we generate an application with Angular CLI; that is, we first have a default project created. More projects can be added to the workspace.

tslint.json

tslint.json is a lint configuration for TypeScript code. This book extensively uses TypeScript. The linting process ensures code quality, adherence to coding standards, and static code analysis. TSLint checks TypeScript and Angular application code against configured rules and warns about any discrepancies.

This is the root configuration. For each project in the workspace, there is a specific lint configuration that extends the configuration from this file at the root directory. Remember, we are in the context of a workspace when we generate an application with Angular CLI; that is, we first have a default project created. More projects can be added to the workspace.

Default Application Directory Root: /src

The first generated Angular application is placed in the /src directory at the root of the project. As mentioned, when you use CLI in a new directory, the first project is generated under the /src folder, and it is the default project in the workspace. As we generate more projects with CLI, they are moved under a /projects folder. The default project remains as the first generated project in /src. You can manually change it.

Consider the following files and directories in the /src folder..

TypeScript Configurations

```
/-
--/src
---/src/tsconfig.app.json
---/src/tslint.json
---/src/tsconfig.spec.json
```

tsconfig.app.json and tsconfig.spec.json extend from /tsconfig.json, which is the workspace-level TypeScript configuration file. The tsconfig.app.json file provides the TypeScript configuration for the application files. tsconfig.spec.json provides the TypeScript configuration for the unit test files, which are post-fixed with .spec.ts.

The tslint.json file in /src extends from tslint.json at the root directory. It provides a specific linting configuration for the default project.

If we create more projects using CLI, each project will have its own tsconfig and tslint configuration files.

index.html

index.html is the primary HTML file. It references the application files and dependencies, style sheets, and so on. This file references the root component for the Angular application. Consider the following code for a body tag, which loads the root component of a generated Angular application called app-root.

```
<body>
 <app-root></app-root>
</body>
```

main.ts

The main.ts file has the code to bootstrap the Angular application. Consider Listing 2-3.

Listing 2-3. Bootstrap the Angular Application

```
platformBrowserDynamic()
  .bootstrapModule(AppModule)
 .catch(err => console.error(err));
```

The file also has code to conditionally enable the production mode (see Listing 2-4). The framework performs assertions in the development mode; for example, an assertion to ensure that a change detection pass does not result in additional unexpected changes. If it notices changes between two change detection patterns, it throws a warning that indicates a possible bug. When production mode is enabled, such assertions are removed.

Listing 2-4. Enable Production Code Based on a Condition

```
if (environment.production) {
 enableProdMode();
}
```

Application Directory: /src/app

Application code—including modules, components, and services—are placed in this directory. I explain each concept in upcoming chapters; however, the following introduces the purpose of each file.

Root Module: app.module.ts

src/app/app.module.ts is the root Angular module for the default project generated with Angular CLI. In Listing 2-5, the Angular module is created by decorating a TypeScript class with NgModule.

Note that the Angular module is different from a JavaScript module. Angular modules may contain one or more components, services, and other Angular code files. It scopes these units of code; that is, if a component in module-1 needs to be used in module-2, it needs to be exported explicitly.

Listing 2-5. Root Module for the Application

```
@NgModule({
  // Removing decorator properties for brevity
})
export class AppModule { }
```

App Component (Root Component)

An app component is a set of files that render the first file and the root component of the application. An upcoming chapter discusses these components in detail.

The following are the files.

- src/app/app.component.ts: The component's TypeScript code file.

- src/app/app.component.spec.ts: The component's unit test file.

- src/app/app.component.css: The component's style sheet.

- src/app/app.component.html: The component's view template. It contains HTML markup and handles presentation for the component.

Routing Module: app-routing.module.ts

src/app/app-routing.module.ts is a module file. Angular CLI generates it only if routing is selected when creating the project. The purpose of this module is to encapsulate routing logic into its own Angular module.

This module is referenced and imported into the main module of the application. In Listing 2-6, the routing module class is available in the main module, and it needs to be imported into JavaScript first (see line 2). Then, it is imported into NgModule (Angular module) (see lines 5, 6, and 7).

Listing 2-6. Import Router Module

```
1. // Import routing module (JavaScript import)
2. import { AppRoutingModule } from './app-routing.module';

3. // Import it into Angular module
4. @NgModule({
5. imports: [
6.   AppRoutingModule,
7.],
8. // Code removed for brevity
9. })
10. export class AppModule { }
```

Scripts

Consider the following scripts in package.json for primary tasks working with an Angular application. These are created using Angular CLI.

Start Script

To run the start script, use

```
yarn start
```

or

```
npm start
```

Refer to the start script in package.json. The start script runs the Angular CLI ng serve command. We can run ng serve directly; however, it is a general practice to run the application using the start script. It is a common convention for Node developers to run the start script to start an application.

The *ng serve* command depends on the configuration in angular.json to start the application. Refer to Figure 2-5 for the configuration to run the application with the script.

```
{} angular.json ✕
  1    {
  2      "$schema": "./node_modules/@angular/cli/lib/config/schema.json",
  3      "version": 1,
  4      "newProjectRoot": "projects",
  5      "projects": {
  6        "superheroes": {
  7          "root": "",
  8          "sourceRoot": "src",
  9          "projectType": "application",
 10          "prefix": "app",
 11          "schematics": {},
 12          "architect": {
 13  ⊞         "build": {⋯
 57            },
 58            "serve": {
 59              "builder": "@angular-devkit/build-angular:dev-server",
 60              "options": {
 61                "browserTarget": "superheroes:build"
 62              },
 63              "configurations": {
 64                "production": {
 65                  "browserTarget": "superheroes:build:production"
 66                }
 67              }
 68            },
 69  ⊞         "extract-i18n": {⋯
 74            },
 75  ⊞         "test": {⋯
 92            },
 93  ⊞         "lint": {⋯
104            }
105        }
106      }
```

Figure 2-5. *Angular CLI configuration for ng serve command (run by script run)*

The build Script

The build script compiles, bundles, and copies resultant files in a dist folder at the root of the project. The angular application output of this command is ready to be deployed on a web server. Consider the following commands to build the application.

```
yarn run build
```

or

```
npm run build
```

Figure 2-6 has "build" listed as one of the scripts. It runs the Angular CLI ng build command. Angular CLI uses the configuration in the angular.json file to build the application. It uses the following information from the configuration file. These are some of the many configuration items in the Angular CLI build process.

- The destination directory in which to place bundled files

- The main file for the Angular application that bootstraps the application

- The index HTML file that loads the Angular JavaScript application

- The TypeScript configuration

- The polyfill configuration used for the application's backward-compatibility requirements

- The assets, such as images and icons, that the application needs

- The style sheets that the application needs

Figure 2-6. *The build command configuration and output*

See Figure 2-6 for the following.

- The build script output in the terminal

- Angular CLI configuration for the build command in the open file

- Output files resulted by the build script (in the left nav)

The categories of the files generated are as follows.

- index.html, the start file of the application

- main.js bundled application

- Other JS files are dependencies that the application needs to run.

- Map files help with the debug process

- The ico file at this stage in the application; however, it copies any images available in the assets

The JavaScript file generated is compiled and bundled; however, it is not minified. There are also additional map files for debugging; hence, this build script is not yet optimized for production deployment. Preferably, it would be used in a development environment deployment, which is an integrated environment with dependent external services yet developer-friendly with debug features.

To get a production-optimized build of the application, run one of the following commands.

```
yarn run build --prod
```

or

```
npm run build --prod
```

The production-optimized code is minified (a lower JavaScript file size), without map files for debugging and tree shaken.

The lint Script

Linting helps you to maintain coding standards and conventions in an Angular project. It warns developers about common mistakes with coding standards, naming, formatting, and so forth.

Use one of the following commands to run the lint script.

```
yarn run lint
```

or

```
npm run lint
```

Angular CLI runs the TypeScript lint process (tslint) with the command. As with the preceding two scripts, the Angular CLI configuration for the lint script begins with angular.json; however, the configuration for tslint is in tslint.json. The angular.json configuration leads to the TypeScript configuration, which in turn leads to tslint.json

Figure 2-7 shows the lint script result.

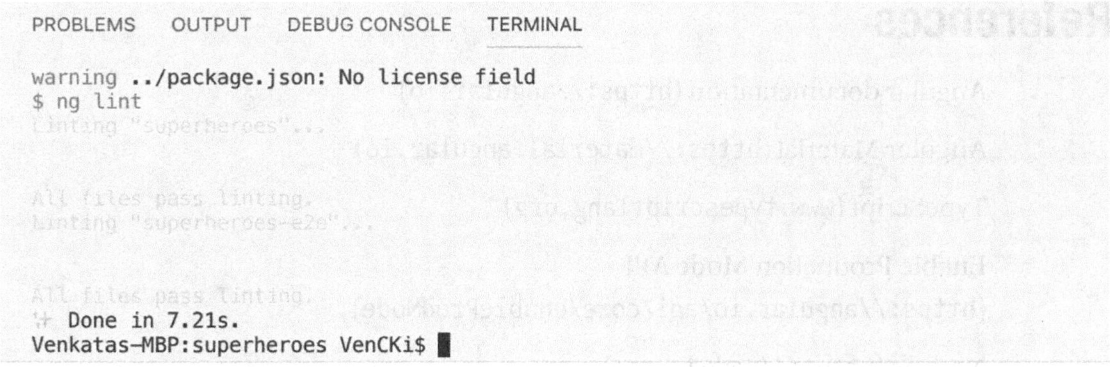

```
PROBLEMS   OUTPUT   DEBUG CONSOLE   TERMINAL

warning ../package.json: No license field
$ ng lint
Linting "superheroes"...


All files pass linting.
Linting "superheroes-e2e"...


All files pass linting.
✨  Done in 7.21s.
Venkatas-MBP:superheroes VenCKi$ █
```

Figure 2-7. The lint script result

Conclusion

This chapter provided instructions on getting started with an Angular application using TypeScript and Material Design. The chapter listed the prerequisites and provided installation instructions.

The chapter described the storyline for the sample application that will be used in all the upcoming concepts.

I prefer to use Angular CLI to build the Angular application. It describes the files and folders generated with CLI. It also describes the pregenerated scripts to perform JavaScript tasks.

Exercise

Create a new Angular application and include an Angular Material reference. Start the application and ensure that a pre-created welcome page comes up.

When the application is up and running on a browser, remove the content from the main component template. Ensure that the application automatically compiles successfully, and refresh the web page.

On the main component (app component), add a toolbar with the title of your choice. Show four Material Design cards with unique content on each card.

References

Angular documentation (`https://angular.io`)

Angular Material (`https://material.angular.io`)

TypeScript (`www.typescriptlang.org`)

Enable Production Mode API
(`https://angular.io/api/core/enableProdMode`)

Node.js (`https://nodejs.org`)

Code Editor or IDE, Visual Studio Code
(`https://code.visualstudio.com`)

CHAPTER 3

Modules

This chapter covers module systems in JavaScript and Angular. Modules are important for Angular code organization and the logical groupings of code. Modules also manage dependencies. An application has many files, classes, functions, and so forth. No code works in a silo or without integrating with other code units. A method in a class calls another method, which creates a dependency. A module system manages the dependency tree.

All modern JavaScript applications use a module system introduced in ES6 (also called ES2015). Angular applications use it, too; however, Angular also uses its own modules system. This chapter explains both modules.

- **The JavaScript module system** is useful for grouping JavaScript functions, classes, constants, and so forth.

- **Angular modules** are containers for Angular components, directives, services, and so forth. You can create a logical grouping of code units in a module and retrieve them using Angular's dependency injection. The Angular module system is used in addition to JavaScript modules.

Figure 3-1 is a visual depiction of the modules.

Note   JavaScript has its own module system from ECMA Script 2015 (ES6). Earlier, JavaScript used custom libraries like RequireJS to implement modules. During the course of this book, however, we use TypeScript. It shares the concept of modules introduced in ES6. For the purposes of this chapter, we will call them JavaScript modules.

© Venkata Keerti Kotaru 2020
V. K. Kotaru, *Angular for Material Design*, https://doi.org/10.1007/978-1-4842-5434-9_3

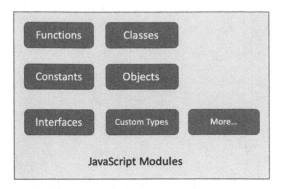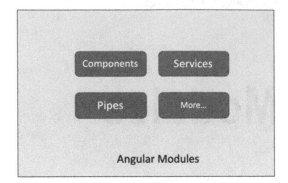

Figure 3-1. *Module system*

JavaScript Modules

JavaScript modules create a logical grouping of JavaScript/TypeScript classes, functions, constants, and so forth. Listing 3-1 is from the Superheroes sample application. It imports classes from a few modules.

Listing 3-1. JavaScript Imports from a Module

```
-- app.module.ts --
import { BrowserModule } from '@angular/platform-browser';
import { NgModule } from '@angular/core';
import { AppComponent } from './app.component';
```

Note   @angular prefixes Angular code components, directives, services, and so forth. The prefix matches with Angular npm monorepo. For example, you may install an Angular library CDK with the command shown in Listing 3-2.

Listing 3-2. Install from npm monorepo

```
npm install @angular/cdk
```

or

```
yarn add @angular/cdk
```

The app.module.ts file exports a class (see Listing 3-3).

Listing 3-3. JavaScript Export

```
-- app.module.ts continued --
@NgModule({
// Removed code for brevity.
})
export class AppModule { }
```

The `ts` file (TypeScript file) acts as a module. You may define more than one class or function in a file. Be sure to export the class or the function so that it is available outside the module.

This information is sufficient for understanding the Angular concepts covered in this book. To learn more about JavaScript modules, refer to the "More About JavaScript Modules" section later in the chapter.

Angular Modules

Angular modules serve a purpose different from JavaScript modules. They act as a container for Angular code. Angular modules create logical groupings of components, directives, pipes, services, and so forth. A typical Angular application includes many modules.

Continuing with the app.module.ts, Listing 3-3 creates an Angular module with @NgModule decorator, which contains metadata for creating the Angular module. The AppModule in the sample application (created by Angular CLI) is the root module of the entire application. AppModule is a class (see Listing 3-4).

Listing 3-4. Root Module app.module.ts

```
--- app.module.ts ----
import { BrowserModule } from '@angular/platform-browser';
import { NgModule } from '@angular/core';
import { AppComponent } from './app.component';
```

```
@NgModule({
 declarations: [
   AppComponent
 ],
 imports: [BrowserModule],
 bootstrap: [AppComponent]
})
export class AppModule { }
```

The JavaScript module imports BrowserModule and NgModule at the beginning of the file.

- **NgModule** is a decorator needed to create a new module in the Angular application. You use the decorator annotated on top of the AppModule module class . It captures the metadata for the module. A decorator is a new feature in both JavaScript and TypeScript. In JavaScript, it was a "proposal" feature at the time of authoring this content.

- **BrowserModule** is a required Angular infrastructure module available with the Angular library. It is required for an Angular application running on a browser like Google Chrome or Firefox. Angular applications can also run outside the context of a client browser on a Node.js server application. These applications do not have to use BrowserModule.

You also import the root component for the entire application, which is typically called AppComponent. This the first component created by Angular CLI.

The ngModule decorator has the following metadata fields.

- **declarations**: An array that declares components and other Angular code to be part of the module (see Listing 3-5), AppComponent is declared on the root module. It is the only component created so far in the application. As we create additional components during the course of this book, we add them to declarations. Angular CLI automatically adds declarations when creating a new component. Listing 3-5 shows how to create a new component with Angular CLI.

- **bootstrap**: Specify the root component of the Angular application here. Only one module can use the bootstrap field for an application. AppModule is the root module when we create the application; it bootstraps with the first component, AppComponent.

- **imports**: As mentioned, an Angular application includes many Angular modules. To use features from other modules, import them to the Angular module by including the module class reference in the imports array. For now, we import the BrowserModule platform module.

For complete list of metadata fields, see the "ngModule Decorator Complete List of Fields" section.

Note   The decorator pattern augments a class with additional features, without modifying the class definition. In this case, the additional features include metadata fields and functions that the module class will carry.

To generate a new component using Angular CLI, run the command in Listing 3-5.

Listing 3-5. Create a Component with Angular CLI

```
ng generate component my-sample-component
```

An Approach to Modules

Modules are containers of Angular code. They are a logical group of classes, functions, components, directives, and so forth. While there is no one approach to logical groupings, in the superheroes code sample, we group all Material Design components and other code units in a module (see Figure 3-2).

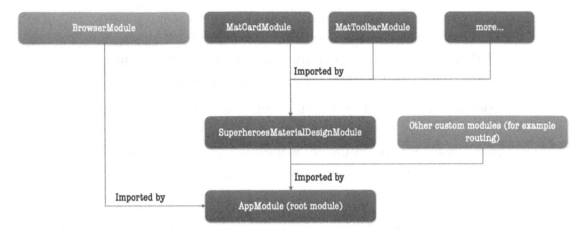

Figure 3-2. *Angular modules and dependencies*

Figure 3-2 describes the dependencies between Angular modules. AppModule is the root module. *It depends on* Angular platform modules like BrowserModule. In other words, AppModule *imports* BrowserModule and other platform-level modules. Notice the dependency with gray boxes in Figure 3-2.

Let's create a new module: SuperheroesMaterialDesignModule. In the Superheroes sample application, consider grouping all Material Design (Angular Material) components into this module. In the code samples so far, you have seen a card and a toolbar. For these components to function, we need to import MatCardModule and MatToolbarModule. As we work with more Angular Material components, we import more modules.

Briefly, AppModule depends on SuperheroesMaterialDesignModule and Angular platform modules. The SuperheroesMaterialDesignModule, in turn, depends on more Angular Material modules. Notice the dark boxes in Figure 3-2.

Create an Angular Module

Use the Angular CLI command in Listing 3-6 to create a new module.

Listing 3-6. Create an Angular Module

```
ng generate module superheroes-material-design
```

If you do not use Angular CLI, create a module TypeScript class (preferably in a separate file and folder) and decorate it with @ngModule.

Angular CLI creates the module file in a new folder: app/superheroes-material-design. The file name matches the folder name: superheroes-material-design.module.ts. The module class is named in pascal case: SuperheroesMaterialDesignModule.

Notice the "Mat" prefix on all Angular Material modules, components, and so forth. Import the Mat∗ (Angular Material) modules to the newly created SuperheroesMaterialDesignModule (see Listing 3-7).

Listing 3-7. Superheroes Material Design Module

```
-- superheroes-material-design.module.ts --
import { BrowserAnimationsModule } from '@angular/platform-browser/
animations';
import { MatToolbarModule } from '@angular/material/toolbar';
import { MatCardModule } from '@angular/material/card';

@NgModule({
 imports: [
   BrowserAnimationsModule,
   MatCardModule,
   MatToolbarModule
 ]
, // ** removed other metadata objects for brevity.
// ** this module definition is not complete. We will create modules and
reference them.
})
export class SuperheroesMaterialDesignModule { }
```

Import MatToolbarModule and MatCardModule from the Angular Material library, which are @angular/material/toolbar and @angular/material/card, respectively. The imports array with the Mat∗ modules allow all exported Angular code from the Mat∗ modules to be used in the newly created module. You can reference and use the components, services, and so forth in SuperheroesMaterialDesignModule's components and services. Creating and using components and services are discussed in other chapters in the book.

Note   We are also importing BrowserAnimationModule because Angular
Material uses animations. If you need to skip animations, you should import
NoopAnimationsModule to avoid errors due to a missing animation API when using
Material Design components.

Pretend that the components that render a superheroes profile on a
card and toolbar are ready and available in the application. Include them in
SuperheroesMaterialDesignModule by importing the component classes and declaring
them on @ngModule (see Listing 3-8).

Listing 3-8. Import and Export Profile and Toolbar Components

```
Import { SuperheroProfileComponent } from "./superhero-profile/superhero-
profile.component";
Import { SuperheroToolbarComponent } from "./superhero-profile/superhero-
toolbar.component";

@NgModule({
  declarations: [
    SuperheroProfileComponent,
    SuperheroToolbarComponent
  ],
  imports: [
    BrowserAnimationsModule,
    MatCardModule,
    MatToolbarModule
  ],
  exports: [
    SuperheroProfileComponent,
    SuperheroToolbarComponent
  ]
})
export class SuperheroesMaterialDesignModule { }
```

Including the SuperheroProfileComponent and SuperheroToolbarComponent
components in the declarations array makes them part of the module.

For these components to be accessible outside the SuperheroesMaterialDesignModule module, you need to export them as well. Notice the exports array in the @ngModule metadata.

Let's now import the new SuperheroesMaterialDesignModule to AppModule so that the exported Angular code from the module is usable in the root module and the rest of the application (see Listing 3-9). Review Figure 3-2 again to better understand the module dependencies.

Listing 3-9. App Module Importing SuperheroesMaterialDesignModule

```
-- app.module.ts --
import { SuperheroesMaterialDesignModule } from './superheroes-material-
design/superheroes-material-design.module';
import { AppRoutingModule } from './app-routing.module';

@NgModule({
  declarations: [
    // ** removed other metadata objects for brevity.
  ],
  imports: [
    BrowserModule,
    AppRoutingModule,
    SuperheroesMaterialDesignModule
  ],
})
export class AppModule { }
```

NgModule Decorator Complete List of Fields

The following is a list of the metadata fields used when creating a module.

Declarations

Declarations are the Angular components, directives, and pipes that belong to a module. We do not include provider services here. In Listing 3-9, we declared two components: SuperheroesProfileComponent and SuperheroesToolbarComponent.

Imports

Imports provide a list of modules in an array so that the given module has access to them. In the sample, we included MatCardModule. It contains a mat-card component. Now, the mat-card component is available to SuperheroesMaterialDesignModule components.

Exports

Not everything defined in an Angular module needs to be publicly available outside the module. The exports array provides a list of the components, pipes, or directives that are available to a module importing the current one.

Providers

Providers are a list of Angular services in an array. An angular service is a reusable class that is injectable into a component or another service. A separate chapter in the book elaborates creating and using services in Angular; however, for now, understand that a service needs to be provided or instantiated. It is done at the application level, module level, or at a component level.

A service provided at the module level instantiates it for the entire module. Hence, the state of the service or the values in the service is retained across multiple components in the module. It is like maintaining data at a global or module level.

Chapter 7 explains more about services.

Bootstrap

In Listing 3-10, notice app.module.ts. The AppModule, which is the root module, or the first main module of the application, bootstraps with AppComponent. Only one module in an application can use the bootstrap field.

Listing 3-10. App Module Bootstraps AppComponent

```
@NgModule({
  declarations: [
    AppComponent
  ],
```

```
imports: [
  BrowserModule,
  AppRoutingModule,
  SuperheroesMaterialDesignModule
],
providers: [],
bootstrap: [AppComponent]
})
export class AppModule { }
```

More About JavaScript Modules

Modules are included in JavaScript and TypeScript files. Each file can have exactly one module. Each file can import and export multiple items such as classes, objects, functions, and constants.

The Primary Ways to Import and Export Code

To export an item, use the export keyword. Each file can have one default export, which can export multiple other items. Listing 3-11 exports an Array object and two other functions. The `superheroes` array is exported as the default.

Listing 3-11. Export JavaScript Modules

```
const superheroes: SuperHero[] = [
    {
        name: "batman",
        creators: ["Bob Kane", "Bill Finger"],
        firstAppearance: "Year 1939",
        livesIn: "Gotham City",
    },
    {
        name: "Chhota Bheem",
        creators: [
            "Raj Viswanadha",
```

```
            "Arun Shendurnikar",
            "Nidhi Anand"
        ],
        firstAppearance: "Year 2008",
        livesIn: "India",
    },

];

export default superheroes;

function findSuperhero(name: string): SuperHero[] {
    return superheroes.find(x => x.name === name);
}

export function getSuperheroLocation(name: string): string {
    return findSuperhero(name).livesIn;
}

export function getSuperheroCreators(name: string): string {
    return findSuperhero(name).creators;
}
```

Notice that we did not export the findSuperhero function. Hence, we cannot access it outside the module or file. It is private to the module. The other functions are APIs exposed for other modules to use.

In another file, import and use the functions and the objects. In Listing 3-12, notice that the syntax, the default export, is not included in parentheses.

Listing 3-12. Import JS Modules

```
import  superheroes, {getSuperheroCreators, getSuperheroLocation} from
'./superhero';
```

In Listing 3-11 and Listing 3-12, getSuperheroCreators and getSuperheroLocation are called *named exports*. There can be multiple named exports. The file importing the JavaScript code (functions, in this case) identifies the function with its name. That means it cannot be an anonymous function.

There is a single default export from a module, however. Hence, it can be anonymous. We can rewrite Listing 3-13 to default export an anonymous array object.

Listing 3-13. Anonymous Default Export of an Array Object

```
export default [
    {
        name: "batman",
        creators: ["Bob Kane", "Bill Finger"],
        firstAppearance: "Year 1939",
        livesIn: "Gotham City",

    },
    {
        name: "Chhota Bheem",
        creators: [
            "Raj Viswanadha",
            "Arun Shendurnikar",
            "Nidhi Anand"],
        firstAppearance: "Year 2008",
        livesIn: "India",
    },
];
```

We import this code with Listing 3-14. The name of the object can by anything.

Listing 3-14. Import an Anonymous Object

```
import aCustomObjectName from './superhero';
```

It also holds well for anonymous functions (see Listing 3-15).

Listing 3-15. Export an Anonymous Function

```
export default function (name: string): string {
    // function definition
}
```

Import All

To import all functions, constants, and classes from a module, use the following syntax.

```
import * as heroApi from './superhero'
```

It creates a variable, heroApi, in the importing TypeScript file. Access the named imports with the function or constant name.

```
heroApi.getSuperheroCreators("batman")
```

Access the default export with the default keyword.

```
heroApi.default
```

You may rename the default import with the following syntax. Notice that getSuperheroCreators was renamed to renamedSuperheroCreators with the "as" keyword.

```
import  superheroes, {getSuperheroCreators as renamedSuperheroCreators,
getSuperheroLocation} from './superhero'
```

Access it in the class or function with the custom name.

```
renamedSuperheroCreators("batman")
```

Conclusion

It is important to understand module systems while developing complex applications with Angular, JavaScript, or TypeScript. In this chapter, we began by introducing the ES6/ES2015 module system. The chapter described the basics of importing and exporting JavaScript and TypeScript classes, functions, constants, and so forth.

Next, the chapter described Angular modules. It explained how to create an Angular module by using the NgModule decorator. It covered the usage of fields within the NgModule decorator. These fields and their values act as metadata for the Angular module.

The chapter described logical groupings and code organization with the Superheroes sample application. At the end, the chapter elaborated on ES6 module syntaxes and usage.

References

Angular Docs (`https://angular.io/docs`)

RequireJS library for modules (`https://requirejs.org`)

Node.js documentation on modules
(`https://nodejs.org/docs/latest/api/modules.html`)

CHAPTER 4

Angular: Components

Components are the building blocks of an Angular application. Components bring reusability to a view. Imagine a view that presents user profiles and order information in the sample application that we are building (a superhero profile). We might need to present the same data in many places. Instead of duplicating the code in each instance, let's create a component and reuse it.

This chapter introduces Angular components. It covers creating new components. An Angular application needs metadata that describes a component. Metadata defines how we use the component in the application. This chapter elaborates the metadata elements, which are typically coded as arguments to the TypeScript decorators on top of the component class.

This chapter also explains how to provide input data to a component and how to receive output from a component. The chapter concludes by discussing lifecycle hooks for a component.

Introduction

In an Angular application, the view is built with a component tree. In a typical HTML page, DOM (Document Object Model) nodes are organized as a tree. It starts with a root node, which has many child nodes. Each child node may have its own child nodes. Listing 4-1 is a small form capturing user input. It has a root div element that has two child nodes—a label and another div, which have more child nodes.

Listing 4-1. DOM Tree

```
<div>
  <label for="heroName">
    <strong>Hero</strong>
    <input type="text" name="heroName"/>
  </label>
```

© Venkata Keerti Kotaru 2020
V. K. Kotaru, *Angular for Material Design*, https://doi.org/10.1007/978-1-4842-5434-9_4

```
<div>
  <strong> Enter the hero name </strong>
  </div>
</div>
```

Figure 4-1 is a visual representation.

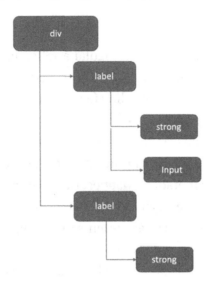

Figure 4-1. *DOM tree*

An Angular component is a custom element—a custom DOM node. It may intermix with HTML nodes. Consider the superhero profile component. It shows a hero's name, superpowers, and other information. Listing 4-2 has the superhero-profile among the HTML elements (see line 2). The superhero-profile component may contain more elements and child components.

Listing 4-2. Angular HTML Template with a Component Among Elements

```
1. <div class="form-group">
2.   <superhero-profile></superhero-profile>
3.   <strong>Hero</strong>
4.     <input type="text" name="heroName"/>
5.   </label>
```

```
6.   <div>
7.     <strong> Enter the hero name </strong>
8.   </div>
9. </div>
```

Now, let's focus on the superhero profile component. Figure 4-2 shows a profile component (or the view) with a title, description, and superpowers, which can be reused throughout the application.

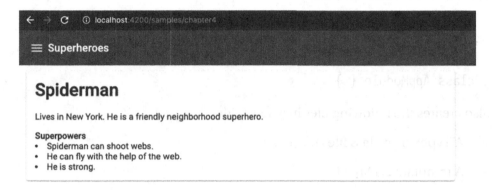

Figure 4-2. *Superhero profile component*

Create a Component

Let's begin by creating a new superhero-profile component using Angular CLI. Run the command shown in Listing 4-3 to create a new component.

Listing 4-3. Angular CLI Command for Creating a New Component

```
ng generate component superheroes-material-design/superhero-profile
```

Note   The path specified, superheroes-material-design/<component-name>, creates the component under the superheroes-material-design folder. It also looks for a module with the name SuperheroesMaterialDesign.module. Without this path reference, the component is created in the root module.

The component is declared in the module (see Listing 4-4).

Listing 4-4. Angular Module with the New Component Declaration

```
@NgModule({
 /* For brevity removed unrelated blocks of code */
  imports: [ ],
  declarations: [
    SuperheroProfileComponent
  ]
 /* For brevity removed unrelated blocks of code */
})
export class AppModule { }
```

It also creates the following files in a new folder.

- A TypeScript class file component

- A template HTML file

- A style sheet/CSS file

- A unit test file

Let's look at the new component's TypeScript class file. In Listing 4-5, the @Component decorator is on top of the class file. This makes a TypeScript class an Angular component. The decorator has a JSON object as an argument. The fields in this object define the metadata for the component. It defines various aspects of the component, such as the name of the component in the HTML markup, references to the HTML template file, references to the CSS file, and so forth.

Listing 4-5. A Component Class in TypeScript

```
@Component({
 selector: 'superhero-profile',
 templateUrl: './superhero-profile.component.html',
 styleUrls: ['./superhero-profile.component.css']
})
export class SuperheroProfileComponent implements OnInit {
```

```
constructor() { }

ngOnInit() { }
}
```

The following are the metadata attributes frequently used with components.

selector

We refer to a component using the selector value. In this example, we provided a value: superhero-profile. To use this component in another component in the application, the template (HTML file) would create a <superhero-profile></superhero-profile> element (see Listing 4-5).

Note   This attribute is inherited from another decorator, Directive. Components are a type of directive. Directives are discussed later.

---

templateUrl

A template defines the view of a component. It is the HTML intermixed with Angular bindings and syntaxes. templateUrl refers to the component's HTML template. Angular CLI places the template in the same directory as the TypeScript file component.

Listing 4-6 is the superhero profile component's HTML template. The result is shown in Figure 4-3.

Listing 4-6. HTML Template for Sample Superhero Profile

```
<mat-card>
  <h1>Spiderman</h1>
  <p>
    Lives in New York. He is a friendly neighbourhood superhero.
  </p>
```

```
<div>
  <strong>Superpowers</strong>
  <li>
    Spiderman can shoot web
  </li>
  <li>
    He can fly with the help of the web.
  </li>
  <li>
    He is strong
  </li>

</div>
</mat-card>
```

template

Typically, the HTML template code is separated in another file; however, if you prefer to keep the template and the TypeScript code in the same file, use the template attribute (instead of templateUrl). It might be a good idea to use the template attribute for a small number of lines of code (perhaps four to six lines of template code); otherwise, it could be convoluted to use template and the TypeScript in the same file.

styleUrls

Style sheets, or CSS, manage a component's look and feel. It takes care of colors, fonts, sizes, the margin width and height, and so forth. Styles are preferably separated into one or more files. Specify the relative path of the styles here.

style

The style attribute is used for inline styles; it is in the same file as the TypeScript component.

encapsulation

Traditionally, it is difficult to scope CSS in a web page. Over time, an application's complexity increases, and a lot of presentation and styling code accumulates. Web pages import styles at the HTML page level. Considering there is a single HTML page that loads at the beginning of an SPA (single-page application), it might mean the style sheet file is used by the entire application. With multiple developers on any typical team, it is very easy to step on one another's toes. Changing the style in one functionality could adversely affect rest of the application.

The encapsulation attribute helps scope CSS for Angular components. Angular provides three options.

- **emulated**: The default option. Angular ensures that the CSS used in a component does not interfere with other components. This is done by adding a surrogate ID to the host element. This host element is added to all CSS selectors that use the styles and elements.

- **shadowDom**: A new web standard popularized by Web Components. It helps scope the styles for natively supported components in a web page. This option works well for all browsers that support Web Components and the standard.

- **none**: Styles are global.

providers

The providers attribute accepts an array of tokens. With DI (dependency injection) in Angular, the injector uses provider to create an instance and supply the object to the decorated class.

Let's simplify this explanation. The decorated class is the component. It is a TypeScript class. Components in Angular typically use a reusable class instance (Angular services). It needs to be "provided"—that is, provide metadata for the injector to create an instance. Once the injector creates an instance, it is readily used by the component.

Note that "providers" is a field in the ngModule decorator mentioned in the Chapter 3. An Angular service (reusable TypeScript class) can be provided at the root, module, or component level.

A TypeScript class can maintain the state. The state is a class level variable or an object with data. If we provide at the root level, the state is shared across the application. It acts as a singleton for the application. If we provide it at the module level, the state is shared within the module, which means that it will provide a single instance throughout the module.

If it is provided at the component level, it acts like a local instance and does not share the value with any components; however, the instance is shared in the child components.

Note   Angular 1.x has services and factories. The state of a service or a factory is maintained across the application. The object and data is shared among controllers (in Angular 1.x). Angular 2+ depends on the provider. By default, the TypeScript classes that act as services are transient. Providers define how data is shared in the application.

Services providing dependency injection is discussed more in Chapter 7.

viewProviders

viewProviders are very similar to providers but have one major difference: they do not provide for projected content. The projected content is the DOM and the components supplied within the component's opening and closing elements (see Listing 4-7).

Listing 4-7. Projected Content

```
<my-component>
  <!-- projected content goes here -->
  <div>
    <child-component></child-component>
  </div>
</my-component>
```

This is useful for allowing the contents of a component to be supplied "on the fly." A component can apply its functionality on any content projected between the opening and closing elements. A component library might extensively use content projection.

The downside, however, is that the author of the component does not have control over which content is projected. It is coded by the component's consumers.

If you need to restrict a provided class to be used by only the real child components and not by the projected content, you may use viewProviders.

Note   Use <ng-content> (a built-in directive in Angular) for projecting content.

An Example to Showcase Projecting Content in Angular

Before we go over using viewProviders, we want to discuss projected content by using an example. Let's review the component tree that we have built so far. At the root of the application, there is the AppComponent. The AppComponent's template uses the SuperheroProfile component. To better understand the projected content, let's create a child component for SuperheroProfile. Let's name it SuperheroProfileFooter. We will include it in the SuperheroProfile template. Figure 4-3 is a visualization of a component tree.

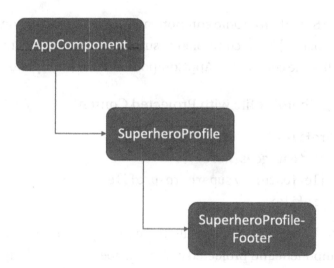

Figure 4-3. *Component tree*

Listing 4-8 is the HTML template for the superhero-profile component. It uses the superhero-profile-footer component directly as a child component.

Listing 4-8. superhero-profile-footer in SuperheroProfile Component Template

```
<mat-card class="custom-style">
 <!—Superhero details go here ⊛
 <superhero-profile-footer></superhero-profile-footer>
</mat-card>
```

On the other hand, we may let the superhero-profile consumers decide what goes into the footer. To do this, we may need to use the footer projected, instead of always using the same child component (hard coded in the component, as in Listing 4-9). Use ng-content in place of the footer component (see line number 4).

Listing 4-9. SuperheroProfile Template with Support to Projected Content

```
1. <mat-card class="custom-style">
2.   <div>Superhero profile.</div>
3.   <!-- Superhero details go here -->
4.   <ng-content></ng-content>
5. </mat-card>
```

While using the SuperheroProfile component, supply the footer component. ng-content projects (replaces) child components supplied by the user of the superhero-profile. Listing 4-10 is the code in the AppComponent HTML template.

Listing 4-10. SuperheroProfile with Projected Content

```
<app-superhero-profile>
 <!-- projected content goes here -->
 <superhero-profile-footer></superhero-profile-footer>
</app-superhero-profile>
```

In this example, both approaches result in the same view because we are using the same child component and projected content: superhero-profile-footer. The "A superhero made in Hollywood!" text is from the footer (see Figure 4-4); however, the later approach (content projection) allows any component or DOM element to be used as the footer; it does not need to be superheroProfileFooter. The footer is supplied to the component externally.

Note   For simplicity, this section does not describe the features of <mat-card>. Positioning content at the bottom of the card makes it look like a footer; however, in a future chapter, I discuss a better way to use a Material Design card.

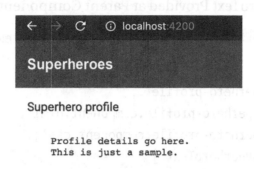

Figure 4-4. *A view with SuperheroProfile and SuperheroProfileFooter components put together*

Using viewProvider

Imagine that the contents of the child component, superhero-profile-footer, are returned by a reusable TypeScript class. Assume that it is a single place for all the superhero data. Eventually, we may use a remote service to get this data from a database. For now, consider Listing 4-11, which returns a string from the class variable.

Listing 4-11. A Reusable Class Providing Contents for the Superhero Components

```
export default class SuperheroText {
    private _footerText: string = "A superhero, made in Hollywood";

    get footerText(): string {
        return this._footerText;
    }
}
```

If you do not want this service to be used by the projected content, but to be used only by the direct child component, provide it with viewProviders. In Listing 4-12, SuperheroText is provided with viewProviders (line 6), but it is not injected (in line 9, the constructor does not inject anything).

Listing 4-12. SuperheroText Provided at Parent Component

```
1. import SuperheroText from '../utilities/superhero-text';

2. @Component({
3. selector: 'app-superhero-profile',
4. templateUrl: './superhero-profile.component.html',
5. styleUrls: ['./superhero-profile.component.css'],
6. viewProviders: [ SuperheroText ]
7. })
8. export class SuperheroProfileComponent {
9. constructor() {
10.  }
11. }
```

SuperheroProfile's child components (i.e., SuperheroProfileFooter) inject SuperheroText (see Listing 4-13).

Listing 4-13. A Child Component Injecting a Class Provided by Parent

```
import SuperheroText from '../utilities/superhero-text';

@Component({
 selector: 'superhero-profile-footer',
 templateUrl: './superhero-profile-footer.component.html'
})
export class SuperheroProfileFooterComponent {
 constructor(private superheroText: SuperheroText) { }
}
```

The superheroText object used by the direct child component referenced in the profile component (viewProvider) works without an error (see Listing 4-14).

Listing 4-14. Direct Child Component Using superheroText Works Well

```
---- superhero-profile.component.html ---
<mat-card class="custom-style">
 <!-- Superhero details go here -->
 <superhero-profile-footer></superhero-profile-footer>
</mat-card>
```

If superhero-profile-footer is projected, and it attempts to inject superheroText, it will return the following error. Hence, it gives control to the author or the superhero-profile component to disallow injecting a service by a projected component.

NullInjectorError: No provider for SuperheroText!

Input to a Component

Components are building blocks of an Angular application. They are reusable blocks of code. A component is expected to be designed with a single responsibility principle in mind. A component should be responsible for a particular view in the application.

So far, we have built a component to show a superhero profile. The same component could be used for any superhero in the system. This means, it expects input. The component processes and presents the data in a uniform manner.

To accept input into a component, Angular follows a natural HTML way: element attributes. As you might have noticed, a div tag can accept additional input, like a CSS class, with a class attribute. It accepts a unique identifier with an id attribute. Similarly, a text field accepts text with a value attribute, and so on.

While building custom elements with Angular, there could be one or more attributes added. The TypeScript code has a reference to the variable, and you can also use it in a template for presentation.

Use the @Input decorator to qualify a Component class field as an input. Import the Input decorator for the Angular core library (see Listing 4-15).

Listing 4-15. Component Class with Input Elements

```
import { Component, OnInit, Input, OnChanges } from '@angular/core';

export class SuperheroProfileComponent {
 @Input() name: string;
 @Input() firstAppearance: string;
 @Input("lives-in") livesIn: string;
}
```

Notice the input to the decorator in the livesIn field. It allows you to rename the component element attribute. In this case, we can use livesIn as lives-in in the template.

Provide input while invoking the component in the HTML template (see Listing 4-16).

Listing 4-16. Input in the Template

```
<app-superhero-profile name="Chhota Bheem" firstAppearance="2008"
lives-in="India">
```

Validate Input with a Setter

We can validate the input if we use the @Input decorator on a setter function instead of a class field. In Listing 4-17, we validate that the first appearance is greater than 1950. Decorate the setter with @Input. Notice that we used a private field in the component class. Getter and a setter allow you to access the private field and set a value to it through input.

Listing 4-17. Use a Setter to Validate Input

```
// create a private field
private _firstAppearance: number;

// use a public setter
@Input()
set firstAppearance(val: number) {
  if (val > 1950){
    this._firstAppearance = val;
```

```
  } else {
    console.error("Superhero is too old");
  }
}

// getter for the use of template.
get firstAppearance() {
  return this._firstAppearance;
}
```

Validate Input with the ngOnChanges Lifecycle Hook

Setters are effective for validating input when the number of input attributes is small. The downside to this approach is that we need a separate function for each attribute. We can combine all validations to a single function with ngOnChanges.

To use ngOnChanges, import and implement the onChanges interface. Override the ngOnChanges function (see Listing 4-18). Notice the SimpleChanges parameter. The object will have the previous value and a new value in each field.

Lifecycle hooks are discussed later in the chapter.

Listing 4-18. ngOnChanges Override

```
import { Component, OnInit, Input, OnChanges, SimpleChanges } from
'@angular/core';
export class SuperheroProfileComponent implements OnChanges {
 ngOnChanges(changes: SimpleChanges) {
   console.log(changes);
 }
}
```

```
◁ ▾{name: SimpleChange, livesIn: SimpleChange, firstAppearance: SimpleChange} 🔢
    ▸firstAppearance: SimpleChange {previousValue: undefined, currentValue: "2008", firstChange: true}
    ▸livesIn: SimpleChange {previousValue: undefined, currentValue: "India", firstChange: true}
    ▸name: SimpleChange {previousValue: undefined, currentValue: "Chhota Bheem", firstChange: true}
    ▸__proto__: Object
```

Figure 4-5. *SimpleChange object with values*

Output from a Component

A component can emit events, which can be tapped into by a consuming component. To demonstrate an output event, consider enhancing the Superhero Profile component. Let's add a button that emits the complete superhero object to the consuming component.

The component using SuperheroProfile will add an event handler to access the data. The event in the example is named flyWithSuperhero. In Listing 4-19, the event is passed to the handler function. The object received from the superhero profile component as an output is accessed in the app component.

Listing 4-19. AppComponent Accessing the flyWithSuperhero New Event

```
--- app.component.html ---
<app-superhero-profile (flyWithSuperhero)="printSuperhero($event)"
name="Chhota Bheem" firstAppearance="2008" lives-in="India">

--- app.component.ts ---
 printSuperhero(hero: Superhero) {
   console.log(hero); // print the received event object.
 }
```

Let's create a Superhero data type for the SuperheroProfile component to help define a strict type to the output object (see Listing 4-20).

Listing 4-20. A Type Representing Output

```
--- superhero-profile.component.ts ---

// Create a type representing superhero
export type Superhero = {
 name: string;
 firstAppearance: number;
 livesIn: string;

}
```

Next, let's create an event emitter and emit the object when the user clicks a button in the component. The event emitter is decorated with Output. In Listing 4-21, the event emitter and Output are imported from @angular/core.

Listing 4-21. Create an Event Emitter and Decorate It

```
import { Component, OnInit, Input, OnChanges, SimpleChanges, Output,
EventEmitter } from '@angular/core';

export class SuperheroProfileComponent implements OnInit, OnChanges {
 @Input() name: string;
 @Input("lives-in") livesIn: string;
 @Output() flyWithSuperhero = new EventEmitter<Superhero>();
 // … rest of the component
}
```

The EventEmitter instance is of a generic type, Superhero. Hence, this event is strictly typed to emit the Superhero type. With the click of a button, the Superhero type object is emitted.

Listing 4-22. Emit the on click Event of the Button in the Component

```
--- superhero-profile.component.html ---
<button (click)="returnSuperheroData()"> Fly with a Superhero</button>

--- superhero-profile.component.ts
 returnSuperheroData(){
   let hero = {
     name: this.name,
     livesIn: this.livesIn,
     firstAppearance: this._firstAppearance
   };
   this.flyWithSuperhero.emit(hero);
 }
```

Lifecycle Hooks

A component's lifecycle is managed by the framework (Angular). It creates an instance of the component, updates data as required, and finally, destroys the component. The framework provides the ability to tap into various moments in the lifecycle and perform additional actions. These functions, which are called at various stages in the lifecycle, are known as *hooks*, or *lifecycle hooks*.

Consider the following list of lifecycle hooks. You may define one or more lifecycle hooks in a component. It is based on the need and the use case. Each lifecycle hook has a TypeScript interface that defines the contract and the signature for the lifecycle hook function. Implement the interface on the component class so that it enforces to define the function.

- **ngOnInit()**: Invoked as the component is initialized. It is in addition to constructor. The constructor is meant for simple initializations, such as setting a default value on class variables. Use ngOnInit for more complex tasks, such as invoking a remote API to obtain data for the component. To define the ngOnInit() lifecycle hook, implement the OnInit interface, which is part of @angular/core (see Listing 4-22).

- **ngOnDestory():** Invoked as the component instance is destroyed. Perform cleanup actions in this function. To define the ngOnDestory() lifecycle hook, implement the OnDestroy interface, which is part of @angular/core (see Listing 4-22).

- **ngOnChanges()**: Invoked as and when the values of the input attributes change. This provides control for the developer to perform additional actions if the input values meet certain criteria.

  Exercise caution when using this lifecycle hook. The number of times that this lifecycle hook is invoked is high. In a typical component, data-bound input attributes change often. If an additional action needs to be performed every time it happens, this could affect the application's performance.

  To define the ngOnChanges() lifecycle hook, implement the OnChanges interface, which is part of @angular/core.

- **ngDoCheck()**: Not all changes to the input attributes are caught by the framework. Use ngDoCheck() for a manual check on all input attributes (or the variables of interest)on the component.

  Exercise caution while using this lifecycle hook. This hook is invoked every time a change occurs in the application. Hence, using this lifecycle has a high cost to the application.

- **ngAfterViewInit() and ngAfterViewChecked():** The Angular application is a tree of parent/child components (or views). The ngAfterViewInit()lifecycle hook is called after the child view of the given component is initialized.

  The ngAfterViewChecked() lifecycle hook is called after data has been changed (updated) for the child views or components. This lifecycle hook is invoked in the parent component. Child components may use their own ngOnChanges() or ngDoCheck().

  To define the ngAfterViewInit() or ngAfterViewChecked() lifecycle hooks, implement the AfterViewInit and AfterViewChecked interfaces, respectively. The interfaces are part of @angular/core.

- **ngAfterContentInit() and ngAfterContentChecked():** These lifecycle hooks are in projected content, which is the markup provided between the component's opening and closing tags. Refer to the "An example to showcase projecting content in Angular" section for more information on projected content. The ngAfterContentInit() lifecycle hook is called after the projected content is initialized. The ngAfterContentChecked() lifecycle hook is called after the projected content data has been changed (updated).

  To define the ngAfterContentInit() or ngAfterContentChecked() lifecycle hooks, implement the AfterContentInit and AfterContentChecked interfaces, respectively. The interfaces are part of @angular/core.

Listing 4-23 defines the ngOnInit() and ngOnDestroy() lifecycle hooks.

Listing 4-23. ngOnInit() and ngOnDestory

```
import { Component, OnInit, OnDestroy, } from '@angular/core';

@Component({
  selector: 'app-superhero',
  templateUrl: './superhero.component.html',
  styleUrls: ['./superhero.component.css']
})
export class SuperheroComponent implements OnInit, OnDestroy {
```

```
constructor(private route: ActivatedRoute) {
    // Constructor for basic initialization of variables or assigning a
    default value.
}

ngOnInit() {
    console.log("ngOnInit Called");
    // Perform component initializations like calling an API here.
 }

 ngOnDestroy(){
    console.log("ngOnDestory called");
    // Perform component clean-up here.
  }
}
```

Note   Implementing an interface for a lifecycle hook is a good practice; however, it is not mandatory. We may define the lifecycle hook function without the interface. It will still be invoked by the framework. If you make a mistake with the signature or function name, the IDE and the compiler cannot highlight the error because we have not used an interface.

Conclusion

Angular components are fundamental to the library. In this chapter, we began by providing DOM tree context on a web page. HTML elements organized as a tree were introduced.

Next, I discussed the components and how to create them using Angular CLI. The ng generate command was used to create a component. It listed the files needed for building a component and their purposes.

Next, I elaborated on the various fields and configurations with the components. I explained the @Component TypeScript decorator. The decorator configures HTML templates and CSS style sheets as parameters. The TypeScript class encapsulates the presentation logic written in the TypeScript language.

Then we covered dependency injection and providing a TypeScript class or a service to the component. The component uses and depends on the TypeScript class or a service. A block of reusable code without a view can be encapsulated in the service.

The chapter concluded by discussing how components accept input, and use @ Input decorator, provide output to the environment, and use @Output decorator with an event emitter.

References

Angular documentation on components (`https://angular.io/ api/core/Component#viewproviders`)

Code Craft blog: NgModule.providers vs. Component.providers vs. Component.viewProviders (`https://codecraft.tv/ courses/angular/dependency-injection-and-providers/ ngmodule-providers-vs-component-providers-vs-component- viewproviders/`)

Exercise

Create a component that shows the following information about four dinosaurs. Use a Material Design card component as a container of the component. Show a Like button that increments a counter every time a user clicks it.

Dinosaur 1

Herrerasaurus

A large predator

Herrerasauridae family

Dinosaur 2

Triceratops

An herbivorous dinosaur

Ceratopsidae family

Dinosaur 3

T. rex

Tyrannosaurus rex is abbreviated as T. rex.

Tyrannosauridae family

Dinosaur 4

Plateosaurus

The name means a broad lizard.

Plateosauridae family

Show a picture of the dinosaur.

CHAPTER 5

Angular: Data Binding and Change Detection

A markup language (like HTML) is better suited for building a view. It is declarative and easy to read. As we build web pages in an Angular application, views are built with HTML. Data and logic stay in the TypeScript classes. Traditionally, the JavaScript API (and JQuery) allows you to query and select an HTML element. The JavaScript code might read the value from the selected element or set a value to it. This becomes error prone and convoluted as the application grows in size and complexity.

Angular solves this problem with data binding. Data binding helps bring data in TypeScript code to the view or HTML, and vice versa. This chapter discusses data binding and its approaches. This chapter also covers Angular's change detection strategy. It is a key Angular feature for data binding. Angular's new approach (compared to the AngularJS 1.x digest cycle) is at the heart of better-performing modern Angular applications.

Let's begin with data binding.

Interpolation

Interpolation is a special syntax to show data in an HTML view. By default, Angular templates use the double curly braces ({{ }}) delimiter to embed a variable, an expression, or a value returned by a function among HTML elements. Listing 5-1 and Figure 5-1 show the result of the interpolation sample. It embeds the value of a variable "name" as an <h2> element. A simple addition was interpolated, which evaluates the sum of two numbers and shows the result. Also, a function call shows the value returned from the function.

© Venkata Keerti Kotaru 2020
V. K. Kotaru, *Angular for Material Design*, https://doi.org/10.1007/978-1-4842-5434-9_5

Listing 5-1. Data Binding: Interpolation

```
<!-- Show value of a variable -->
  <h2>{{name}}</h2>

  <!-- Shows sum of two numbers, evaluated -->
  <strong> {{ 1243 + 232 }} </strong>

  <!-- Calls a function and shows the returned value -->
  <div> First appeared in {{getFirstAppearance()}} </div>
```

Figure 5-1. *Result of interpolation sample in Listing 5-1*

The context of data binding is the TypeScript class component. That is, variables and functions are class-level properties and methods on the component (see the variable "name" and the getFirstAppearance() function in Listing 5-1). It is possible that the values of these variables change on the fly. Data binding automatically updates the value of the view in DOM.

Note   We can override the default interpolation delimiter ({{ }}) with a different string value by using the interpolation field on a component decorator.

Property Binding

Property binding allows you to bind a dynamic value to a DOM property. It is easy and natural as we continue to use the HTML element properties that we have always used. For common tasks like enabling or disabling a control, setting a dynamic value for a text field, or setting a dynamic path on an image, you do not need to use any special Angular keywords (see Listing 5-2).

Listing 5-2. Property Binding

```
<!-- disable a dropdown -->
<select type="text" [disabled]="isOptionsDisabled" >
  <option selected>Blue</option>
  <option>Red</option>
</select>

<!-- set a dynamic path on an image -->
<img [src]="imageUrl" />

<!-- set a dynamic value to a text field -->
<input type="text" [value]="textValue">
```

The property is enclosed in square brackets for data binding. That is all it takes to apply property binding. We use the fields defined in the TypeScript class as values. Listing 5-3 has the values that are used: isOptionsDisabled, imageUrl, and textValue. Listing 5-3 defines these variables in the TypeScript file component.

Listing 5-3. TypeScript Class Component with Fields

```
@Component({
  selector: 'app-sample,
  templateUrl: './sample.component.html',
  styleUrls: ['./sample.component.css']
})
```

```
export class SampleComponent
{
          isOptionsDisabled: boolean = true;
         imageUrl: string = "/assets/angular-image.png";
          textValue: string = "welcome";

         constructor() {}
}
```

You can dynamically change the values of these fields. It enables the drop-down on the fly, changes the image, and sets a new value to the text field.

Alternate Syntax for Property Binding

As an alternative to enclosing a property in square brackets, you may prefix the property name with bind-. For example, you may use bind-disabled instead of [disabled]. There is no difference in how it works. It is just a matter of preference. Some developers may feel one way is more readable than the other. Listing 5-4 uses the bind-disabled syntax instead of [disabled].

Listing 5-4. Property Binding with bind-property Name

```
<input type="text" bind-disabled="isTextDisabled" />
```

Note   The "bind-" syntax is not often used. Enclosing a property in square brackets is a popular approach. The alternate syntax is described for information only.

Notice that the direction of data binding is one way. It goes from the component class to the HTML template. As values change in the component, the view is updated. Various events, such as server-side API calls and DOM (Document Object Model) events could cause the values to change. Data binding ensures updating the view.

With property binding, the binding target is an element's DOM properties; not the HTML elements' attributes. Please note that the DOM's objects are different from HTML elements. The latter are created in the HTML web page when it loads. DOM properties are initialized by the HTML elements and attributes. The DOM element properties can change while using the web page.

In many cases, attribute names match property names, but there are exceptions, and Angular property bindings depend on DOM properties.

Consider a colspan example with an attribute on <td> in an HTML table. The property is named colSpan (with an uppercase S). Listing 5-5 shows the results in an error. It attempts to use the attribute name with a lowercase s. Please note that spanTwoCells is a variable defined in the TypeScript class. The value is set to an arbitrary number.

Listing 5-5. Incorrect Usage of an Attribute in Property Binding

```
<td [colspan]="spanTwoCells">2.b</td>
```

Note the following error.

```
compiler.js:2427 Uncaught Error: Template parse errors:
Can't bind to 'colspan' since it isn't a known property of 'td'.
```

To fix the problem, use the property name with an uppercase S.

Listing 5-6. Property Binding with colSpan Property Name

```
<td [colSpan]="spanTwoCells">2.b</td>
```

There could be scenarios in which attribute names need to be used. Use attribute binding to bind an element attribute with a variable. Prefix the attribute name with attr. In Listing 5-7, the attribute name with colspan (lowercase s) does not return an error.

Listing 5-7. Attribute Binding

```
<td [attr.colspan]="spanTwoCells">2.b</td>
```

Class Binding (CSS classes)

Class binding allows you to apply a CSS class on an element on the fly. Typically, CSS classes define the various style aspects of an element, including the font, foreground/ background colors, border styles, and so forth.

Use data binding to apply one or more CSS classes on an element. It also provides the ability to change the CSS class, and hence, change the styles of an element.

When using class binding, we combine all the CSS classes into a single string that is separated by spaces. In Listing 5-8, like property binding, the "class" element property is enclosed in square brackets. A myCssClass variable holds a list of CSS classes to apply on the <div> element.

Listing 5-8. Class Binding Sample

```
<div [class]="myCssClass">
  Welcome to data binding
</div>
```

The declaration of the myCssClass class variable is in Listing 5-9. The show-border and show-bg-color CSS classes are in a single string separated by a space.

Listing 5-9. Class with CSS String on a Variable

```
myCssClass: string = "show-border show-bg-color"
```

We could add more CSS classes or remove an existing CSS class from this string. This would change the look and feel of the element.

Editing a string is convoluted and error prone, however. There is an alternate approach to changing CSS classes on the fly: use boolean variables that can be toggled to turn a CSS class on or off. When true, the CSS class is applied (and vice versa). Listing 5-10 has boolean variables declared in the component class. These values are initialized. The value can change dynamically based on user interaction, service calls, or any other criteria.

Listing 5-10. Boolean Variables that Control to Show or Hide a CSS Class on an Element

```
showBorder: boolean = false;
showBgColor: boolean = true;
applyMargin: boolean = true;
```

In the template, use the [class.class-name] syntax to bind with the boolean variables (see Listing 5-11).

Listing 5-11. Bind Boolean Variables with Class Binding

```
<div [class.show-bg-color]="showBgColor" [class.show-border]="showBorder"
[class.apply-margin]="applyMargin">
  <!-- Content goes here -->
</div>
```

Figure 5-2 shows that when the value of showBorder is false, showBgColor and applyMargin are true.

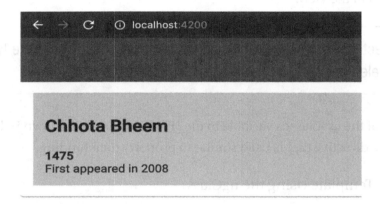

Figure 5-2. *A div with CSS classes applied with class binding*

ngClass Directive

In addition to the class binding described in the previous section, Angular provides an easier and better way to apply a CSS class on the fly. The framework provides an out-of-box directive—ng-class—with ready-made functionality to easily update CSS classes. It allows encapsulating class names in a TypeScript object. In Listing 5-12, the individual class names are put together in an object.

Listing 5-12. An Object Encapsulating CSS Classes for Data Binding

```
cssClasses: {[key: string]: boolean} = {
  'show-border': false,
  'show-bg-color': true,
  'apply-margin': true
}
```

Note the data type for the cssClasses variable, {[key: string]: Boolean}. Let's decode the anonymous TypeScript type defined in this sample. On the outset, it is an object with key/value pairs. The key is a string. The values in Listing 5-13 (show-border, show-bg-color, etc.) use a hyphen in the key name. A typical JSON object does not use a hyphen in the key name or field name. Considering that we are defining a CSS class, it is a general practice to use a hyphen in CSS class names.

We toggle each key (which is nothing but the CSS class name) as true or false. The values can change on the fly. With the data binding applied by the directive, the CSS class is reflected in the view.

Note   A directive in Angular enables adding a custom behavior to the HTML markup and elements. I discuss directives in an upcoming chapter.

The usage of the cssClasses variable in the HTML template is shown in Listing 5-13. It is an attribute directive that is used similar to property data binding.

Listing 5-13. Template Using the ngClass

```
<div [ngClass]="cssClasses">
        <!-- content goes here -->
</div>
```

Style Binding

Style binding allows you to change the style of an element on the fly. While class binding works on CSS classes, which encapsulates multiple CSS styles into a single CSS class, style binding helps with in-line styles (see Listing 5-14).

Listing 5-14. Style Binding

```
<div [style.font-size.pt]="fontSize" [style.color]="fontColor">{{name}}
</div>
```

Style bindings are prefixed with the word *style*. In Listing 5-15, fontSize and fontColor are the fields in the TypeScript class component; the values can be changed on the fly (see Listing 5-15).

Listing 5-15. Styles Values Defined in the Component

```
fontSize: number = 16;
fontColor: string = "red";
```

Note   font-size is followed by a unit as well. In Listing 5-15, it is pt (points). You can use other measurements, like % or px.

It is a common practice to change the values of a style based on a condition. We can do it in the template or in the component file. Listing 5-15 applies red text if the hero's weight is more than 180.

```
<div [style.font-size.pt]="fontSize" [style.color]="heroWeight > 180 ?
'red' : 'black'">{{name}}</div>
```

Figure 5-3 shows the result. The inline styles are applied in the developer tools.

Figure 5-3. *Result of style binding*

ngStyle Directive

Angular provides another easy and better way to apply CSS styles on the fly. Use the ngStyle directive to encapsulate all style values into an object. Listing 5-16 is in the TypeScript class component. The styles object is created with all the necessary inline styles. The values are conditional and can change and update the style in the element.

Listing 5-16. Style Object For Inline Styles

```
styles: {[key: string]: string} = {
  'font-size.pt': this.fontSize,
  'color': this.heroWeight > 180 ? 'red': 'black',
  'font-weight': this.heroWeight > 180 ? 'bold': 'normal',
  'text-decoration': this.heroWeight > 180 ? 'underline': 'none'
}
```

Listing 5-17 is the template using the ngStyles directive.

Listing 5-17. ngStyle Directive for Inline Styles

```
<div [ngStyle]="styles">{{name}}</div>
```

Figure 5-4 shows the result. Refer to the developer tools with the desired styles added inline.

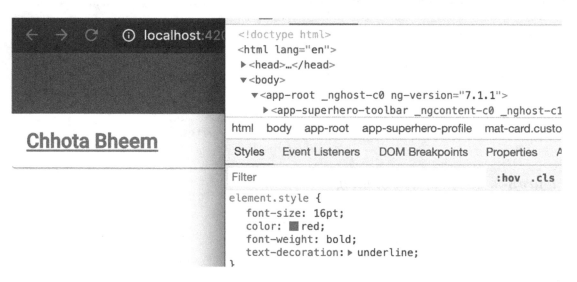

Figure 5-4. *Result with ngStyles*

Event Binding

When a user changes the values of a text field, clicks a button, or submits a form, TypeScript code needs to capture the user's actions and data input. Event binding is used for this. Each action, key stroke, and button click generates events. The direction of the binding is from the view or the HTML template to the TypeScript file component. It goes in the opposite direction of property bindings.

We bind events on an element with a function in the TypeScript file component. The context of the binding remains in the TypeScript class component (like property binding).

Angular captures the event emitted by the element and creates an $event object. Since there are many types of events, raised by various controls, the structure of an $event object differs. Depending on the event, we can capture the necessary information from the object.

In Listing 5-18, there is a text field. We will capture an input event in the text field. To capture the input event, enclose the event name in braces. We can invoke a handler function defined in the TypeScript class component. This function typically processes the event. For this example, we will print the event object.

Listing 5-18. Input Event and Handler

```
--contents in HTML template file---
<input type="text" (input)="handleEvent($event)" />

--TypeScript event handler---
 handleEvent(event) {
   console.log("$event object", event);
   console.log(`event type`, event.type);
   console.log("Value on the event target element", event.target.value);
 }
```

Note   For binding, an event can be enclosed in braces or prefixed with on-eventName. (click)="handlerName()" is the same as on-click="handlerName".

There are three console.log statements printing the event object.

- The first statement prints the complete event object.

- The second statement prints the event type information, which is different for the various types of events that HTML elements can generate.

- The third statement prints the value of the element, which is useful for input controls like text fields, drop-downs, and so forth. On the other hand, elements like buttons do not change values often.

We access the value by using the value field in the target object. The target is on the event object raised by the element.

Figure 5-5 shows the result.

Figure 5-5. *Event handler output for input text field*

The event type is "input" and the value is the data keyed into the text field.

Let's test this handler function on various other events. Listing 5-19 and Figure 5-6 show a drop-down change event.

Listing 5-19. Drop-down with Change Event

```
<select type="text" (change)="handleEvent($event)">
  <option selected>Blue</option>
  <option>Red</option>
</select>
```

Figure 5-6. *Event handler output for drop-down*

The event type is "change" and the value is the selected value in the drop-down. Listing 5-20 and Figure 5-7 show a button click event.

Listing 5-20. Button with Click Event

```
<button (click)="handleEvent($event)">Click me</button>
```

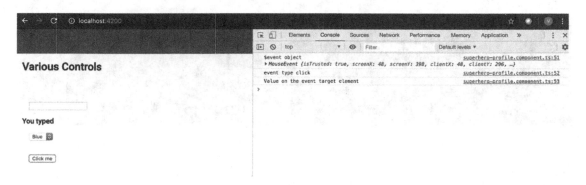

Figure 5-7. *Event handler output for button*

Typically, the event type is "click" and the value of the button is not significant.

The event handler in this example is for demonstration purposes. A typical handler might update the model object associated with the component. The model object may eventually be sent to a server API for insert or update operations in a database.

Property binding and interpolation provide values *to the view* (HTML template) *from the model object* (component fields).

Event binding captures user input in the view or HTML template. It provides values *to the model object* (component fields) *from the view* (HTML template).

So far, data binding has been one way—either toward the view from the model object or toward the model object from the view.

In Listing 5-21, we combine the two and update the value captured in a text field to a variable using the event binding. It shows the value in an element using the property binding.

Listing 5-21. Combine Property Binding and Event Binding

```
<div class="apply-margin">
  <input type="text" (input)="superheroName=$event.target.value;" />
  |
  <strong [innerText]="superheroName"></strong>
</div>
```

We captured the input value of a text field using $event.target.value to a variable called superheroName. We used the innerText property binding to show the input field value in an element. It updates the label when the input event is raised, which is every keystroke. Figure 5-8 shows the result.

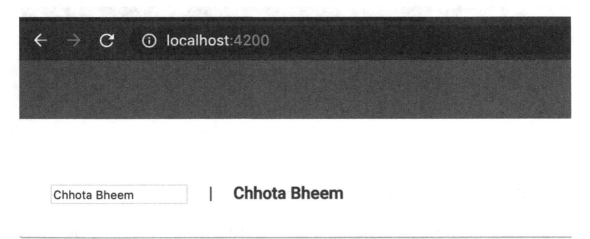

Figure 5-8. *Result of combining property binding with event binding*

Two-Way Data Binding

Two-way data binding simplifies updating model objects as the user changes the view; and updating the view as model objects change; hence, it is called two-way.

For simplifying two-way data binding, Angular provides a directive—ngModel, which comes out of the box with FormsModule in @angular/forms. Follow these next steps to implement two-way data binding.

1. Import the forms module.

    We have been building superhero components as part of the
    superheros Material Design module. Import the forms module in
    it, so that we can use ngModel for two-way data binding. Make the
    changes shown in Listing 5-22 in superheroes-material-design.
    module.ts.

    Notice that we imported FormsModule from @angular/forms.
    Next, we added it to the imports array on the @NgModule
    decorator of the TypeScript class.

Listing 5-22. Import Forms Module for ngModel

```
import { FormsModule } from '@angular/forms';
@NgModule({
 declarations: [
   // For brevit, removed code
 ],
 imports: [
   // For brevit, removed code
   FormsModule
 ],
 })
export class SuperheroesMaterialDesignModule { }
```

2. Use ngModel in the component for two-way data binding. As
    described in the prevoius section, two-way data binding is about
    combining

    a. Property binding, which is used with syntax enclosing the variable in
        square brackets and

    b. Event binding, which is used with syntax enclosing the variable in round
        brackets.

The ngModel directive enables you to combine the two with the directive name in
the middle: [(ngModel)]. It is colloquially referred to as *banana in a box*.

Consider the following changes to the input text field in the Superhero profile component (see Listing 5-23).

Listing 5-23. ngModel for Two-Way Data Binding on a Text Field

```
<input type="text" [(ngModel)]="superheroName"/>
```

Use the superheroName variable (model variable) on a different element in the view with the interpolation or property binding. As changes are made to the text field, the value is reflected in the other element (see Listing 5-24).

Listing 5-24. Show the ngModel value with Interpolation or Property Binding

```
<!-- Interpolation -->
<strong> {{superheroName}} </strong>
```

    OR

```
<!-- property data binding -->
<strong [innerText]="superheroName"></strong>
```

The ngModel directive internally raises an ngModelChange event every time there is a change to the text field. The event sets a value on the model object. Angular adds the directive in the input elements.

Change Detection

So far, you have seen data binding and its approaches. You know that Angular updates the view from the model and vice versa. A model refers to a field or an object in the TypeScript class component. A model is an object representation (of data) for the view.

Change detection plays an important role in data binding. There may be changes to the data due to various reasons, including

- **User interactions::** Edit the fields and perform actions using controls such as buttons, swipes, and so forth.

- **Ajax calls:** XHR and fetch calls that retrieve data from a remote server using RESTful API calls.

- **JavaScript API:** Timeouts, like setTimeout and setInterval.

The change detection process identifies a change and synchronizes the view and model.

Angular uses Zone.js in the change detection process. It is a JavaScript library included with Angular. It provides the execution context for change detection. Facilitated by Zone.js, Angular taps into the browser API to identify a change. As the user interacts with the view, or an Ajax call returns data, the change detection occurs for each component.

As described in Chapter 4, components are organized as a tree. Angular begins with a root component on a primary Angular module, which bootstraps the application. There are child components in it, and the child components have more components. Figure 5-9 is a hypothetical example demonstrating a component tree. It depicts a root component that has three components facilitating page navigation, left navigation, tabs, and a toolbar. The tabs component has two child components to add and show superheroes. The toolbar component has a single header component.

Angular creates a change detector for each component. The change detector is not generic for the whole application, but rather created specifically for each component, which makes the change detection process faster. The change detector identifies changes to the template expression and updates the view and model objects. Figure 5-9 depicts a separate change detector in each component.

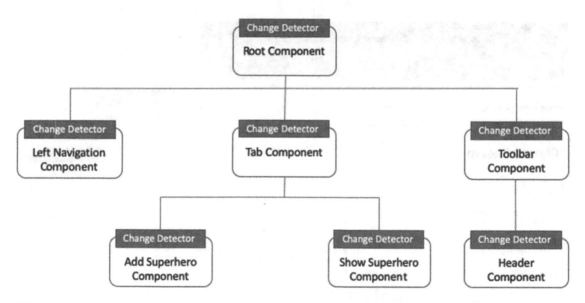

Figure 5-9. *Component tree and change detector with each component*

Angular emphasizes a unidirectional data flow from the parent to the child components through input attributes. When a change is detected, it is propagated to all child components, which is further sent down to the other nodes.

Detecting change is a simple process of comparing a component's previous input with the new input. If a change is identified, in the complete tree under the component, verify and synchronize the template expressions with the model.

Change Detection Strategy

A change detection strategy is applied at the component level. We can specify the strategy as part of a component decorator. It affects the component and its children. Angular provides two change detection strategies: the default and OnPush.

A change could be caused by user interaction, such as the click of a button or API calls. The change is propagated from parent to child components. Often change is identified with an input parameter value change.

In Figure 5-10, AppComponent has two child components: Toolbar and SuperheroProfile. AppComponent includes a form that moves a superhero from one city to another. When the change is identified in AppComponent, and the user clicks the Go button, the change needs to propagate to the SuperheroProfile component so that the city name in the profile is updated.

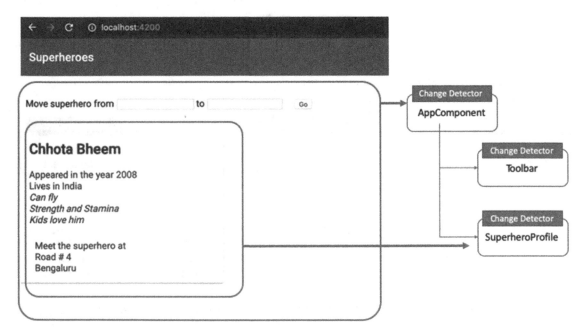

Figure 5-10. *Change detection sample*

Default Change Detection Strategy

As the name suggests, Default Change Detection Strategy is the default strategy on a component and its children. In Figure 5-10, the SuperheroProfile component has the input attributes shown in Listing 5-25. The property data binding and fields in AppComponent are shown in Listing 5-25.

Listing 5-25. Input Attributes on SuperheroProfile Component

```
<app-superhero-profile
[superpowers]="superpowers"
[address]="address"
[name]="name"
[firstAppearance]="year"
[lives-in]="country">
</app-superhero-profile>
```

Listing 5-26 features the name, address, and superpowers attributes declared in the component class.

Listing 5-26. Class Fields That Are Input Attributes to the Superhero Profile Component

```
export class AppComponent {
 title: string = "Superheroes";

 name: string = "Chhota Bheem";
 firstAppearance: number = 2008;

 superpowers: Array<string> = [
   "Can fly",
   "Strength and Stamina",
   "Kids love him"
 ];
```

```
address: AddressType = {
  firstLine: "Road # 4",
  city: "Bengaluru"
};
```

```
// Remaining code removed for brevity
}
```

As mentioned, a separate change detector is generated for each component. When an event that can cause change is raised, it compares input attributes, the previous value, and the new value. If there is a difference, the change is identified and the component template is updated.

For the SuperheroProfile component, each of the input attribute values—superpowers, address, name, firstAppearance, and lives-in—are compared.

With the default change detection strategy, for example, name and firstAppeared is compared between previous and new value. The value types are a string and a number, respectively. If there is a value change, a simple === comparison identifies the change; however, it is different with reference types, for example, an address. If we update the address object, the equals (===) comparison will fail. The reference comparison checks the memory address of the object. We updated the same object, and hence, no change is identified. Here, the address is a mutable type object.

Note   There are also immutable type objects that do not change their value. We need to create a new object at a different memory location to update a value of these types.

Hence, Angular has to compare all the fields in the object. In a default change detection strategy, that's exactly what is done by a component-specific change detector; however, it compares fields if they are part of the template in the superhero profile component. In the previous example, the address field, the city field, and the firstLine variable values are compared.

When the user changes the value in the AppComponent's text field, the new values are propagated to the SuperheroProfile component.

This approach is costly because the code has to compare child objects and fields, but it is effective in identifying the change.

Note   Overall, the Angular's component-specific change detector is efficient and fast compared to the AngularJS 1.x digest cycle performance.

Listing 5-27 explicitly states the default change detection strategy. It is not required to be explicitly specified because it is the default.

Listing 5-27. Default Change Detection Strategy

```
@Component({
  selector: 'app-superhero-profile',
  templateUrl: './superhero-profile.component.html',
  changeDetection: ChangeDetectionStrategy.Default
})
export class SuperheroProfileComponent implements OnInit, OnChanges {
// Removed rest of the code for brevity
```

OnPush Change Detection Strategy

OnPush compares values by reference. It does not compare individual fields on reference types; hence, it is faster than the default approach.

In Listing 5-28, the address object is compared by reference. The two address fields (firstLine and city) are not compared, even though they are part of the template in the SuperheroProfile component.

If the OnPush strategy is used (for better performance), we need to use immutable objects. As mentioned, immutable objects can never be mutated or updated. A new instance is created every time there is a change. As a consequence, a new instance has a new memory location. This ensures that the reference comparison identifies the change, and it is done faster because individual fields do not need to be compared.

Listing 5-28 is the OnPush change detection strategy.

Listing 5-28. OnPush Change Detection Strategy

```
@Component({
 selector: 'app-superhero-profile',
 templateUrl: './superhero-profile.component.html',
 changeDetection: ChangeDetectionStrategy.OnPush
})
export class SuperheroProfileComponent implements OnInit, OnChanges {
// Removed rest of the code for brevity
```

Conclusion

This chapter covered Angular's data binding and change detection features. It began with an explanation of data binding and how it eases web application development.

Interpolation and property binding help show the values of TypeScript component fields in the template. It works toward the template or view, away from the model.

Event binding allows changes made by the user to reflect in model objects. The latter are defined in TypeScript component classes. These are the fields and objects defined with the component.

CSS class binding and style binding combine the power of data binding with web page style features.

Change detection is crucial for performant and fluid web UI applications. Two strategies of change detection were discussed: default and on-push.

Exercise

Create a form that allows the user to input the following information about a dinosaur.

- Dinosaur name

- Description

- Family drop-down menu: the values are Herrerasauridae, Ceratopsidae, Tyrannosauridae, and Plateosauridae

- Submit button

The user should see the dinosaur information in a separate section of the page. The section could be to the side of or below the form. Use interpolation to show the dinosaur values in this section.

Use ngModel and two-way data binding to persist the form's values in a model object.

When the Submit button is clicked, the console logs the values provided by the user.

References

Angular documentation on templates and data binding
(https://angular.io/guide/template-syntax#template-syntax)

Angular University blog on change detection
(https://blog.angular-university.io/how-does-angular-
2-change-detection-really-work/)

CHAPTER 6

Angular: Directives

Angular helps build views that are declarative and use HTML markup. Angular helps reuse most HTML elements and features. It helps extend functionality, making it a powerful framework.

This chapter describes various types of directives. It lists some of Angular's most popular built-in directives. The directives help code conditional logic in the HTML template, iterate through the collections, and apply the styles dynamically.

Directives

Angular provides the ability to augment the HTML template and provide additional features and functionalities. Directives play an important role. There are three categories of directives in Angular.

- **Components**: This type of directive allows you to create custom elements. It is a powerful feature that provides maximum reusability of the Angular application. It is arguably the most widely used feature in Angular. There is an entire chapter dedicated to components in this book.

- **Structural directives**: This type of directive allows you to customize and modify the structure of a view. For example, a list of the superheroes is a view. You may use a directive to iterate through an available list of superheroes and show them in an ordered list. As another example, imagine that the contact information about a superhero is hidden by default. You can show it conditionally when the user requests it.

  Conditionally showing or hiding contact information is a structural change to the superhero view. Iterating through the superhero list and showing the available superheroes in a list is structural.

© Venkata Keerti Kotaru 2020
V. K. Kotaru, *Angular for Material Design*, https://doi.org/10.1007/978-1-4842-5434-9_6

- **Attribute directives**: Attribute directives augment an element's behavior and view. It may add additional functionalities to the element. ngStyle is an example of an attribute directive. A section in this chapter describes this directive.

This chapter discusses the built-in directives in Angular. They are powerful and used often in building web applications.

Using the ng-template Directive in the HTML Template

ng-template is an Angular element. You may use it to refer to a block in an HTML template. It is useful for showing or hiding a section of the component or for using a block of HTML in one or more places in the template.

You may use a *template reference variable* to provide a name for a block of HTML. In Listing 6-1, a component that shows superhero information, a section of contact information is wrapped in ng-template (see lines 8 to 13). A template reference variable is provided to refer to the contents (see #heroContactDetails in line 8).

Note   Refer to the @ViewChild() implementation in Chapter 4 to learn about using a template reference variable in a TypeScript file component.

The block of HTML in lines 8 to 13 do not show when the page loads. It is a block of HTML waiting to be used. Refer to line 5, which has the ngTemplateOutlet structural directive. It refers to heroContactDetails, the template reference variable defined in line 8. Hence, the block of HTML for the superhero contact information is rendered in line 5.

We placed the template between the <hr> elements to highlight that the location template has been rendered. The result is shown in Figure 6-1.

Listing 6-1. Usage on ng-template in the Superhero Component

```
1.    <div class="hero">
2.       <div>
3.        <h2>Chhotta Bheem</h2>
4.        <div>Loves laddu. Grows strong everyday</div>
5.        <hr /><div *ngTemplateOutlet="heroContactDetails"></div> <hr />
6.       </div>
7.    </div>
```

```
8.    <ng-template #heroContactDetails>
9.
10.        <h3>Contact Details</h3>
11.        Email: ChhottaBheem@angularsample.com
12.        Meet him in Dholakpur Villege in India.
13.   </ng-template>
```

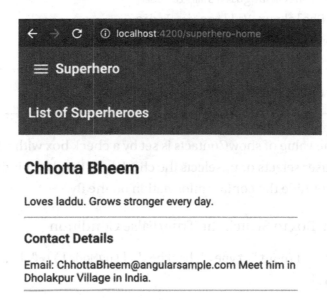

Figure 6-1. *Contact information template*

Using if…else Conditions in the HTML Template

To incorporate conditional logic in the HTML template, we can use the *ngIf directive. It is a structural directive. Imagine that we want to show or hide part of a component conditionally. Let's enhance Listing 6-2. Consider showing the superhero contact information when the user explicitly selects a check box. By default (or when the user unselects the check box), contact information is hidden.

We can achieve this functionality with the *ngIf directive. In line 1 of Listing 6-2, when the showContacts value is true, the contact details template is shown. The contact details template is written in lines 2 to 7.

Listing 6-2. Show Elements When Conditional

```
1. <div *ngIf="showContacts; then contactDetails"></div>
2. <ng-template #contactDetails>
3.   <hr />
4.   <h3>Contact Details</h3>
5.   Email: ChhottaBheem@angularsample.com
6.   Meet him in Dholakpur Villege in India.
7. </ng-template>
```

Note   Structural directives are prefixed with an asterisk (*).

In Listing 6-3, the value of showContacts is set by a check box with ngModel data binding. When the user selects or unselects the check box, the data binding updates *ngIf. We can show or hide the contact information on the fly.

Listing 6-3. Check Box to Switch the True/False Condition

```
<input class="specialInput" type="checkbox" [(ngModel)]="showContacts">
Show contact details
```

Let's improve this sample code by adding an else condition. Show a message that the contact information is hidden when the check box is unselected. Listing 6-4 adds an else condition to the directive. Note the else condition that uses the hiddenText template. The HTML code between lines 8 and 11 is for the message text.

Notice the syntax to use if...else with the *ngIf directive in the first line (see Listing 6-4). We use two template reference variables: the first variable, contactDetails, followed by the "then" keyword, when the condition is true; and the second variable, hiddenText, followed by the "else" keyword, when the condition is false.

Listing 6-4. Else Condition for Superhero Contact Details

```
1. <div *ngIf="showContacts; then contactDetails else hiddenText"></div>
2.   <ng-template #contactDetails>
3.     <hr />
4.     <h3>Contact Details</h3>
```

```
5.      Email: ChhottaBheem@angularsample.com
6.      Meet him in Dholakpur Villege in India.
7.    </ng-template>
8     <ng-template #hiddenText>
9.      <hr />
10.     *Contact information is hidden.
11.   </ng-template>
```

Note   Listing 6-4 uses a Boolean variable, showContacts, which can be true/false. Any conditional statement that returns true/false can be used with *ngIf.

Using the ng-container Directive in the HTML Template

ng-container wraps HTML elements. Typically, HTML elements are wrapped in elements like <div>, <span>, <p>, and so forth; however, applications might use specific styles that are predefined when these elements are used. For example, there could be a global style on a web application that applies certain margins and padding to a div element. This style might interfere when attempting to wrap a set of elements in your component. To address this scenario, you could use ng-container. It does not show as an element in HTML when rendered in a browser; hence, there is no style applied that interferes with the set of elements it encapsulates.

Refer to the first lines of Listing 6-3 and Listing 6-4. A div is used as a placeholder for the conditional logic; either #contactDetails template or #hiddenText template is shown in its place. If the div uses a global style, it is applied here as well. You may use ng-container instead of a div here.

You may simplify the code sample another level by showing the content within the ng-container instead of using a separate template for it. This removes #contactDetails as a separate section (see Listing 6-5).

Listing 6-5. Simplified Conditional Logic

```
1.    <ng-container *ngIf="showContacts else hiddenText">
2.      <hr />
3.      <h3>Contact Details</h3>
```

```
4.        Email: ChhottaBheem@angularsample.com
5.        Meet him in Dholakpur Villege in India.
6.      </ng-container>

7.      <ng-template #hiddenText>
8.          <hr />
9.          *Contact information is hidden.
10.     </ng-template>
```

Note that *ngIf="showContacts; then contactDetails else hiddenText" is simplified to *ngIf="showContacts else hiddenText".

Figure 6-2 shows the result.

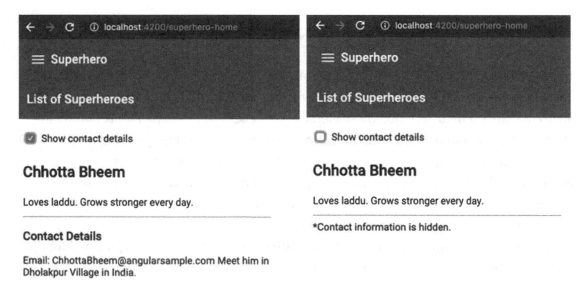

Figure 6-2. *Contact details shown/hidden conditionally*

In Figure 6-3, the ng-container does not show as an element in the rendered HTML.

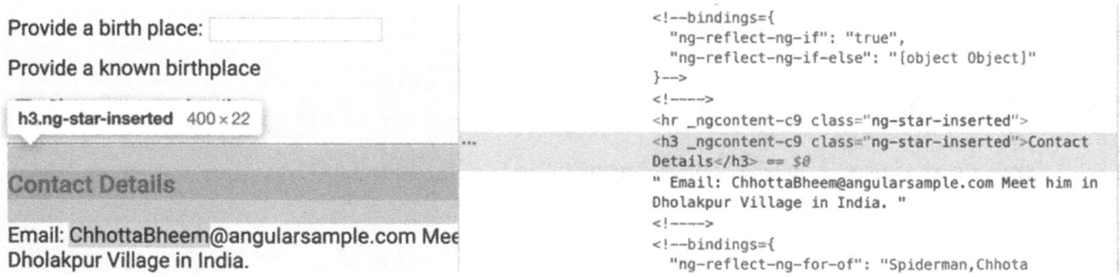

Figure 6-3. *HTML rendered while using ng-container*

Using a Switch Case in the HTML Template

*ngIf is useful for a simple if/else condition. Use the following directives if the condition includes comparing multiple values.

- **ngSwitch**: The variable to be compared with values.

- **ngSwitchCase**: One of the many values to be compared. Typically, a series of ngSwitchCase directives are used.

- **ngSwitchDefault**: The default value when none of the values matches.

To better understand usage, consider birthplace as an input text field. If the user inputs places on Earth, we show an Earthling label. For alien places, we show an Alien label. If it does not match any known values, show a default message to provide a known value. Listing 6-6 uses the ngSwitch, ngSwitchCase, and ngSwitchDefault directives.

Listing 6-6. Switch/Case to Conditionally Verify Multiple Values

```
1.      Provide a birth place: <input type="text" [(ngModel)]="birthplace">
2.    <div [ngSwitch]="birthplace">
3.      <span *ngSwitchCase="'Dholakpur'">Earthling</span>
4.      <span *ngSwitchCase="'Kryptonopolis'">Alien</span>
5.      <span *ngSwitchCase="'Asgard'">Alien</span>
6.      <span *ngSwitchCase="'New York'">Earthling</span>
7.      <span *ngSwitchCase="'Gotham'">Earthling</span>
8.      <span *ngSwitchCase="'Dholakpur'">Earthling</span>
9.      <span *ngSwitchDefault>Provide a known birthplace</span>
10.   </div>
```

Refer to line 2 in Listing 6-7. The ngSwitch directive checks the equality condition in the birthplace variable. If the value provided in the text field (line 1) matches any value provided between lines 3 and 8, the respective value is shown. The ngSwitch variable is compared to the ngSwitchCase value. In the sample, we are using string values. The values Dholakpur, Kryptonopolis, and so forth, are not data bound with a variable.

A default message, "Provide a known birthplace", is shown when none of the values match (see line 9). Figure 6-4 shows the result.

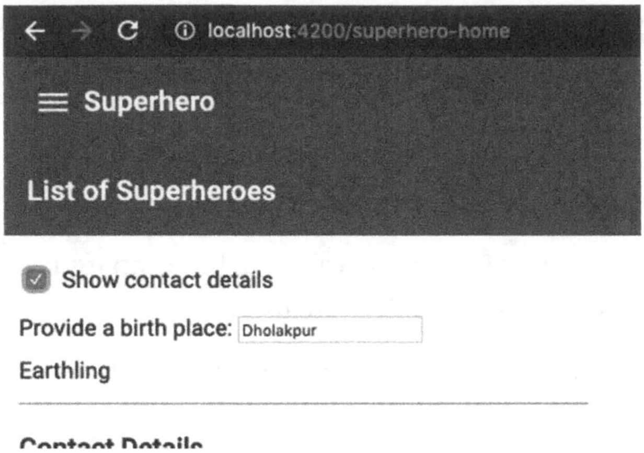

Figure 6-4. *Result of using Switch/Case*

Iterate Through an Array in the HTML Template

Use the *ngForOf structural directive to iterate through an array of elements. Consider an example. There is a list of superheroes to show in the component. We can iterate through the objects to process and show each of them. For simplicity, let's consider using an array of simple strings, as shown in Listing 6-7.

Listing 6-7. List of Superheroes in the TypeScript File Component

```
@Component({ //  Removed code for brevity })
export class HomeComponent implements OnInit {

  superheroes =[
    "Spiderman",
    "Chhota Bheem",
    "Superman",
    "Batman"
  ]

  constructor() { }
  ngOnInit() {  }
}
```

A shorthand form of *ngForOf directive is often used. Listing 6-8 iterates through the superheroes and shows the values in a list. We create a hero variable that represents each hero string with *let hero of superheroes*. Considering that a hero is a simple string, we show the value with interpolation data binding ({{hero}}).

Note   If superheroes is an array of objects, the hero local variable would be an individual object in the array. You may use the hero.fieldName syntax to show a field.

Listing 6-8. Iterate Through Superheroes in HTML Template

```
<div>
  <li *ngFor="let hero of superheroes"> {{hero}} </li>
</div>
```

Figure 6-5 shows the result.

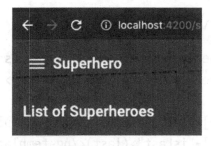

Figure 6-5. *List of superheroes*

Listing 6-9 is the shorthand form of ngFor. This form simplifies the syntax. We can expand the *ngFor shorthand form to ngForOf syntax (see Listing 6-9).

Listing 6-9. ngForOf with Superheroes Array

```
<ng-template ngFor let-hero [ngForOf]="superheroes">
  <li > {{hero}} </li>
</ng-template>
```

Local Variables with ngFor

You may use the following local variables with the directive.

- *index*: Stores a zero-based index number for each iteration

- *first*: Sets to true if it is the first iteration.

- *last*: Sets to true if it is the last iteration.

- *even*: Sets to true if it is an even iteration.

- *odd*: Sets to true if it is an odd iteration.

Listing 6-10 makes use of these variables. In the first line, each local variable is aliased to be used; for example, index is i. Line 2 shows item numbers. We increment by one because it is a zero-based index.

In lines 3 to 6, there is a conditional check if a local variable value is set to true. If yes, we show the string identifying whether it is a first item or a last item, or an even item or an odd item.

Listing 6-10. Show Local Variables

```
1.   <div *ngFor="let hero of superheroes; index as i; first as isFirst;
     last as isLast; even as isEven; odd as isOdd">
2.   {{i+1}}. {{hero}}
3.   <ng-template [ngIf]="isFirst">(first)</ng-template>
4.   <ng-template [ngIf]="isLast">(last)</ng-template>
5.   <ng-template [ngIf]="isEven">(even)</ng-template>
6.   <ng-template [ngIf]="isOdd">(odd)</ng-template>
7.  </div>
```

Note   Note [ngIf]="expressionOrBoolean". The *ngIf="expressionOrBoolean" directive syntax does not show the value as the page loads. With the latter, the template is expected to be referenced and used elsewhere.

Figure 6-6 shows the result.

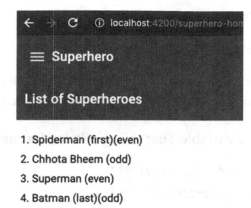

Figure 6-6. *List of superheroes with local variables on ngFor*

Change Styles On the Fly with ngStyle

We use the ngStyle directive to update the styles on an element on the fly. Typically, styles are predefined, and we do not need a directive to update them. However, consider a requirement to update the style as the user chooses to select and unselect values on the screen. We can use ngStyle, an attribute directive for grouping styles, to apply on the element. Figure 6-7 is a use case.

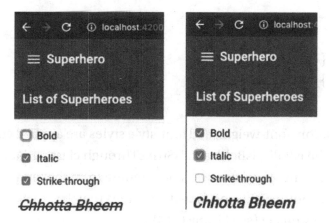

Figure 6-7. *ngStyle for updating styles on the fly*

The options include bold, italic, and strike-through.

Use the ngStyle directive to apply the combined derived styles on the title element, Chhotta Bheem. In Listing 6-11, the titleStyle variable holds the grouped style values.

Listing 6-11. ngStyle Usage

```
<div [ngStyle]="titleStyle">Chhotta Bheem</div>
```

Listing 6-12 groups the styles (in the TypeScript file component) and exposes them to the HTML template with a getter function. The getter function is used in Listing 6-12.

Listing 6-12. titleStyle, a Variable That Groups Styles for the Superhero Title

```
@Component({// removed code for brevity})
export class HomeComponent implements OnInit {
  isItalic = false;
  isBold = false;
  isStrikeThrough = false;

  get titleStyle(){
    return {
      'text-decoration': this.isStrikeThrough ? 'line-through' : 'none',
      'font-weight': this.isBold ? 'bold': 'normal',
      'font-style': this.isItalic ? 'italic': 'normal',
      'font-size': '24px'
    };
  }

  constructor() { }
  ngOnInit() {  }
}
```

The text-decoration, font-weight, and font-style styles are applied conditionally. They are based on the isItalic, isBold, and isStrikeThrough class variables. These variables are used with ngModel two-way data binding from the template HTML file. The text-decoration, font-weight, and font-style names match the CSS style names. They are wrapped in a JSON object (see Listing 6-13).

Listing 6-13. HTML Template with ngStyle

```
1. <div>
2.     <input class="specialInput" type="checkbox" [(ngModel)]="isBold">
       Bold
3. </div>
```

4. `<div>`

5.   `<input class="specialInput" type="checkbox" [(ngModel)]="isItalic">` Italic

6. `</div>`

7. `<div>`

8.   `<input class="specialInput" type="checkbox" [(ngModel)]="isStrikeThrough"> 9.    Strike-through`

10. `</div>`

11. `<div [ngStyle]="titleStyle">Chhotta Bheem</div>`

The ngStyle attribute directive was applied in line 11. When the user changes values, the component rerenders to apply the new styles with the ngStyle directive. It translates styles in the JSON object to the styles on the element. Figure 6-8 shows the directive applying selected CSS styles on the element.

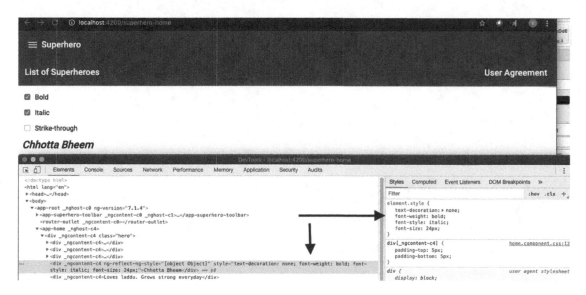

Figure 6-8. *ngStyle modifies styles on the DOM*

Conclusion

This chapter introduced you to directives. It described the types of component directives, structural directives, and attribute directives.

It described the purpose and usage of two Angular elements: ng-template and ng-container.

It lists a few important and often-used directives that help code conditional logic in a template: *ngIf and *ngSwitch with *ngSwitchCase and *ngSwitchDefault.

The chapter also described *ngForOf, which helps you to iterate through arrays.

Exercise

Create a list screen that shows a dinosaur's listing. Also iterate through the following dinosaur family list to show check boxes next to each item. When the user selects a family, show only the dinosaurs that belong to the selected family.

- Abelisauridae

- Noasauridae

- Megalosauridae

Reference

Angular documentation (`https://angular.io/`)

CHAPTER 7

Angular: Services and Dependency Injection

Angular provides features that help encapsulate reusable logic into a service. An Angular service does not have a view. It is the logic and the code that runs in the background (still in the browser).

Along with Angular services, this chapter introduces asynchronous constructs. It begins with simple callback functions in JavaScript, and then describes promises and observables. RxJS is used for observable implementation.

The chapter describes dependency injection in Angular and introduces Angular services, which are powerful and frequently used features.

Asynchronous Function Calls

Asynchronous programming and function calls are powerful and widely used. They help build applications that are fluid and responsive to user interactions. When building a user interface, a long-running process can adversely affect the user experience. It is important that the application is usable and responds to user clicks and keyboard input when a function call takes multiple seconds to finish.

A typical function executes a set of statements and returns a value. The calling function waits for the return value. This is a traditional and synchronous model. This model does not scale for long-running functions; for example, remote service calls (server-side API/HTTP calls) may take multiple seconds to return. As another example, user prompts that need user interaction and decisions could be time-consuming. It could be a prompt to confirm that a record was deleted. Users typically take a second or two to respond by clicking yes or no. In a synchronous model, the application does not run other statements while waiting for user input.

© Venkata Keerti Kotaru 2020
V. K. Kotaru, *Angular for Material Design*, https://doi.org/10.1007/978-1-4842-5434-9_7

Before we get into the details of asynchronous programming in JavaScript and TypeScript, let's discuss function callbacks. This is a widely used paradigm. JavaScript programming (including Angular and TypeScript) extensively uses callbacks, which are a function passed in by the calling function. The *called function* invokes a callback when the task is complete or a result is available. Listing 7-1 is an example of using callback functions. It uses the setTimeout() API, which runs after a prescribed number of milliseconds.

Listing 7-1. setTimeout, an Example of an Asynchronous Function Callback

```
1. console.log("message 1");
2. setTimeout(
3.    function(){ console.log("callback invoked after 3 seconds") }
4.    , 3000);
5. console.log("message 2");
```

Listing 7-1 has three JavaScript statements: lines 1, 2, and 5. The setTimeout function spans three lines: 2, 3, and 4.

We pass a function as a parameter in the setTimeout() function. It is a simple function that prints a console log message. The second parameter to the setTimeout is the number of milliseconds after which the callback function needs to be invoked. We pass 3000 milliseconds/3 seconds. setTimeout, the *called function*, asynchronously invokes a callback after the timeout. The called function does not wait for the timeout to occur. It executes lines 1, 2, and 5 and finishes the task. After three seconds, the callback is asynchronously invoked to print the final console message.

The result prints as follows.

> message 1
>
> message 2
>
> callback invoked after 3 seconds

JavaScript Promises

Function callbacks allow you to run statements out of order, which opens the possibility that one or more lines of code can run when the data is ready. The statements do not need to run in order and block the remaining statements.

Promises are progressive succession in asynchronous programming. A function can return a promise object. The calling function assigns the returned value to a variable. The returned value is not the real value, rather it is a promise (object). It is a promise that the task will be attempted (see Listing 7-2).

Listing 7-2. Promise Returned by a Function Call

```
let promiseRef: Promise = aTimetakingTask(false);
```

Listing 7-3 shows the Promise constructor, which is natively supported by browsers.

Listing 7-3. Promise Constructor

```
Promise(executorCallback(resolve, reject));
```

Whenever a piece of code is run, there are two possibilities: the statements run successfully and the result is obtained, or there is an error and the function fails to run completely. An asynchronous function returning a promise either resolves the promise or rejects it. Listing 7-4 successfully resolves if the input parameter is true; otherwise, the promise fails with a reject.

Listing 7-4. A Function Returning Promise

```
1. aTimetakingTask (input){
2.    return new Promise( (resolve, reject) => {
3.      if(input){
4.        resolve("job well done");
5.      }else{
6.        reject("job failed");
7.      }
8.    })
9. }
```

Line 2 returns the promise. The conditional logic in lines 4 and 6 either resolve or reject the promise.

Going back to the calling function in Listing 7-4 to retrieve the data out of promiseRef, we call a then() function. It expects two callback functions: one for resolve when the asynchronous function has been successful, and another for reject when the asynchronous function fails (see Listing 7-5).

Listing 7-5. Promise Reference Used by the Calling Function

```
1.   let promiseRef: Promise = this. aTimetakingTask (false);
2.   promiseRef.then(
3.       (result) => console.log(result),
4.       (error) => console.log(error)
5.       );
```

Alternatively, we may chain success and error handlers using the catch() function. Listing 7-5 is effectively similar to Listing 7-4. However, the then() function returns a promise. The catch() function is called on the promise returned by then(). In the earlier sample, the success and error handler are both defined on the then() function.

The alternative approach is useful to chain success and error handlers. It handles the errors not only in resolve or reject, but also in the success handler of then(). Consider Listing 7-6. If the error occurs between lines 4 and 7, the catch() function handles the error. Control is passed to line 9 because catch() is working on the promise returned by then().

Listing 7-6. Error Handling with catch()

```
1.    promiseRef
2.      .then(
3.       (result) => {
4.              console.log(result)
5.              /* More lines of code
6.                  making use of data returned by the promise. */
7.      })
8.      .catch(
9.       (error) => console.log(error)
10.     );
```

Figure 7-1 is a visual representation of using promises.

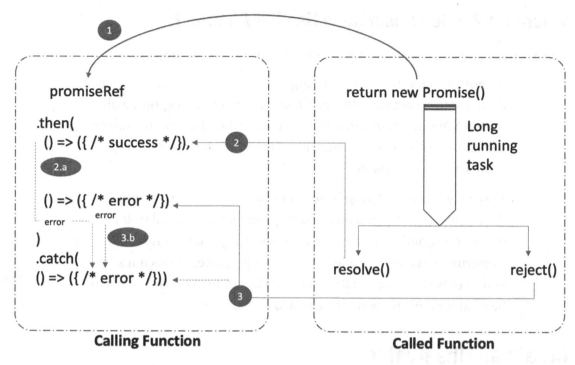

Figure 7-1. *Using promises*

Reactive Programming with RxJS

RxJS (Reactive Extensions for JavaScript) is an open source library that uses reactive programming techniques in JavaScript and TypeScript. Angular extensively uses RxJS.

This section introduces RxJS and provides enough information for you to understand the Angular concepts described in the book. The concepts are vast, and complete coverage is out of the scope of this book.

Observable

Observable provides a collection of values asynchronously, as and when available. RxJS has an implementation of an observable. The observable streams values to the subscriber.

Note   A promise returns a value and the promise is closed. On the other hand, an observable can stream a series of values.

Where Do We See Observable Used in Angular?

The following are two common use cases for an observable in Angular.

- ***Remote Service API***. When an Angular application makes HTTP calls to a remote server, the API could take a long time to respond with results. We can create and return an observable. The calling function subscribes with a callback function. The callback is invoked as the results become available.

- ***User prompts and dialog boxes***. Angular components prompt data from the user, open model dialogs, create alerts, and so forth; the user responds with input or a choice. The parent component subscribes to an observable. The parent component does not stop and freezes the screen or the browser. The application continues to be fluid until the response is returned by the user.

Create an Observable

Import and use the Observable constructor to create an observable. In Listing 7-7, we import Observable from the rxjs module.

Listing 7-7. Create Observable

```
1.  import { Observable } from 'rxjs';
2.  observableSample(input): Observable<string>{
3.    return new Observable((observer) => {
4.      let values = ["value1", "value2", "value3", "value4"];
5.      if(input){
6.        values.map( value => observer.next(value));
7.      }else{
8.        observer.error("error");
9.      }

10.     observer.complete();
11.   });
12.  }
```

The observableSample function returns an observable of generic type String. The Observable constructor in line 3 accepts a callback function as a parameter. The callback has an observer parameter. Every time the observer invokes next(), a value from the collection is returned to the subscriber (see line 6). The observable streams the values.

In Listing 7-8, we continue with the promise code example from the previous section. For simplicity, if the input parameter value for the observableSample() function is false, observer errors out (see line 8).

Finally, in line 10, the observable completes (finished the job) for the subscriber.

In Listing 7-8, line 1 sets a returned Observable reference to a variable. It invokes the subscribe() function on the observable. The subscribe() function has three callback functions: line 3 is a success callback, line 4 is an error callback, and line 5 is when the observable has completed and closed.

Listing 7-8. Observable Subscription

```
1.    let observableRef: Observable<string> = this.observableSample(true);
2.    observableRef.subscribe(
3.        (result) => console.log(result),
4.        (error) => console.log(error),
5.        () => console.log("complete")
```

Angular Services

Services are reusable units of code in an Angular application. The feature could be a value, a function, or a class. Services are separate from components and other directives. They do not have a user interface or a view. The code runs behind it, but still in the browser.

Let's review some use cases for a service in Angular.

- Consider a class that abstracts the logic to obtain superhero data from the components. It could be reused throughout the application, and hence, it is a potential service.

- A function that aggregates and transforms data objects could be a service. We might receive data shown in a component from multiple sources. A service could stitch the data together and provide a structure that a component can instantly show on the screen (with data binding features).

115

We could build services to encapsulate cross-cutting concerns like logging, auditing, and so forth. This reuses the feature across the application.

Create a Service

To create a service with Angular CLI, run the command shown in Listing 7-9.

Listing 7-9. Create a Service with Angular CLI

```
ng g service data-services/superhero-data
```

Note   The first parameter of the Angular CLI command, g, stands for generate. You may alternatively run this command as ng generate service my-service-name.

The command creates a service file under the data-services folder. In the superheroes code sample, data-services is not a module; it is just a folder under which we created the new service. If a module with the same name existed, the service would have been added to the module.

Dependency Injection in Angular

One of the salient features of Angular has been dependency injection. Angular creates and maintains instances of classes and types. This process defines the reusability of an instance.

What is a dependency? A component uses a service for reusable functionality. As discussed, a Superhero List component could use a superhero data service to get a list of superhero objects. Here, the service is a dependency for the component.

Angular uses the metadata defined in the decorators as instructions for dependency injection. Angular with TypeScript uses decorators almost everywhere with modules, components, services, and so forth.

Provider for a Service

Angular, the framework, creates injectors. They are typically application wide. The injector creates and maintains instances. Provider is another object that instructs an injector on how to create and obtain an instance of the service to be reused.

The metadata gives us choices to "provide" a service at any of the following levels. Again, it creates an instance at this level.

- **Root**: For a service provided at root, the instance is created once and is reused throughout the application.

- **Module**: The service instance is reused within the module.

- **Component**: The service instance is specific to the component. Angular creates as many instances of the service as that of the component.

In Figure 7-2, the Service-1 instance is reused throughout the entire application, without reinstantiating. The Service-2 instance is reused in Component-1 and Component-2 of Module A. The Service-3 instance is specific to Component-3.

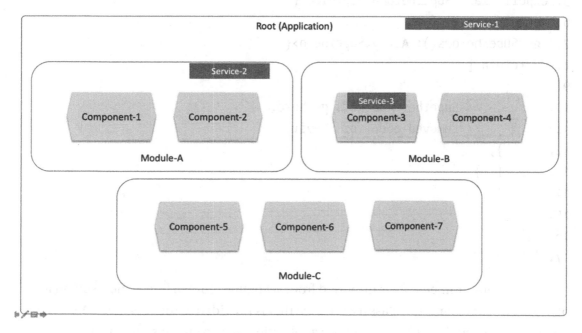

Figure 7-2. *Service provided at various levels*

By default, the Angular CLI command in Listing 7-10 creates and provides the service at the root level. Refer to Listing 7-10 for the new service in which we add a getSuperheroes() function that returns a list of superhero objects.

Note   getSuperheroes() returns a list of superheroes hardcoded in this function. It is for the simplicity of the code sample. A real-world application might invoke an HTTP service and a server-side API that returns a list of superheroes. You learn to do this in Chapter 16.

Listing 7-10. Service Created by Angular CLI

```
1. import { Injectable } from '@angular/core';
2. @Injectable({
3.   providedIn: 'root'
4. })
5. export class SuperheroDataService {
6.   constructor() { }
7.   getSuperheroes(): Array<Superhero>{
8.     return [
9.       {
10.         // Superhero objects go here.
11.         // removed code for brevity
12.       },
13.       { }, {
14.       }
15.     ];
16.   }
17. }
```

The decorator injectable is imported from @angular/core in line 1 and used on top of the class. This marks the class as a service that is provided at the root level. A single instance is reused throughout the entire application. It also enables the injector to not create an instance unnecessarily if the service is not used.

As depicted in Figure 7-3, let's provide the service at various levels. To inject the service at the module level, consider removing providedIn: 'root' and doing so in the superheroes Material Design module in the @NgModule() decorator. Consider Listing 7-11 and note the providers array in line 10. With this change, the service is available at the module level.

Listing 7-11. Provide at the Module Level

```
import { SuperheroDataService } from '../data-services/superhero-data.
service';
```

```
1. @NgModule({
2.   declarations: [
3.     // Removed code for brevity
4.   ],
5.   imports: [
6.   ],
7.   exports: [
8.   ],
9.   providers:[
10.     SuperheroDataService,
11.   ],
12.   entryComponents: [
13. // removed code for brevity
14.   ]
15. })
16. export class SuperheroesMaterialDesignModule { }
```

We may inject the service at the component level. Consider including it in the @component decorator for the component (see line 7 in Listing 7-11).

Whichever level the component has been provided, it needs to be injected into a component or another service. In Listing 7-12, it is injected into the constructor so that a reference is available for the component to use. At this point, the service is a dependency for the component.

We use the service reference in line 14 by calling the getSuperheroes() function.

Listing 7-12. Provide Service at the Component Level

```
1. import { Component, OnInit, ViewChild } from '@angular/core';
2. import { SuperheroDataService } from 'src/app/data-services/superhero-
   data.service';

3. @Component({
4.   selector: 'app-superhero-new-list',
```

```
5.  templateUrl: './superhero-new-list.component.html',
6.  styleUrls: ['./superhero-new-list.component.css'],
7.  providers: [SuperheroDataService]
8.  })
9.  export class SuperheroNewListComponent implements OnInit {
10.   private heroes: Array<Superhero>;

11.   constructor(private bottomsheet: MatBottomSheet,
12.     private heroData: SuperheroDataService) { }

13.   ngOnInit() {
14.     this.heroes = this.heroData.getSuperheroes();
15.   }
16. }
```

If we remove providedIn at all levels in the application, it results in the error seen in Figure 7-3.

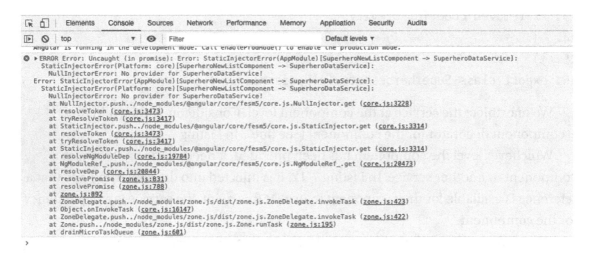

Figure 7-3. *Removing a provider results in an error*

Typically, data is retrieved from a remote service, which is a time-consuming task. Hence, we return an observable. For simplicity, we return the hard-coded data wrapped in an observable. Listing 7-13 returns superhero data from the getSuperheroes() service function through an observable.

Listing 7-13. Return Observable from the Service

```
getSuperheroes(): Observable<Array<Superhero>>{
  return new Observable<Array<Superhero>>( observer => {
    observer.next([
      {
        name: "Chhotta Bheem",
        email: "ChhottaBheem@angularsample.com",
        details: "A hero in Dholakpur village",
        country: "India",
        cardImage: "/assets/chhottabheem.png",
        specialPowers: ["a very strong boy!"],
        favFood: ["Laddu"]
      },
      {
        // removed code for brevity
      },
      {
      }
    ]);
    observer.complete();
  })
}
```

The return type function is updated to Observable<Array<Superhero>>. A new Observable object is created and returned. The hard-coded data is successfully sent to the subscriber with the next() function.

Listing 7-14 uses this data by assigning it to a class variable in ngOnInit(). The "heroes" class variable is used in the HTML template, so that the result is shown in the component.

Listing 7-14. Component Uses the Data from the Observable

```
ngOnInit() {
  this.heroData
    .getSuperheroes()
    .subscribe( data => this.heroes = data);

}
```

An Example to Differentiate "Providing" at the Module Level vs. the Component Level

Let's use an example to better understand the difference by creating a counter TypeScript class to maintain a hit count for a component or a page. It is a simple class with a class field to maintain the counter. We can increment the value as we go (see Listing 7-15).

Listing 7-15. A Counter Implementation

```
Import { Injectable } from '@angular/core';

@Injectable()
export default class HitCounter {
    private _counter: number;

    constructor() {
        this._counter = 0;
    }

    // It's a getter on the class. Notice there is no setter, that means the class
    // controls changing the private variable _counter.
    // We cannot set counter value from outside the class.
    get counter(): number {
        return this._counter;
    }

    incrementCounter() {
        this._counter += 1;
    }
}
```

We will begin by providing the counter service at the module level. An instance of the class is created at the module level. The same counter value will be used by all the components in the module (see Listing 7-16).

Listing 7-16. Hit Counter Provided at the Module Level

```
import HitCounter from './utilities/hit-counter';

@NgModule({
 /* For brevity removed unrelated blocks of code */
 exports: [
 ],
 providers: [HitCounter]
})
export class SuperheroesMaterialDesignModule { }
```

We will use the HitCounter component in the SuperheroProfileComponent component (see Listing 7-17). We inject HitCounter in the constructor.

Listing 7-17. Counter Injected into the Component

```
import HitCounter from "../utilities/hit-counter.service"

@Component({
 selector: 'app-superhero-profile',
 templateUrl: './superhero-profile.component.html',
 styleUrls: ['./superhero-profile.component.css'],
})
export class SuperheroProfileComponent implements OnInit {
 constructor(public hitCounter: HitCounter) {
 }
}
```

We show the value of the counter in the template (see Listing 7-18). The double curly braces syntax is interpolation data binding. It shows the value of the variable in the component. Also notice (click)="incrementCounter()" on the button. It calls the incrementCounter function in the TypeScript class component.

Listing 7-18. Template with Counter Values

```
<mat-card class="custom-style">
  <div>Superhero profile.</div>
  <button (click)="incrementCounter()">Increment Counter</button>

  <div>You have visited {{hitCounter.counter}} times.</div>
</mat-card>
```

When the user clicks the Increment Counter button, the function shown in Listing 7-19 is invoked. It is defined in the component class. In turn, it invokes the function on the HitCounter service class instance, which increments the private variable.

Listing 7-19. Increment Counter on the Click of a Button

```
incrementCounter(){
  this.hitCounter.incrementCounter()
}
```

Let's create two instances of SuperheroProfile components on a page. When the user clicks the button in one component, it updates the value for the second component as well. Remember, the hit counter is provided at the module level. One instance is shared for both components (see Figure 7-4).

Figure 7-4. *Clicking the Increment Counter button anywhere, the first or second instance of the component will increment both the values*

Provide the TypeScript class at the component level (see Listing 7-20). With this change, an instance of HitCounter is maintained at each component level.

Listing 7-20. Provided at the Component Level

```
@Component({
  selector: 'app-superhero-profile',
  templateUrl: './superhero-profile.component.html',
  styleUrls: ['./superhero-profile.component.css'],
  providers: [HitCounter]
})
export class SuperheroProfileComponent {
}
```

Figure 7-5 shows how the behavior of the component changes. There is a different counter value maintained for each instance of the component. The counter value is shown in Figure 7-5.

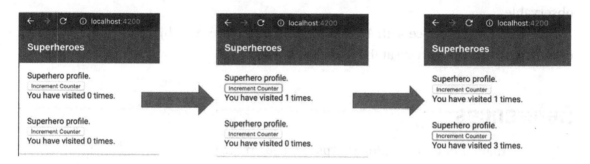

Figure 7-5. *HitCounter provided at the component level*

The injected instance is used by all the child components in the tree. The state is maintained for all SuperheroProfile child components.

Conclusion

Angular services are one of the building blocks of an Angular application. Angular services help bring reusability to an Angular application and abstract complex functionalities from rest of the application.

Angular services extensively use the dependency injection, which is a powerful and highly used feature in the framework. The feature helps abstract object creation logic and extensively reuses service instances.

This chapter introduced asynchronous programming constructs, and described callbacks, promises, and observables (with the help of RxJS library). It also explained how to create a service with Angular CLI and the various possibilities of providing a service at the root, module, or component level.

The chapter used an asynchronous, reactive, programming construct observable with the service to obtain superhero data for a component.

Exercise

Create a new data service for the dinosaur data. Use Angular CLI to create the service. Update the components showing the dinosaur data; use the newly created service by injecting into it. Provide this service at the module level.

Ensure that the dinosaur data is returned asynchronously with a promise or an observable.

Create a logger service with Angular CLI that logs the given object information to the console. Provide this service at the root level.

References

Angular documentation (`https://angular.io/`)

RxJS documentation (`https://rxjs-dev.firebaseapp.com/guide/observable`)

Documentation on promises (`https://developer.mozilla.org/en-US/docs/Web/JavaScript/Reference/Global_Objects/Promise`)

Article: "JavaScript promises, mastering the asynchronous" (`www.codingame.com/playgrounds/347/javascript-promises-mastering-the-asynchronous/the-catch-method`)

CHAPTER 8

Material Design: User Input

One of the important aspects of an application is accepting user input. Users key in data through controls like text fields, single select or multiselect drop-downs, radio buttons, date controls, and so forth. The Angular Material library provides many such ready-made components that confine to Material Design guidelines.

This chapter explains how to use input fields for accepting user input. We begin with the design aspects of input elements. We discuss using text field and text area controls that confine to Material Design guidelines. Next, we cover using Material Design drop-downs, which are both single select and multiselect. We conclude by talking about chips, a Material Design component for multiselect drop-downs that can add values on the fly.

Material Input Elements

Material Design aesthetics define input elements like the text field, text area, drop-downs, and so forth, with the characteristics shown in Figure 8-1. The text field is an example.

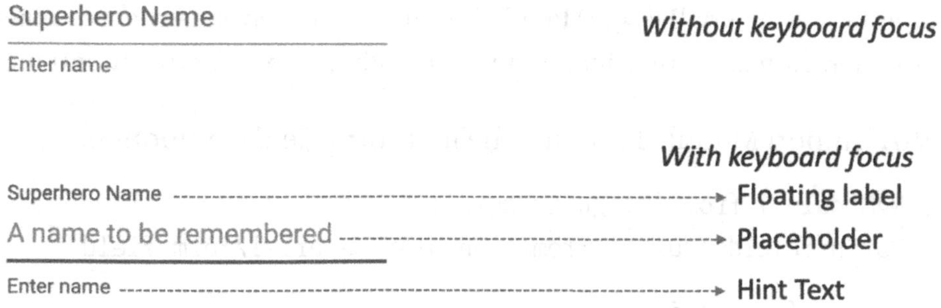

Figure 8-1. *Sample Material Design input element*

V. K. Kotaru, *Angular for Material Design*, https://doi.org/10.1007/978-1-4842-5434-9_8

Notice that the text field is underlined. The behavior of the control is such that underlining is emphasized as the user focuses the cursor on the text field. The floating label shows the title of the text field. It moves away as the user focuses the cursor on the text field. The placeholder text shows in its place until the user types a value into the text field.

Material Design Form Fields

The Angular Material library provides the mat-form-field component, which is typically used to enclose the following controls.

- Text field

- Text area

- Drop-down

- Chip input (used for selecting multiple items for an input field)

On these controls, mat-form-field encapsulates the appearance, floating labels, hint text, and placeholders.

Note   The Angular Material library components and directives that are provided out of the box are prefixed with mat. We can identify Material components easily with this naming convention.

To use mat-form-field, import MatFormFieldModule from material/form-field in @ angular monorepo. In the code sample we created in Chapter 1, notice that we created a separate module for Material Design components. The TypeScript class module was named SuperheroesMaterialDesignModule (located in src/app/superheroes-material-design/superheroes-material-design.module.ts). Listing 8-1 x is for the import module.

Listing 8-1. Import Module for Using the mat-form-field Component

```
import { NgModule } from '@angular/core';
import { MatFormFieldModule } from '@angular/material/form-field'

// Removed code for brevity
```

```
@NgModule({
 declarations: [
// Removed code for brevity

 ],
 imports: [
   BrowserAnimationsModule,
   MatFormFieldModule
 ],
  exports: [
    CreateSuperheroComponent
  ],

// Removed code for brevity
})
export class SuperheroesMaterialDesignModule { }
```

Note the exports array with createSuperheroComponent. We use the newly generated component in the main module (named AppModule); hence, it needs to be exported.

To use the component, add it to the AppComponent template file. This is temporary. Eventually, we will be able to use multiple components on different URLs in the application. See Listing 8-2.

Listing 8-2. Using the Create Superhero Component in the Main Module

```
--- app.component.html ---
<app-create-superhero></app-create-superhero>
```

Appearance

Appearance is an input attribute. The component provides the following options (also see Figure 8-2).

- legacy

- standard

- fill

- outline

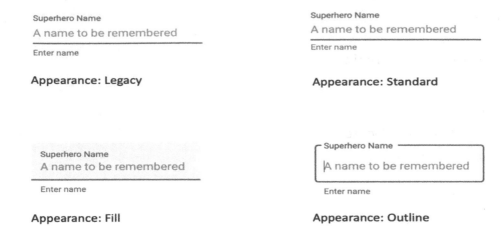

Figure 8-2. *Text field with various appearances*

Listing 8-3 is for the appearance input attribute in mat-form-field.

Listing 8-3. mat-form-field with the appearance Attribute

```
<mat-form-field appearance="legacy">
        <!-- code for input field goes here -->
</mat-form-field>
```

Text Field Within mat-form-field

You saw the look and feel and behavior of mat-form-field with a text field in Figure 8-1 and Figure 8-2. Let's review creating a Material Design text field.

Angular provides the matInput directive out of the box. This directive is used in the <input /> element (text field). All Angular Material components and directives are prefixed with mat.

To use the directive, you need to import the module that the directive is available in. Listing 8-4 imports matInputModule from @angular material's monorepo. It expands what we saw in Listing 8-3.

Listing 8-4. Import MatInputModule

```
import { NgModule } from '@angular/core';
import { MatFormFieldModule } from '@angular/material/form-field'
import { MatInputModule } from '@angular/material/input';
// Removed code for brevity
```

```
@NgModule({
 declarations: [
  // Removed code for brevity

 ],
 imports: [
   MatInputModule,
   MatFormFieldModule,
// Removed code for brevity

 ],// Removed code for brevity
})
export class SuperheroesMaterialDesignModule { }
```

Superheroes Code Sample

Before we start using the directive and other components, consider enhancing the superheroes code sample. Since we are working with user input in this chapter, let's create a component that accepts superhero data as input. Let's call it the create-superhero component. Use the command in Listing 8-5 to create the component.

Listing 8-5. Generate the create-superhero Component

```
ng g c superheroes-material-design/create-superhero
```

Here we are using Angular CLI to generate a new component; hence, the ng command. Use the g flag to generate it. The c flag refers to a component. The component is under the superheroes-material-design module and folder; hence, the create-superhero component name is prefixed with superheroes-material-design/.

The Angular CLI command in Listing 8-5 is abbreviated. For clarity, if you prefer to use the complete command, consider the following:

ng generate component superheroes-material-design/create-superhero

---

The command creates a new component with the files shown in Figure 8-3.

Figure 8-3. *The Angular CLI generated create-superhero component*

Now that we have created a new component for a *superhero input form,* and the directive is available to use, edit the create-superhero.component.html template file. Add the matInput directive in the <input /> element. Remember, mat-form-field encloses input elements and form fields. Include the input element as part of the mat-form-field component (see Listing 8-6 and Figure 8-4). It gives the Material Design look and feel and adds an underline, which is emphasized on focus (keyboard cursor). The placeholder text shows until the user types.

Listing 8-6. Use matInput to Create the Material Text Field

```
<div>
 <mat-form-field appearance="standard">
   <input type="text" matInput placeholder="A name to be remembered" />
 </mat-form-field>
</div>
```

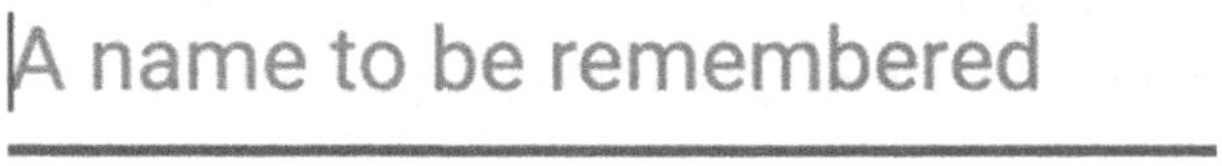

A name to be remembered

Figure 8-4. *Material text field*

Floating Label

Within mat-form-field, use mat-label to add a title or a floating label. It is part of MatFormFieldModule, which is already imported. By default, a floating label shows within the text field and moves away as the user focuses the keyboard cursor to type text (see Listing 8-7 and Figure 8-5).

Listing 8-7. Material Text Field with the Float Label

```
<mat-form-field floatLabel="float" appearance="standard">
  <mat-label>Superhero Name</mat-label>
  <input type="text" required matInput placeholder="A name to be
  remembered" />
</mat-form-field>
```

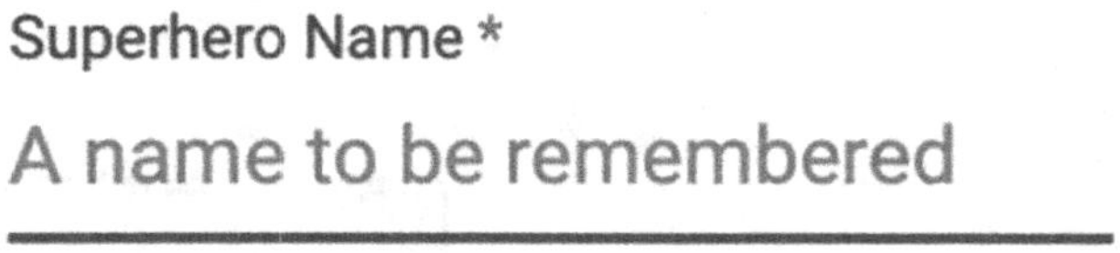

Superhero Name *

A name to be remembered

_____

Figure 8-5. *Material text field with float label*

Note the floatLabel input attribute. In Listing 8-7, it has a default value float. You may change it to one of the following.

- **always** to float on top of the text field, even when the keyboard cursor is not focused on the text field.

- **none** to never float. It can only be used with the appearance value legacy in mat-form-field.

- **float** is the default value. It floats to the top when the keyboard cursor focuses on the text field.

When the appearance value (in the mat-form-field component) is a legacy, the placeholder text in the input element (text field) substitutes as a floating label. This behavior doesn't apply to other appearances, or standard, fill, and outline. The latter needs an explicit mat-label component that is used for a floating label.

Required Field

Use the required attribute in the input element to mark the required input field. It adds an asterisk to the floating label (see Listing 8-8 and Figure 8-6).

Listing 8-8. Required Input Field

```
<div>
 <!-- Appearance: Outline -->
 <mat-form-field appearance="outline">
   <mat-label>Superhero Name</mat-label>
   <input type="text" matInput required placeholder="A name to be
   remembered"/>
   <mat-hint>Enter name</mat-hint>
 </mat-form-field>
</div>
```

Superhero Name *

Enter name

Superhero Name *

A name to be remembered

Enter name

Figure 8-6. *Required field adds asterisk to floating label*

If you do not wish to show the required field indicator (asterisk), use the hideRequiredMarker input attribute in mat-form-field (see Listing 8-9). The form field is still a required field. You can hide the asterisk if there is a custom implementation to highlight the required fields.

Listing 8-9. Hide Asterisk, Indicating a Required Field

```
<mat-form-field hideRequiredMarker appearance="standard">
   <!-- removed code for brevity -->
   <input type="text" matInput required placeholder="A name to be
   remembered"/>
</mat-form-field>
```

Hint Text

Use the mat-hint component to provide hint text. It is part of MatFormFieldModule, which is already imported. The component has two input attributes.

- **align**: Uses an "end" value to right align the hint text. The default value is start.

- **id**: The unique ID for the hint text.

Note   Optionally, you may use the hintLabel input attribute in mat-form-field instead of using a separate mat-label component; however, you cannot position the label's start or end with this input attribute.

Listing 8-10 is the complete code snippet of a text field. Figure 8-7 shows the hint text and floating label.

Listing 8-10. Input Text Field with Floating Label and Hint Text

```
<div>
 <!-- Appearance: Standard -->
 <mat-form-field appearance="standard">
   <mat-label>Superhero Name</mat-label>
   <input type="text" matInput placeholder="A name to be remembered" />
   <mat-hint>Enter name</mat-hint>
 </mat-form-field>
</div>
```

Note   You may use the matPrefix and matSuffix directives to show a prefix and a suffix. For a currency value, the dollar symbol could prefix the text field.

Input Types with matInput

You have seen using the matInput directive with <input type="text" />. The following are other types that are supported by the directive.

- Date and time–related types

  - date

  - datetime-local

  - month

  - time

  - week

- User data types

  - password

  - email

  - tel

  - url

- Other frequently used types

  - number

  - search

  - color

The following input types are not supported.

- checkbox

- file

- hidden

- image

- radio

- range

- reset

- submit

Note   Even though the matInput directive does not support check boxes, mat-check box, which is an Angular Material component, provides this functionality with Material Design look and feel and behavior. You need to import MatCheckboxModule to use this component.

Text Area Within mat-form-field

You can have a text area with mat-form-field and the matInput directive. In Listing 8-11, the explanation of superhero powers needs more than a single-line text field. You can use textarea for this.

Listing 8-11. Text Area with mat-form-field and matInput

```
<mat-form-field appearance="outline">
  <mat-label>Powers</mat-label>
  <textarea rows="6" matInput></textarea>
  <mat-hint>Explain superhero powers</mat-hint>
</mat-form-field>
```

Figure 8-7 shows the result.

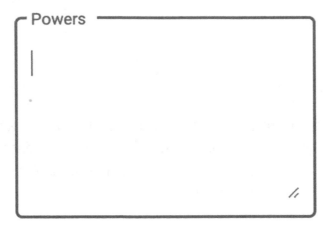

Explain superhero powers

Figure 8-7. *Text area with matInput*

Autosize the Text Area

You can enter more than one line (or rows) of text in a text area. To configure a number of rows, use the "rows" attribute in the <textarea /> element. For example, if we use a value of 5 for the number of rows, textarea adds a scrollbar when the user types the sixth row of text.

It is useful if the text area grows and shrinks as the user types. Use the *cdkTextareaAutosize* directive to add or remove rows, depending on the text. However, it might be inconvenient if the text area starts very small and grows indefinitely. You can set a minimum and maximum number of rows. To do this, use cdkAutosizeMinRows and cdkAutosizeMaxRows, respectively. The text area in Listing 8-12 starts with four rows and grows to a maximum height of ten rows. It adds a scrollbar at the eleventh row.

Listing 8-12. Textarea with cdkTextareaAutosize

```
<div>
  <mat-form-field appearance="outline">
    <mat-label>Powers</mat-label>
    <textarea cdkTextareaAutosize cdkAutosizeMinRows="4"
    cdkAutosizeMaxRows="10" rows="6" matInput></textarea>
    <mat-hint>Explain superhero powers</mat-hint>
  </mat-form-field>
</div>
```

In Figure 8-8, the text area starts with a height of four rows, even though the text is only in two of the rows. It grows to ten rows without a scrollbar.

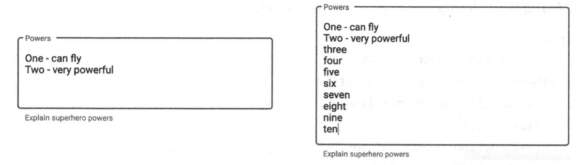

Figure 8-8. *The text area with a minimum of four rows height and a maximum of ten rows*

Material Drop-downs

Form controls for data input commonly select a value from a drop-down. The Angular Material library provides mat-select and mat-option components that confine to the Material Design look and feel. Components are wrapped in mat-form-field (same as the text field).

To begin, import MatSelectModule, which makes the mat-select and mat-option components available in the application (see Listing 8-13).

Listing 8-13. Import Module for Material Design Select Component

```
import { MatSelectModule } from '@angular/material/select';
@NgModule({
  // removed code for brevity
  imports: [
    BrowserAnimationsModule,
    MatSelectModule,
    MatInputModule,
    MatFormFieldModule
  ],
})
export class SuperheroesMaterialDesignModule { }
```

In Listing 8-14, the mat-select component encapsulates all available options. The mat-option component is repeated to show each component.

Listing 8-14. Using mat-select and mat-option

```
<div>
 <!-- Appearance: Outline -->
 <mat-form-field appearance="outline">
   <mat-label>Country</mat-label>
   <mat-select>
     <mat-option>India</mat-option>
     <mat-option>United States</mat-option>
     <mat-option>Outer space</mat-option>
   </mat-select>
 </mat-form-field>
</div>
```

The result is shown in Figure 8-9. Notice that the mat-form-field appearance is set to outline.

Figure 8-9. *Material Design drop-down*

Note the Material Design look and feel and behavior in the drop-down. The "Country" mat-label value shows by default in the drop-down. When the user selects a value, it moves up to a floating label.

Use the value field in the mat-select and mat-option components.

- In the mat-option component, it uniquely identifies an option or a value. Typically, you use an ID for the option (see Listing 8-15).

- In mat-select, notice the two-way data binding with a variable in the component class.

Listing 8-15. Using the value Attribute in a Select Box

```
1. <div>
2. <!-- Appearance: Outline -->
3. <mat-form-field appearance="outline">
4.    <mat-label>Country</mat-label>
5.    <mat-select [(value)]="country">
6.       <mat-option>None</mat-option>
7.       <mat-option value="in">India</mat-option>
8.       <mat-option value="us">United States</mat-option>
9.       <mat-option value="os">Outer Space</mat-option>
10.    </mat-select>
11. </mat-form-field>
12. <strong>Superhero comes from " {{country}} "</strong>
13. </div>
```

Note that a label within a strong element is shown for demonstration purposes (see line 12). The selected value is shown on the label instantly—as soon as the user selects an option on the drop-down. The value attribute on mat-select acts like ng-model, as seen in data binding (see Figure 8-10). The "os" label is the value in mat-option (see line 9).

Superhero comes from " os "

Figure 8-10. *Two-way data binding with a value field*

Note   The None mat-option is without a value. After selecting a value, if the user needs to reset the country, an option without a value could be used. It is useful because the user can't delete a selected value (unlike a text field). We may show one or more options disabled. Add the disabled attribute in mat-option.

Categorize Options

Grouping options can be useful, especially when there are too many options to select from. Use the mat-optgroup component to group options. Use the label attribute in mat-optgroup to label the group.

Consider line 7 and line 11 in Listing 8-16. Note the category title specified in the component. Figure 8-11 shows the result.

Listing 8-16. Group Options

```
1. <div>
2. <!-- Appearance: Outline -->
3. <mat-form-field appearance="outline">
4.   <mat-label>Country</mat-label>
5.   <mat-select placeholder="select country" [(value)]="country">
6.     <mat-option>None</mat-option>
7.     <mat-optgroup label="Earth">
8.       <mat-option value="in">India</mat-option>
9.       <mat-option value="us">United States</mat-option>
10.    </mat-optgroup>
11.    <mat-optgroup label="Outer Space">
12.      <mat-option value="os">Asgard</mat-option>
13.    </mat-optgroup>
14.   </mat-select>
15. </mat-form-field>
16. </div>
```

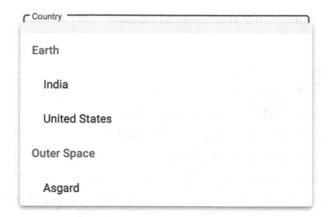

Figure 8-11. *Categorized options*

Multiselect

By default, a drop-down is used to select one item for a field. You may use it for multiselect. While the drop-down is expanded, the component uses check boxes that indicate the selected options (see Figure 8-12). When done (collapsed), it shows all the selected options.

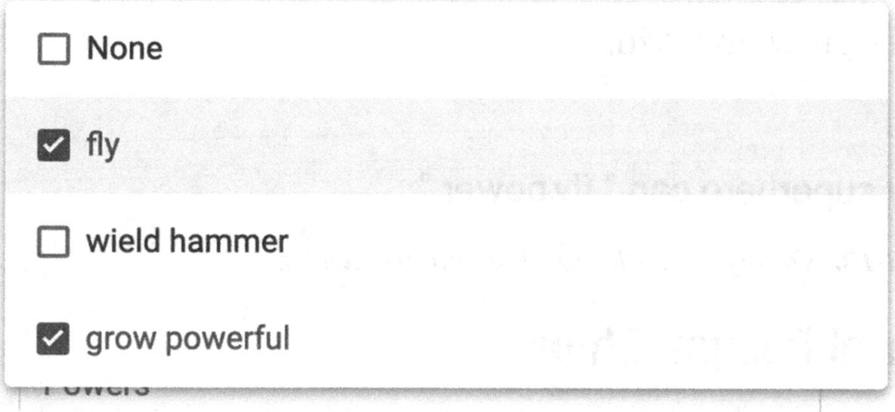

☐ None

☑ fly

☐ wield hammer

☑ grow powerful

Figure 8-12. *Multiselect drop-down*

To use multiselect add the "multiple" attribute on the mat-select element (see line 5 in Listing 8-17).

Listing 8-17. mat-select with Multiselect Enabled

```
1. <div>
2.   <!-- Appearance: Outline -->
3.   <mat-form-field appearance="outline">
4.     <mat-label>Special Powers</mat-label>
5.     <mat-select [(value)]="powers" multiple>
6.       <mat-option>None</mat-option>
7.       <mat-option value="fly">fly</mat-option>
8.       <mat-option value="hammer">wield hammer</mat-option>
9.       <mat-option value="power">grow powerful</mat-option>
10.     </mat-select>
11.   </mat-form-field>
12.   <strong> My superhero can " {{powers}} "</strong>
13. </div>
```

Figure 8-13 shows the result. The value binding captures multiple selected values as a comma separated string.

Figure 8-13. *Value field with multiple options selected*

Material Design: Chips

Chips is an interface for selecting one or more items in a list. It is used similarly to a multiselect drop-down. The chips component allows entering a new value. The presentation of selected items is different. In Figure 8-14, the cross button lets you easily remove a selected item.

Likes to eat

Figure 8-14. *Material Design: Chips*

The chip values are in a text field. A new value can be typed in there.

As with any other Angular Material library component, to use chips, you import the required modules. In Listing 8-18, we need mat-chips-module and mat-icons-module to use chips in the application.

Listing 8-18. Import Chips Modules

```
import { MatChipsModule } from '@angular/material/chips';
import { MatIconModule } from '@angular/material/icon';

@NgModule({
 // Removed code for brevity
 imports: [
   MatChipsModule,
   MatIconModule
 ],)
export class SuperheroesMaterialDesignModule { }
```

Chips are enclosed in mat-form-field, similar to the input element's matInput directive and the mat-select component. Chips are a list of items; hence, they are enclosed in a mat-chip-list directive. Each chip item is rendered by a mat-chip element (see Listing 8-19).

Listing 8-19. Basic Chip List

```
1. <div>
2.     <mat-form-field appearance="standard">
3.       <mat-label>Likes to eat</mat-label>

4.       <mat-chip-list #favFood>
5.         <mat-chip >
6.           Laddu
7.         </mat-chip>
```

```
8.          <mat-chip >
9.            Cheeseburger
10.         </mat-chip>
11.       </mat-chip-list>

12.       <input
13.         [matChipInputFor]="favFood" />
14.       </mat-form-field>

15. </div>
```

Note #favFood. It is a template reference variable. It is discussed in detail in an upcoming chapter. For the moment, know that a chip list is identified with a template-level variable named favFood. We use the matChipInputFor directive in an input element, and map the variable to the element. Figure 8-15 shows the result. It is basic compared to the original chips shown in Figure 8-14.

Likes to eat

Laddu   Cheeseburger

Figure 8-15. *Basic chip list*

Add Items to a Chip List

In Listing 8-20, the two values (Laddu and Cheeseburger) are coded in the HTML template. In the sample, they are static, and the list does not change. See the lines between 4 and 11.

You may use a dynamic list in an array in the TypeScript class component (see Listing 8-20). For simplicity, the array variable in the TypeScript file component has hard-coded values. However, in a real scenario, you might retrieve these values from a remote service.

Listing 8-20. A Dynamic Chip List

```
--- create-superhero.component.ts ---
1. items: Array<string> = ["Laddu", "Cheeseburger", "Pizza" ];

--- create-superhero.component.html ---
1.      <mat-form-field appearance="standard">
2.        <mat-label>Likes to eat</mat-label>

3.        <mat-chip-list #favFood>
4.          <mat-chip *ngFor="let item of items">
5.            {{item}}
6.          </mat-chip>
7.        </mat-chip-list>

8.        <input
9.          [matChipInputFor]="favFood"
10.          (matChipInputTokenEnd)="add($event)"
11.          matChipInputAddOnBlur />

12.      </mat-form-field>
```

Note line 4 in the component's HTML file. Use the *ngFor directive in mat-chip to iterate through the array. For each value in the array, a mat-chip element is created. We look at the ngFor directive in another chapter. For the moment, understand that it is a for-loop in the HTML template.

As described earlier, a chip list allows you to add custom dynamic values to a list. The user may enter a new value in the text field. It will be added to the chip list. To do so, add a *matChipInputTokenEnd* event handler to the text field. Note line 10 in Listing 8-20. The event is raised as the user adds a new value to the list. In other words, it is triggered when the user submits or presses Enter in a text field.

Use the *matChipInputTokenEnd* event to capture a new value entered by the user. Create a new chip by adding it to the item array. (In the preceding example, the array variable is named *items*). Listing 8-21 pushes the new item added by the user into an array object.

Listing 8-21. Capture the Event Value from matChipInputTokenEnd

```
--- create-superhero.component.ts ---
  addItem(event){
    this.items.push(event.value);
  }
```

An additional input attribute, *matChipInputAddOnBlur*, triggers the *matChipInputTokenEnd* event on a blur (losing focus), in addition to pressing the Enter key.

Remove Items from a Chip List

So far, we have created chips that do not have a remove option. Revisit Figure 8-14 and Figure 8-15. The former comes with a remove icon, which isn't shown in Figure 8-15. Without this option, the user cannot remove an item that was accidentally selected.

Let's add the remove option to the chips. To show a cancel button, add a cancel icon to each chip (see Listing 8-22). Note line 4 in the HTML template file. It adds the cancel icon. It is enclosed in the mat-chip component; hence, the Cancel button becomes part of the chip. Remember, we already imported MatIconModule.

Listing 8-22. mat-icon for Cancel Added

```
--- create-superhero.component.ts ---
1.  removeHandler(item: string){
2.    this.items.splice(this.items.indexOf(item), 1);
3.  }
```

```
--- create-superhero.component.html ---
1.  <mat-chip-list #favFood>
2.    <mat-chip *ngFor="let item of items" (removed)="removeHandler(item)">
3.      {{item}}
4.      <mat-icon matChipRemove>cancel</mat-icon>
5.    </mat-chip>
6.  </mat-chip-list>
```

In the HTML template, the "removed" event handler is added to mat-chip (line 2). We use it to handle remove actions. It raises MatChipEvent. However, in the example, we pass the selected chip item as the value. Note the removeHandler code in the TypeScript file component. Line 2 in this file splices the items array (which was used to show the chip list). In other words, it removes the item from the list.

With this addition of code, we achieve the intended result, as shown in Figure 8-15.

Note   We can mark some or all of the chips as removable. By default, all chips are removable. We can add a removable field in mat-chip and set the value as false to disable the ability to remove a chip.

Conclusion

The chapter covered the basics of accepting user input text and values. It explained how to use Angular Material library components. The chapter began with the look and feel and behavior of a Material Design input field. This section included floating labels, hint text, placeholder text, and so forth.

The chapter also introduced mat-form-field, which encapsulates text fields, text areas, drop-downs, and chips. It discussed using textfield and textarea with the matInput directive for providing a Material Design look and feel. Next, it detailed building input fields with Material Design drop-down components, mat-select, and mat-options. It described many features, including multiselect with drop-downs.

The chapter introduced chips and chip lists, which allow dynamic and custom multiselection with values created on the fly. It introduced mat-chip and mat-chiplist components and various input and output attributes and directives to build chips.

Exercise

Build a "create dinosaur" form. Allow the user to provide the following input.

- Dinosaur name: Build a text field with a standard appearance.

- Dinosaur family: Build a drop-down with the following values.

    - Abelisauridae

    - Noasauridae

    - Megalosauridae

- Timeframe: Build a text field and a postfix with Mil-yrs-ago (Millions of years ago)

- Dinosaur description: Build a text area with a minimum of 6 rows and a maximum of 20.

- Continents they lived in: Use a chip list that accepts dynamic values from the user.

Reference

Angular Material documentation (`https://material.angular.io/`)

CHAPTER 9

Angular: Building Forms

Traditionally, forms are an important aspect of a web application. Data is input through a form, which is validated and saved in the back end. Angular has a sophisticated approach to handling forms and user data. The framework provides two choices for creating forms.

- **Template-driven forms**: Simple and easy to build
- **Reactive forms**: Model driven and useful for creating complex forms.

Template-Driven Forms

Template-driven forms address many typical use cases for handling user data. They are easy to build, asynchronous, and the data is mutable (changes to the form to update the model object or the TypeScript class field).

Note Mutable JavaScript objects allow you to update the value after it was created. It is good practice to use immutable objects that do not allow an object value to change. For reliability, especially when comparing objects, using immutable JavaScript objects is advised. They create a new object for each change.

Getting Started with Template-Driven Forms

In the Superhero application, SuperheroesMaterialDesignModule's components have Angular Material dependencies. To implement template-driven forms, we use directives and providers that are defined in an Angular module called FormsModule.

To get started, import FormsModule to SuperheroesMaterialDesignModule. In Listing 9-1, note lines 1 and 5.

© Venkata Keerti Kotaru 2020
V. K. Kotaru, *Angular for Material Design*, https://doi.org/10.1007/978-1-4842-5434-9_9

Listing 9-1. Import Forms Module

```
1. import { FormsModule } from '@angular/forms';

2. @NgModule({
3. // Removed code for brevity
4. imports: [
5.     FormsModule
6. ],
7. exports: [
8.    // Removed code for brevity
9. ],
10. providers:[]
11. })
12. export class SuperheroesMaterialDesignModule { }
```

Approach to Building Forms

In the sample application, we built a component (named app-create-superhero) to create a superhero. Consider creating a model object that represents the create superhero form. This is a TypeScript object representing a superhero form. We use two-way data binding and the ngModel directive to bind each control in the template file with the TypeScript model object. Figure 9-1 visualizes the model object representing the form.

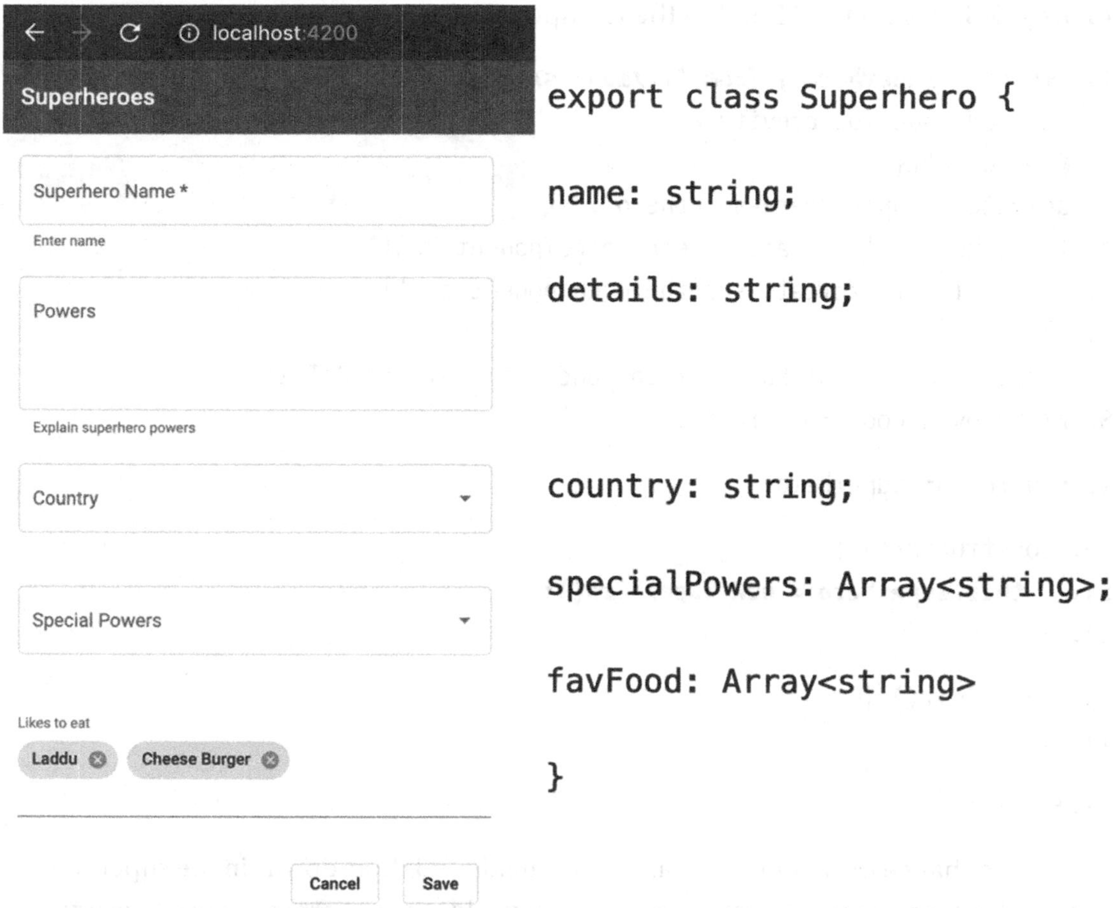

```
export class Superhero {

name: string;

details: string;

country: string;

specialPowers: Array<string>;

favFood: Array<string>

}
```

Figure 9-1. *Model representing the form*

To create a TypeScript class (that will be used as a model) with Angular CLI, use the command in Listing 9-2.

Listing 9-2. Create TypeScript Class Used as a Model

```
ng g class superheroes-material-design/models/superhero
```

In the superhero class, add fields that represent controls on the form (see Figure 9-1). The multiselect controls drop-down (for special powers) and chips (for favorite food) use an array in the model. In this form, the remaining fields are strings.

Import the class to the CreateSuperheroComponent (TypeScript class for app-create-superhero) component. Create a class field and instantiate it. In Listing 9-3, note lines 1 and 11.

Listing 9-3. Using the Model in the Component

```
1. import { Superhero } from '../models/superhero';
// Removed code for brevity
2. @Component({
3. selector: 'app-create-superhero',
4. templateUrl: './create-superhero.component.html',
5. styleUrls: ['./create-superhero.component.css']
6. })
7. export class CreateSuperheroComponent implements OnInit {
8. // Removed code for brevity

9. superhero: Superhero;

10. constructor() {
11.   this.superhero = new Superhero();
12. }

13.  ngOnInit() {
14. }

15.}
```

Next, enhance the template. Wrap the text fields and drop-downs in the superhero form with a form element. Angular automatically adds the ngForm directive to every form element. The directive is part of FormsModule, which we imported earlier.

Listing 9-4 adds a template reference variable, #superheroForm, which we will use later to refer to the form.

Listing 9-4. Wrap Form Controls in a Form

```
<form #superheroForm="ngForm">
   <div>
       <!-- Mat Form Field for name goes here
            Removed code for brevity -->
   </div>
   <div>
       <!-- Mat Form Field for details goes here
            Removed code for brevity -->
   </div>
```

```
<div>
    <!-- Mat Form Field for country goes here
        Removed code for brevity -->
</div>
<div>
    <!-- Mat Form Field for special powers goes here
        Removed code for brevity -->
</div>
<div>
    <!-- Mat Form Field for favorite food goes here
        Removed code for brevity -->
</div>
</form>
```

Next, use two-way data binding with model object to the text fields and drop-downs in the template.

The ngModel is a directive available in FormsModule (see Listing 9-4). The module has already been imported. It is ready to use in SuperheroesMaterialDesignModule. Remember, the app-create-superhero component is part of the same module.

Listing 9-5 (line 5) shows two-way data binding with ngModel in the text field. We use a name field as an example. The name field is in the superhero object in the TypeScript class component.

Listing 9-5. ngModel on Text Field

```
1. <div>
2.     <!-- Appearance: Outline -->
3.     <mat-form-field appearance="outline">
4.     <mat-label>Superhero Name</mat-label>
5.     <input type="text" name="name" [(ngModel)]="superhero.name" matInput
        required placeholder="A name to be remembered" />
6.     <mat-hint>Enter name</mat-hint>
7.     </mat-form-field>
8. </div>
```

Note   The text field also uses the matInput directive, which gives it a Material Design look and feel. In Listing 9-5, the input type is "text". As long as the input type is supported by matInput, ngModel can be used in conjunction (see Chapter 6's *"Input Types with Matinput"* section for a list of input types supported by matInput.

When building forms with template-driven forms, we use two-way data binding on all the form controls. In a drop-down's mat-select elements, we can use the value field for two-way data binding. Listing 9-6's line 3 is an attribute provided by the mat-select component.

Listing 9-6. Two-Way Data Binding with Value Field on mat-select Component

```
1.        <mat-form-field appearance="outline">
2.          <mat-label>Country</mat-label>
3.          <mat-select placeholder="select country" [(value)]="superhero.
            country">
4.            <mat-option>None</mat-option>
5.            <mat-optgroup label="Earth">
6.              <mat-option value="in">India</mat-option>
7.              <mat-option value="us">United States</mat-option>
8.            </mat-optgroup>
9.            <mat-optgroup label="Outer Space">
10.             <mat-option value="os">Asgard</mat-option>
11.           </mat-optgroup>
12.         </mat-select>
13.       </mat-form-field>
```

Note   For consistency, you may use [(ngModel)] with mat-select. If FormsModule has already been imported, use ngModel. The value is useful when ngModel is not available.

To demonstrate two-way data binding, let's print the model object in the template. For debugging purposes, it is temporary; we will delete it eventually.

To print a stringified version of the model object, write a getter function in the component class (see Listing 9-7).

Listing 9-7. Getter Function Printing Model Object

```
get model(){
  return JSON.stringify(this.superhero);
}
```

Use this function in the component template (see Listing 9-8).

Listing 9-8. Show Stringified Version of the Model Object

```
    <strong>
      {{model}}
    </strong>
```

Note   Alternatively, we may use {superhero | json} in the HTML template. It will print the superhero JSON object.

Figure 9-2 shows a user entering values into the form fields.

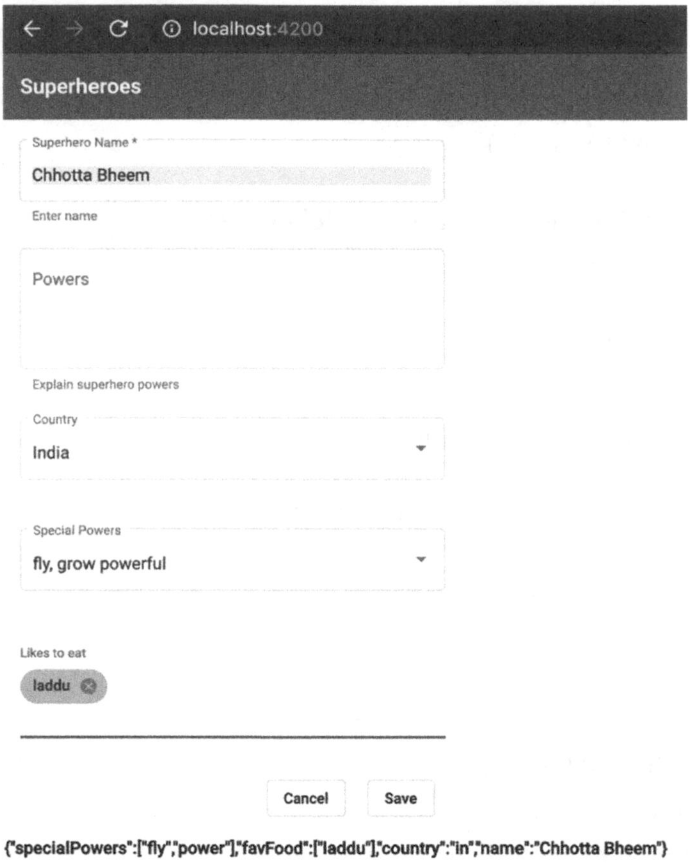

Figure 9-2. *Two-way data binding with ngModel*

Note the stringified model object at the bottom of the screen. The text is updated as the user enters data in real time. Let's say that we reset the model object when the cancel button is clicked, and all the text fields are cleared. No additional action needs to be performed on the DOM.

Form Validation and Errors

Consider the following validators in template-driven forms. They are available out of the box to use along with form fields. They ensure the validity and correctness of the form and the data keyed in by the user.

Required

In the HTML template, the mandatory fields are marked with the required attribute (see Listing 9-8). The name and specialPowers fields are marked as required (see lines 6 and 28). The form is invalid without a value in these fields.

Email

Add the email attribute to validate that the provided text is an email. Let's add email fields to the template and modify the Superhero model object to reflect the same (see Listing 9-8 line 13). The form is invalid without a valid email address in the emailname@domainname.com format.

Minlength

Enforce a minimum length for the text in a form field by using the minlength attribute. In the example, the details field enforces a minimum length of four characters. The form is invalid without a minimum of four characters in it (see Listing 9-8 line 20).

Maxlength

Enforce a maximum length for the text in a form field by using the maxlength attribute. In the example, consider the details field, which has a maximum length of 100 characters. The form is invalid if the text length exceeds this. A control with maxlength does not allow users to enter more than 100 characters (see Listing 9-9 line 20).

Listing 9-9. Template-driven Forms, Validators

```
1. <form #superheroForm="ngForm">
2.    <div>
3.        <!-- Appearance: Outline -->
4.        <mat-form-field appearance="outline">
5.          <mat-label>Superhero Name</mat-label>
6.          <input type="text" name="name" [(ngModel)]="superhero.name"
             matInput required placeholder="A name to be remembered" />
7.          <mat-hint>Enter name</mat-hint>
8.        </mat-form-field>
9.    </div>
```

```
10.     <div>
11.         <mat-form-field appearance="outline">
12.           <mat-label>Email</mat-label>
13.           <input type="text" name="email" email [(ngModel)]="superhero.
            email" matInput  />
14.           <mat-hint>How do I contact the superhero for help?</mat-hint>
15.         </mat-form-field>
16.     </div>

17.     <div>
18.       <mat-form-field appearance="outline">
19.         <mat-label>Powers</mat-label>
20.         <textarea name="details" [(ngModel)]="superhero.
          details" minlength="4" maxlength="10" cdkTextareaAutosize
          cdkAutosizeMinRows="4" cdkAutosizeMaxRows="10" rows="6"
          matInput></textarea>
21.         <mat-hint>Explain superhero powers</mat-hint>
22.       </mat-form-field>
23.     </div>

24.     <div>
25.       <!-- Appearance: Outline -->
26.       <mat-form-field appearance="outline">
27.         <mat-label>Special Powers</mat-label>
28.         <mat-select required name="powers" [(ngModel)]="superhero.
          specialPowers" multiple>
29.           <mat-option>None</mat-option>
30.           <mat-option value="fly">fly</mat-option>
31.           <mat-option value="hammer">wield hammer</mat-option>
32.           <mat-option value="power">grow powerful</mat-option>
33.         </mat-select>
34.       </mat-form-field>
35.       <!-- <strong> My superhero can " {{powers}} "</strong> -->
36.     </div>
37. </form>
```

Using the State Field in Form Controls

When we use ngModel on a form, it tracks the state of the form fields. Form fields could be drop-downs, text fields, and so forth. The following states are possible.

- ***Touched/untouched***: If the user touched, visited, or focused the keyboard in the form field, it is touched. By default, all form fields are untouched, and Angular applies the ng-untouched CSS class on them. When the user focuses on the form field, it is replaced with an ng-touched CSS class.

- ***Dirty/pristine***: If the user attempts to change a value in a form field, it is in a dirty state. By default, all form fields are pristine. Angular applies the ng-prisitine CSS class. When the user brings the focus to the form field, it's replaced with an ng-touched CSS class.

- ***Valid/invalid***: As you saw in the previous section, validations can be applied on form fields. When there is no validation error identified, a form field is valid. Angular applies the ng-valid CSS class; otherwise, the form could be invalid. For example, when a required field is touched but does not have a value, an ng-invalid CSS class is applied.

Angular Material's mat-form-field component adds behavior when working with forms. It adds a highlighted color border to an invalid form field, which indicates that something is wrong with the field. Figure 9-3 is an email field with an invalid email value.

```
┌─ Email ──────────────────────────────────────┐
│                                               │
│  test                                         │
│                                               │
└───────────────────────────────────────────────┘
   How do I contact the superhero for help?
```

Figure 9-3. *mat-form-field indicating invalid status*

In the default theme, floating labels, the cursor, and the border are marked red.

In Figure 9-3, the highlighted border indicates that something is wrong with the form field, but it does not present a friendly message to the user. Listing 9-10 line 3 uses the #email template reference variable assigned to ngModel. Now, the reference variable represents the form field status.

161

Listing 9-10. Input Element with Template Reference Variable Assigned with ngModel

```
1.          <mat-form-field appearance="outline">
2.          <mat-label>Email</mat-label>
3.          <input #email="ngModel" type="text" name="email" email
            [(ngModel)]="superhero.email" matInput  />
4.          <mat-hint>How do I contact the superhero for help?</mat-hint>
5.          </mat-form-field>
```

The following describe a status in the form field.

- ***valid***: This is true when the form field is valid. The usage is email. valid results in true/false.

- ***pristine***: This is true when the user did not attempt to change the form field's value. The usage is email pristine. It is true when it's not dirty.

- ***touched***: This is true when the user did not focus the keyboard in the form field. The usage is email touched. It is true when the user focuses on the field.

Listing 9-11 shows a message if the user touches the field and the state is invalid (notice line 2, in which the negation is on email.valid). We check the touched status since most form fields load with an invalid status when the form loads first. It needs to be valid by the time the user is ready to submit the form.

Listing 9-11. Show a Friendly Error Message to the User

```
1.  <!-- Show error message to the user -->
2.  <div class="error-message" *ngIf="!email.valid && email.touched">
3.    Please enter a valid email address.
4.  </div>
```

The result is shown in Figure 9-4.

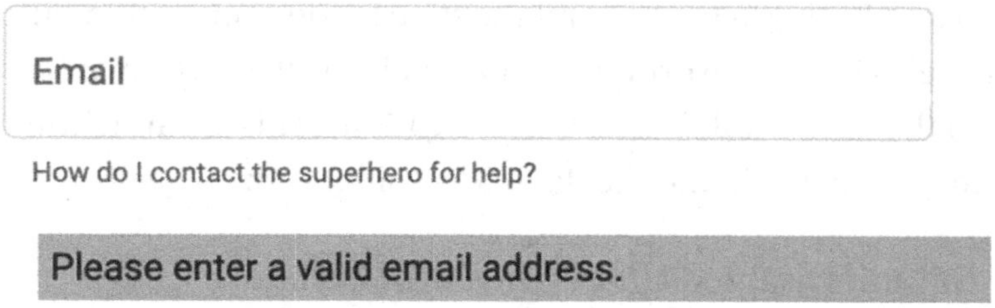

Email

How do I contact the superhero for help?

Please enter a valid email address.

Figure 9-4. *Email field with friendly error message*

Note   In Figure 9-4, the initial fields on the class did not include email. Add an email field of type string in the TypeScript class component.

State of the Form

Note the first line in Listing 9-11. We created a template reference variable for the entire form element. All the state flags described in the previous section are also available in the form reference. The previous section described state fields in form fields, not the form itself. Listing 9-12 prints a form's state fields.

Listing 9-12.   Print Form Status

```
<form #superheroForm="ngForm">

 <strong>
   Form Status, Valid- {{superheroForm.valid}}. Pristine- {{superheroForm.
   pristine}}. Touched- {{superheroForm.touched}}
 </strong>

<!-- removed code for brevity -->
```

The result is shown in Figure 9-5. The form loads with an invalid status because most form fields do not have data. It is pristine because no form field is edited. The touched status is false because the keyboard focus was not brought onto any form field.

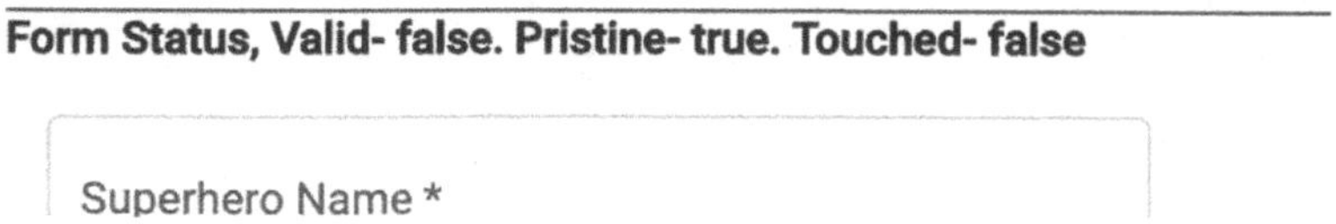

Form Status, Valid- false. Pristine- true. Touched- false

Superhero Name *

Figure 9-5. *Default status of a form*

In Figure 9-5 and Listing 9-12, we print the state for demonstration purposes. How do we use these fields in a real-world scenario? In Listing 9-13, we enable the form's submit buttons if the form is valid (notice the negation). This is part of the validation to ensure that good data makes it into the database from the form.

Listing 9-13. Submit Disabled Unless the Form Is Valid

```
<div>
  <button mat-stroked-button> Cancel </button>
  <button mat-stroked-button [disabled]="!superheroForm.valid"> Save
  </button>
</div>
```

Figure 9-6 shows the result.

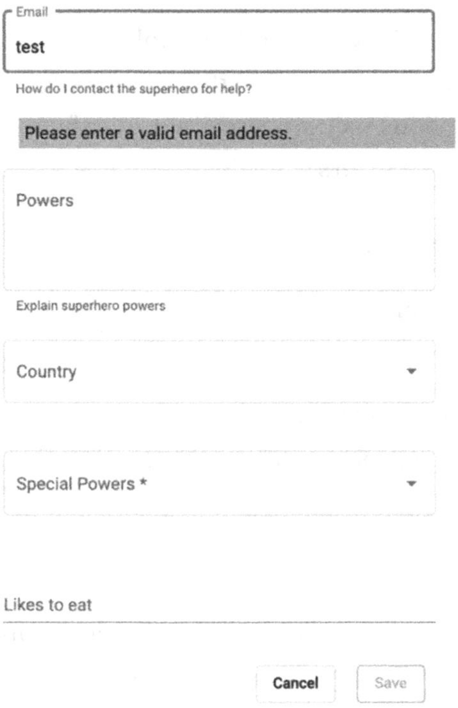

Figure 9-6. *Disable submit/save on an invalid form*

Note   Listing 9-12 and Listing 9-13 used various Angular Material components and directives, mat-select, mat-button/mat-stroked-button, MatInput, and so forth. So far, we have imported Angular modules, such as MatSelectModule, MatButtonModule, MatInputModule, and so forth. Import respective modules to SuperheroesMaterialDesignModule, if you have not done so already.

Reactive Forms

Reactive forms are model driven, immutable, and synchronous.

- **Model driven**: A data object maintained in the component representing the form.

- **Immutable**: Every change to the form creates a new state of the form and maintains the integrity of the model (in the component).

- **Reactive forms**: Easily unit testable as data, or the form state is predictable and can be easily accessed through the component.

Getting Started with Reactive Forms

In the Superhero application, SuperheroesMaterialDesignModule's components have Angular Material dependencies.

To start using reactive forms, import ReactiveFormsModule to SuperheroesMaterialDesignModule (see Listing 9-14 lines 1 and 7).

Listing 9-14. Import ReactiveFormsModule

```
1. import { ReactiveFormsModule } from '@angular/forms';

2. @NgModule({
3. declarations: [
4.   // Removed code for brevity
5. ],
```

```
6. imports: [
7.     ReactiveFormsModule
8. ],
9. exports: [
10.    ],
11. providers:[HitCounter]
12. })
13. export class SuperheroesMaterialDesignModule { }
```

Create a new component to experiment with reactive forms. We will build the same create-superhero component as a reactive form. To do this, run the Angular CLI command shown in Listing 9-15.

Listing 9-15. Create a Component to Demonstrate reactive forms with Angular CLI

```
ng g component superheroes-material-design/create-superhero-reactive-form
```

Reactive forms are model driven, which is part of the component class. It is bound to the component template.

Create a Form Control with Form Builder

A form control represents a form field. An instance of a form control is created in the Angular component's TypeScript file. It could represent a form field like a text field, a drop-down, or a radio button.

FormBuilder is an Angular service in the @angular/forms Angular monorepo. It simplifies creating form controls in Angular's reactive forms.

Reactive forms are model driven. We will create a model in the TypeScript class. Let's create it by adding the name field (Superhero name). The name field is a text field in the HTML template. It is an instance of the FormControl class in the model.

Listing 9-16 imports and injects FormBuilder. The FormBuilder instance creates a form control representing the name of the superhero. It creates an instance of FormControl by using a helper function named *control*. The control function initializes the form control with a value. In Listing 9-16, we initialize it with an empty string (see line 11).

Listing 9-16. Using FormBuilder to Create a FormControl

```
1. import { Component, OnInit } from '@angular/core';

2. // Import FormBuilder and FormControl
3. import { FormBuilder, FormControl } from '@angular/forms';

4. @Component({
5. selector: 'app-create-superhero-reactive-form',
6. templateUrl: './create-superhero-reactive-form.component.html',
7. styleUrls: ['./create-superhero-reactive-form.component.css']
8. })
9. export class CreateSuperheroReactiveFormComponent implements OnInit {

10. // Create an instance of FormControl using the FormBuilder
11. name: FormControl = this.fb.control("");

12. // Inject FormBuilder
13. constructor(private fb: FormBuilder) { }

14. ngOnInit() {
15. }
16. }
```

In the HTML template, we use a formControl directive to refer to the model object from TypeScript class (see line 3 in Listing 9-17).

Listing 9-17. Using formControl Directive to Refer to the Model (in TypeScript Class)

```
1.    <mat-form-field appearance="outline">
2.      <mat-label>Superhero Name</mat-label>
3.      <input type="text" name="name" [formControl]="name" matInput
4.        placeholder="A name to be remembered" />
5.      <mat-hint>Enter name</mat-hint>
6.    </mat-form-field>
```

Note   Using FormBuilder is not mandatory. We may directly create a FormControl instance with a new keyword as well. As you will see in upcoming sections, FormBuilder provides syntactic sugar that simplifies creating reactive forms. Listing 9-18 uses a new keyword to create an instance of FormControl.

Listing 9-18. Create FormControl with New Keyword

```
export class CreateSuperheroReactiveFormComponent implements OnInit {

// Create an instance of FormControl using the FormBuilder
 name: FormControl = new FormControl("Chhotta Bheem by default");

// Inject FormBuilder
 constructor(private fb: FormBuilder) { }

ngOnInit() {
 }
}
```

The constructor for FormControl is initialized with a default value, "Chhotta Bheem by default". The result is shown in Figure 9-7. The form shows the default value.

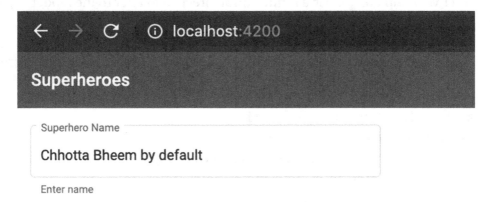

Figure 9-7. *FormControl initialized with a new keyword*

Capture Changes to the Form Control

Forms are built for users to enter data or select values. Users are expected to make a series of changes in the form controls. When users input data, it is never a one-time activity. User interactions are a stream and a series of changes.

Angular applications use an observable to stream changes. In this case, changes made by the user are streamed by the observable. In the FormControl instance, access the observable with valueChanges (see Listing 9-19).

Listing 9-19. Observable for Changes Made to the Text Field

```
ngOnInit() {
  this.name.valueChanges.subscribe( result => console.log(result));
}
```

Listing 9-19 subscribes to the observable and prints the result values to the console (see Figure 9-8). It is just a sample to demonstrate the observable. A real-world example might transform the data and send it to a remote service on a server.

Figure 9-8. *Result logged by the observable*

Access a Snapshot

The preceding sample accesses an observable; however, it is possible to access a single value. Use the change handler in the text field. The form control provides a snapshot of the value at that point in time. It is different from a stream, as you saw in the previous sample (see line 5 in Listing 9-20).

Listing 9-20. Template with Change Handler Attached to the Form Field

```
1.    <mat-form-field appearance="outline">
2.      <mat-label>Superhero Name</mat-label>

3.      <!-- Change handler on the input field below -->
4.      <input type="text" name="name" [formControl]="name" matInput
5.        (change)="changeHandler()"

6.        placeholder="A name to be remembered" />
7.      <mat-hint>Enter name</mat-hint>
8.    </mat-form-field>
```

The changeHandler function is invoked on a change to the text field. The snapshot of the FormControl field is available in the value field. The code sample logs the snapshot to the console.

Listing 9-21. Change Handler Function Invoked on Change

```
changeHandler(){
   console.log("Log the snapshot at a point in time, ", this.name.value);
 }
```

Figure 9-9 shows the result.

Figure 9-9. *A snapshot value of the text field logged to the browser console*

Set a Value on FormControl

In the prior example, a value set by the user in a form control is read by the Angular TypeScript code component. We initialized the form control with a default value; however, we did not set a value.

Imagine that a value needs to be set on the form control when a server-side API returns a value. To mimic the scenario, and without complicating the sample with a server-side API call, we use setTimeout. This is just for the sample. We set a value on the form control after a stipulated number of milliseconds.

To set a value on a form control, use the setValue API (see Listing 9-22).

Listing 9-22. Set a Value on a Form Control

```
ngOnInit() {
  setTimeout( () => this.name.setValue("Value set on timeout"), 1000);
}
```

The sample times out after a second (1000 milliseconds). this.name is an instance of FormControl. It sets a sample string, "Value set on timeout", which is set on the text field in the form.

Create a Form Group with Form Builder

In the prior example, a single FormControl instance was created (superhero name). This approach works well for a small number of form controls. As the form grows larger, to represents a group of controls use Form Group. When using a form group, actions like reset can be performed at the form level. Instead of reading the values on the form from separate variables, they can be read on a form-level object.

Let's continue with the Create Superhero component; for the complete superhero form, create FormGroup. Use FormBuilder instance's helper function, group, to create a form group. We provide a JSON object with key/value pairs to represent the model object or the form with all the fields required to create a superhero. Listing 9-23 creates a FormGroup instance and assigns it to a class-level field—superheroFormGroup (see lines 3 and 7 to 14).

Listing 9-23. Create FormGroup with FormBuilder

```
1.export class CreateSuperheroReactiveFormComponent implements OnInit {

2. // Class variable representing FormGroup.
3. superheroFormGroup: FormGroup;

4. // Inject Form Builder
5. constructor(private fb: FormBuilder) { }
```

```
6. ngOnInit() {
7.    // Create FormGroup object with FormBuilder.
8.    this.superheroFormGroup = this.fb.group({
9.      name:",
10.      email:",
11.      details: ",
12.      powers: ",
13.      country: "

14.  });

15. }
16. }
```

Each field name—email, details, and so forth—is initialized with empty an string. We can specify default values to initialize.

In the HTML template, identify the form as a form group and the individual form controls in it as child elements. Listing 9-24 is the complete HTML template for the form. Note the highlighted formGroup directive in the form element (line 1). Each form control is identified with the formControlName attribute in the input elements (see lines 6, 14, 21, 29, and 46).

Listing 9-24. Form Group and Form Controls in the HTML Template

```
1. <form #superheroForm="ngForm" [formGroup]="superheroFormGroup">
2. <div>
3.    <!-- Appearance: Outline -->
4.    <mat-form-field appearance="outline">
5.      <mat-label>Superhero Name</mat-label>
6.      <input type="text" name="name" formControlName="name" matInput
7.        placeholder="A name to be remembered" />
8.      <mat-hint>Enter name</mat-hint>
9.    </mat-form-field>
10. </div>
```

```
11.   <div>
12.    <mat-form-field appearance="outline">
13.      <mat-label>Email</mat-label>
14.      <input type="text" name="email" formControlName="email" matInput />
15.      <mat-hint>How do I contact the superhero for help?</mat-hint>
16.    </mat-form-field>

17.   </div>

18.   <div>
19.    <mat-form-field appearance="outline">
20.      <mat-label>Powers</mat-label>
21.      <textarea name="details" formControlName="details"
           cdkTextareaAutosize matInput></textarea>
22.      <mat-hint>Explain superhero powers</mat-hint>
23.    </mat-form-field>
24.   </div>

25.  <div>
26.    <!-- Appearance: Outline -->
27.    <mat-form-field appearance="outline">
28.      <mat-label>Country</mat-label>
29.      <mat-select formControlName="country" placeholder="select country" >
30.        <mat-option>None</mat-option>
31.        <mat-optgroup label="Earth">
32.          <mat-option value="in">India</mat-option>
33.          <mat-option value="us">United States</mat-option>
34.        </mat-optgroup>
35.        <mat-optgroup label="Outer Space">
36.          <mat-option value="os">Asgard</mat-option>
37.        </mat-optgroup>
38.      </mat-select>
39.    </mat-form-field>
40.    <!-- <strong>Superhero comes from " {{country}} "</strong> -->
41.  </div>
```

```
42. <div>
43.    <!-- Appearance: Outline -->
44.    <mat-form-field appearance="outline">
45.      <mat-label>Special Powers</mat-label>
46.      <mat-select name="powers" formControlName="powers" multiple>
47.        <mat-option>None</mat-option>
48.        <mat-option value="fly">fly</mat-option>
49.        <mat-option value="hammer">wield hammer</mat-option>
50.        <mat-option value="power">grow powerful</mat-option>
51.      </mat-select>
52.    </mat-form-field>
53.    <!-- <strong> My superhero can " {{powers}} "</strong> -->
54. </div>

55. <div class="pull-right">
56.    <button mat-stroked-button> Cancel </button>
57.    <button mat-stroked-button> Save </button>
58. </div>

59. </form>
```

Note that the Form Builder is again syntactic sugar that simplifies creating the form control and the form group. The same code could be written to create an instance of FormGroup that combines multiple FormControl objects instantiated using the new keyword (see Listing 9-25).

Listing 9-25. Create Form Group Object with a Collection for FormControl Objects Instantiated with the New Keyword

```
ngOnInit() {

  this.superheroFormGroup = new FormGroup( {
    name: new FormControl("),
    email:new FormControl("),
    details: new FormControl("),
    powers: new FormControl("),
    country: new FormControl(")
  });
}
```

174

Read Form Group Values as a Stream

Before we read the values in the form group, let's create a model object representing the form. Listing 9-26 is a Superhero form. The model class refers to each control in the form group.

Listing 9-26. Model Object Referring to the Form Group

```
export class Superhero {
    name: string;
    email: string;
    details: string;
    country: string;
    specialPowers: Array<string> = [];
}
```

Similar to the form control, we can subscribe to changes to the form group. Angular applications use an observable to stream changes. This observable streams changes made by the user. In the form group, you can access the observable with valueChanges. In Listing 9-27, see lines 11 to 16.

Listing 9-27. Observable for Changes Made to the Form Group

```
1. ngOnInit() {

2.   // Create FormGroup object
3.   this.superheroFormGroup = this.fb.group({
4.     name:",
5.     email:",
6.     details: ",
7.     powers: ",
8.     country: ",
9.     favFood: "

10.   });
```

```
11.    // Subscribe to the changes to form group
12.    this.superheroFormGroup
13.    .valueChanges
14.    .subscribe(item =>
15.      console.log("Stream as form changes, ", item as Superhero));

16. }
```

Listing 9-27 subscribes to the observable and prints the result values to the console (see the result in Figure 9-10). Considering it is a stream, a series of values are printed on the console for each change. It is just a sample to demonstrate the observable. A real-world example might transform the data and send it to a remote service on a server.

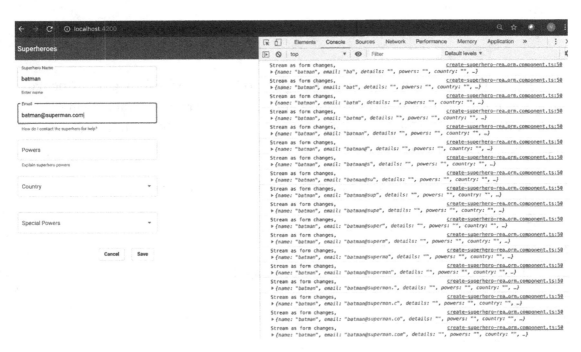

Figure 9-10. *Changes to the form group are streamed. The handler prints the change on browser console*

Also notice that the subscribe success function handler receives each change. The data is available on a variable named item. The received form group value instance is type cast to the Superhero class (see line 15 in Listing 9-27).

Read Form Group Values as a Snapshot

Similar to form control, form group values can also be read as a snapshot. You can use the submit event on the form. It provides a snapshot of the form and all of the controls' values when the user clicks submit.

See the changes to the template file to add a handler in the form submit (see Listing 9-28 and Listing 9-29).

Listing 9-28. Form Submit Handler Added

```
<form #superheroForm="ngForm" [formGroup]="superheroFormGroup"
(submit)="submitHandler()">
</form>
```

Refer to the contents of the handler function. It prints a snapshot of the form group. The snapshot is available on value variable. As in the previous section, we type cast snapshot to the Superhero model object.

Listing 9-29. Print Snapshot of the Form Group to the Console

```
submitHandler(){
  let superhero = this.superheroFormGroup.value as Superhero;
  console.log("Superhero model object ", superhero);
}
```

The result is shown in Figure 9-11. It prints a snapshot of the form group to the browser console.

Figure 9-11. *Print snapshot of a form group*

Form Validation

Consider the validators in reactive forms (see Listing 9-30). They are available out of the box to use along with form fields. They ensure the validity and correctness of the form and the data entered by the user.

To use validators in a reactive form, import the validator from the @angular/forms monorepo.

Listing 9-30. Import Validator

```
import { Validators } from '@angular/forms';
```

Required

When creating the form control, qualify mandatory field as required. The required validator is available out of the box in validators.

You have seen two ways to create form controls: Form Builder and the new keyword. Listing 9-31 uses the required validator.

Listing 9-31. Using a Required Validator

```
// 1. If FormControl constructor is used, pass the validator as the second
parameter
name= new FormControl(", [Validators.required])

// 2. With FormBuilder, provide validator as the subsequent object to the
initial value in the array
this.superheroFormGroup = this.fb.group({
  name:[", Validators.required],
  // more form controls on the form group
});
```

In the form control constructor (line 1), the second parameter is an array. If there are multiple validations in the form control, provide all validators in the array.

Email

Add the email validator to ensure that the provided text is an email. Add the email validator to the email form control. In Listing 9-32, the form is invalid without a valid email address in the emailname@domainname.com format.

Listing 9-32. Using a Required Validator

```
// 1. If FormControl constructor is used, pass the email validator as the
second parameter
    this.superheroFormGroup = new FormGroup( {
      name: new FormControl(", Validators.required),
      email:new FormControl(", [Validators.required, Validators.email]),
    });

// 2. With FormBuilder, provide validator as the subsequent object to the
initial value in the array
    this.superheroFormGroup = this.fb.group({
      name:[", Validators.required],
      email:[", Validators.required, Validators.email],
```

The email form control in the example is required, and the email is validated.

Note When using the new keyword, the form control could be part of form group. Validators still apply. It is a similar scenario with form builder. The form control could be created as part of the group or with the control function.

---

minLength

Use the minLength validator to ensure that the user provides at least the stipulated number of characters in the field. Listing 9-33 shows minlength applied in the *details* form field.

Listing 9-33. Minimum Length Validator

```
// If FormControl constructor is used, pass the minlength validator as the
second parameter
    details= new FormControl(", Validators.minLength(5)),

// 2. With FormBuilder, provide validator as the subsequent object to the
initial value in the array (see details field below.
    this.superheroFormGroup = this.fb.group({
      name:[", Validators.required],
      email:[", Validators.required, Validators.email],
      details: [", Validators.minLength(5)],
```

maxLength

Use the maxLength validator to ensure that the user provides, at most, the stipulated number of characters in the field. Listing 9-34 shows the maxlength applied in the *details* form field.

Listing 9-34. Minimum Length Validator

```
// 1. To the FormControl constructor, pass the validator
    this.superheroFormGroup = new FormGroup( {
      name: new FormControl(", Validators.required),
      email:new FormControl(", [Validators.required, Validators.
      maxLength(100)]),

    });

// 2. With FormBuilder, provide validator as the subsequent object to the
initial value in the array (see details field below
    this.superheroFormGroup = this.fb.group({
      name:[", Validators.required],
      email:[", Validators.required, Validators.email],
      details: [", Validators.minLength(5), Validators.maxLength(100)],

    });
```

Show Form Status and Errors

Angular Material components indicate an error when the validation fails. The components use validators to show the error status. Consider the form in Figure 9-12. The name, email, and details fields show an error because their respective validators— required field validation, email format validation, and minimum character length validation—failed. The error is indicated by a red border around the form field.

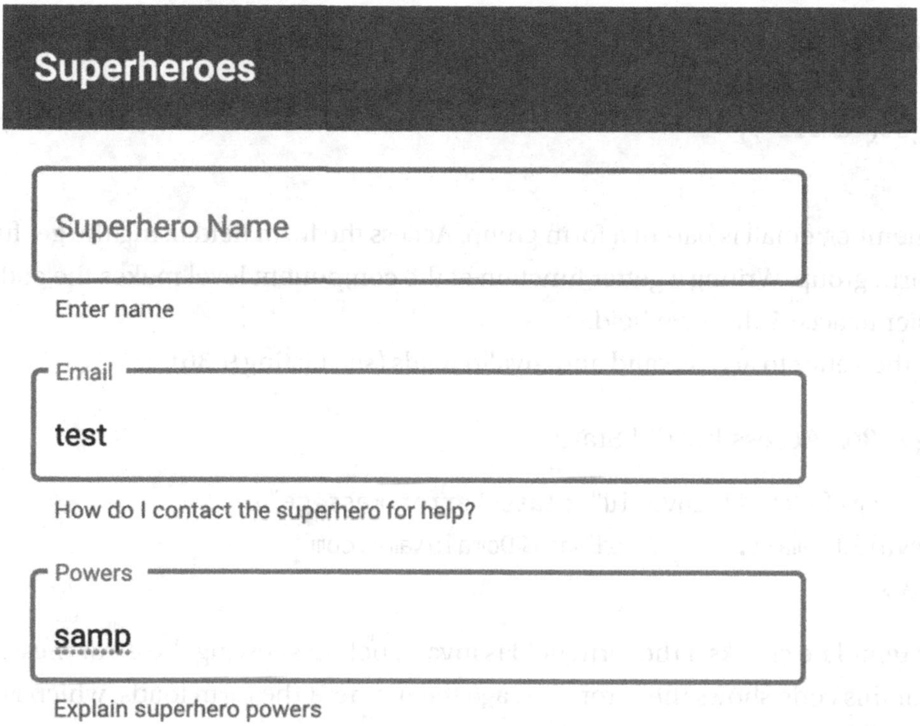

Figure 9-12. *Angular Material shows error state. Field has a red border around the field*

Note   The error is shown only after the form field is touched (receives a keyboard focus).

As you have seen with template-driven forms, a field can be in one of the following states.

Valid/Invalid

If a form field validator condition is met, it is valid. Consider an example with an email validator. If the user provided a valid email in the emailaddress@domainname.com format, it is valid; otherwise, it is invalid.

To access the field and the validity status, see Listing 9-35 and Listing 9-36.

Listing 9-35. Getter for Email Field

```
get email(){
  return this.superheroFormGroup
    .get("email");
}
```

Remember, email is part of a form group. Access the form field using the get function in the form group. Writing a getter function at the component level makes the code clean and easier to access the form field.

Use the getter to access valid and invalid fields (see Listing 9-36).

Listing 9-36. Access Invalid Status

```
<div *ngIf="email.invalid" class="error-message">
  Invalid email. Use YourEMail@DomainName.com
</div>
```

The template checks if the form field is invalid before showing the error message. Note that this code shows the error message the moment the form loads, which is not ideal. We will fix this in the next section.

We may also use the valid status field, if required. Listing 9-37 shows an indicator, which is a Material Design icon that shows that the validation was successful.

Listing 9-37. Access Valid Status

```
1.   <mat-form-field appearance="outline">
2.     <mat-label>Email</mat-label>
3.     <input type="text" name="email" formControlName="email" matInput />
4.     <mat-icon *ngIf="email.valid" matSuffix >check_circle</mat-icon>
5.     <mat-hint>How do I contact the superhero for help?</mat-hint>
6.   </mat-form-field>
```

Figure 9-13 shows the result.

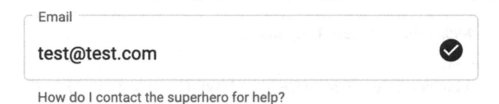

How do I contact the superhero for help?

Figure 9-13. *Indicate valid status with a Material Design icon*

Note   Listing 9-37's line 4 uses the mat-icon component in Angular Material. In an earlier code sample, we imported MatIconModule into SuperheroesMaterialDesignModule. Import it now, if not done already.

---

touched/untouched

If the user brought keyboard focus onto the form field, it is touched; otherwise, it is untouched. Use the touched and untouched fields in the form field.

Typically, when showing form validation status messages, just checking the valid/invalid status in a form field is not effective. After the user attempts to enter a value, it is logical to show or hide an error message. When the form loads, most fields are blank or preloaded with the current data. The form code and the user do not yet have control.

In Listing 9-38, we modify the code in Listing 9-38 to show the error message only if the field is touched.

Listing 9-38. Access in-Valid Status

```
<div *ngIf="email.touched && email.invalid" class="error-message">
  Invalid email. Use YourEMail@DomainName.com
</div>
```

pristine/dirty

If the user attempted to edit a field, it is marked as dirty; otherwise, it is pristine (either blank or with the default data). A common use case for these flags is to enforce users to save the form data if any field is dirty. You may show an alert that indicates the data might be lost if the user navigates away without saving. When all fields are pristine, such an error does not need to be shown in Listing 9-39 and Figure 9-14.

Listing 9-39. Print Pristine or Dirty Status

```
<strong>
  Pristine: {{ email.pristine }}. Dirty: {{ email.dirty }}
</strong>
```

Email

How do I contact the superhero for help?

Pristine: true. Dirty: false

Figure 9-14. *Print pristine or dirty status. This is just to showcase the flag*

Validator Error Flags

We have used valid/invalid, touched/untouched, pristine/dirty flags to get a form field status at a point in time. For each validator, Angular adds error flags as well.

Remember the email flag in Listing 9-39. The form control was created with two validators: required and email.

```
email:[", Validators.required, Validators.email],
```

If either of these validators return false, an error flag is added. It is added to the errors object in the form control.

In Listing 9-40, separate error flags provide the ability to show specific error messages. If the required field is empty, specify that it is a required field. If the email format failure occurs, show that the email needs to follow the provided format. See Figure 9-15.

Listing 9-40. Show Error Message Based on the Error Flag

```
<div *ngIf="email.errors.required" >
  *Email is a required field
</div>
```

```
<div *ngIf="email.errors.email" >
  *Invalid email. Use YourEMail@DomainName.com
</div>
```

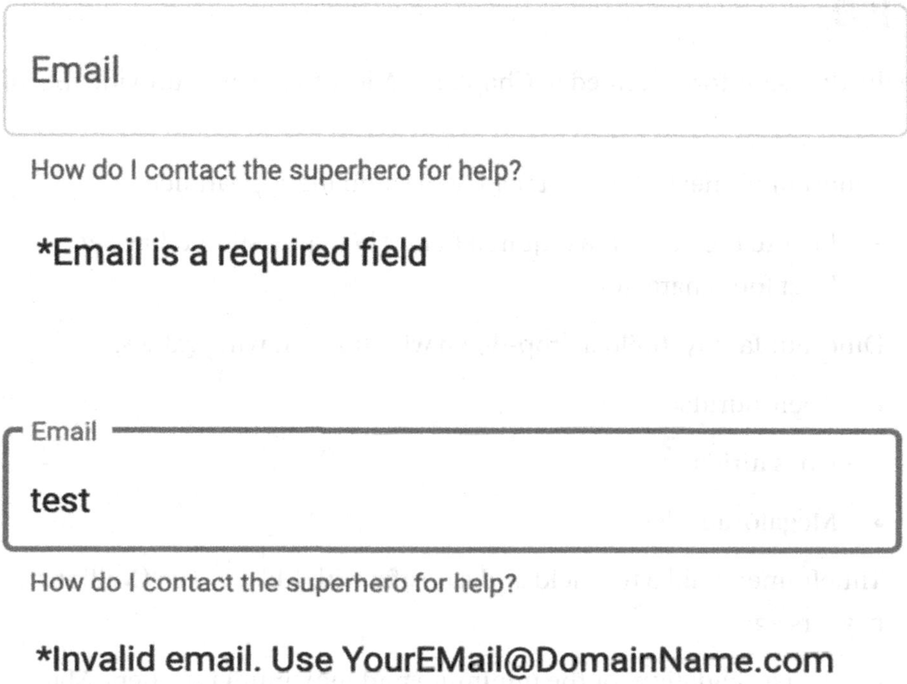

Figure 9-15. Show specific error messages based on the error

Conclusion

Angular provides two ways to build forms. This chapter discusses both approaches: template-driven forms and reactive forms. Template-driven forms are easy to build, and use ngModel and two-way data binding. Template-driven forms are mutable. Reactive forms are sophisticated and best fit for complex forms.

In this chapter, we imported the Angular module for template-driven forms, FormsModule. We used Angular Material components to build the form. We used two-way data binding, primarily using the ngModel directive. Form data in the template was matched with the model object in the TypeScript class component.

Some of the built-in form validation features were discussed. These validations were performed on the client in the browser's Angular code. Hence, they are quick and validate data correctness.

Angular Material component features and Angular form features to show errors when validation fails were also discussed.

Exercise

Enhance the dinosaur form created in Chapter 8. Allow the user to provide the following input.

- Dinosaur name: Build a text field with standard appearance.

    - Ensure the name is a required field. The name should have at least four characters.

- Dinosaur family: Build a drop-down with the following values.

    - Abelisauridae

    - Noasauridae

    - Megalosauridae

- Timeframe: Build a text field and a postfix with Mil-yrs-ago (Millions of years ago)

    - Add a validation for the minimum and maximum numbers. Make it a required field.

- Dinosaur description: Build a text area with a minimum of 6 rows and a maximum of 20 rows.

- Continents they lived in: Use a chip list that can accept dynamic values from the user.

Reference

Angular Material documentation (`https://material.angular.io/`)

CHAPTER 10

Material Design: Additional Form Fields

In the previous chapters, you used Material form fields such as text fields, text area, single select, and multiselect drop-downs. You explored Angular forms, such as template-driven and reactive forms. When building the forms, we need controls in addition to the basic text fields, drop-downs, and so forth. This chapter covers other commonly used Angular Material form fields: the date picker, the slider (for selecting a value in a range), toggle switches, and check boxes. They are a Material Design implementation of Angular components.

This chapter explains importing Angular Material components and discusses common usage with the help of the Superheroes sample application.

Material Design Date Picker Control

Date is a commonly used input field in a form. The Angular Material library provides a date component confined to the Material Design look and feel. The component provides the functionality to easily select a date or switch between previous months and years. For reference, see Figure 10-1, Figure 10-2, and Figure 10-3.

© Venkata Keerti Kotaru 2020
V. K. Kotaru, *Angular for Material Design*, https://doi.org/10.1007/978-1-4842-5434-9_10

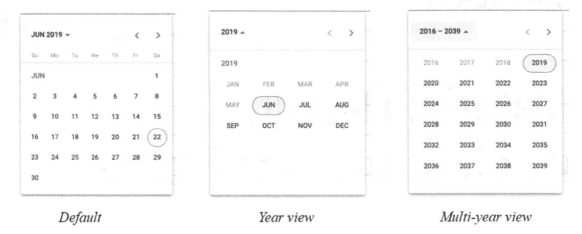

Default   *Year view*   *Multi-year view*

Figure 10-1. *Angular Material date picker*

Getting Started

Similar to other Angular Material components, to use Angular Material's date picker, import the module containing the component (see Listing 10-1). In the Superheroes code sample, all the Material Design components are encompassed in superheroes-material-design.module.ts.

Listing 10-1. Import Modules for Date Picker

```
import { MatDatepickerModule } from '@angular/material/datepicker';
import { MatNativeDateModule } from '@angular/material/core';

@NgModule({
  declarations: [
      // Removed code for brevity
  ],
  imports: [
      // Removed code for brevity
    MatDatepickerModule,
    MatNativeDateModule,
  ],
```

```
  exports: [
  ],
  providers:[]
})
export class SuperheroesMaterialDesignModule { }
```

We are importing two modules.

- **MatDatepickerModule**: Contains the Angular Material components and directives for Material Design.

- **MatNativeDateModule**: Contains the date implementation. Components in MatDatepickerModule provide the UI control. It is agnostic of the date implementation underneath. To begin, you may use MatNativeDateModule.

It is imported from @angular/material/core. It uses the JavaScript Date object implementation.

Alternative for MatNativeDateModule

The JavaScript default implementation does not include all locales around the world. Hence it is preferable to use a Moment.js-based implementation named MatMomentDateModule. Moment.js is a popular library for handling the date and time in JavaScript.

To use MatMomentDateModule, install two packages—moment and @angular/material-moment-adapter—with the following command.

```
npm install --save moment @angular/material/moment-adapter
```

or

```
yarn add moment @angular/material-moment-adapter
```

Next, modify the imports in the Angular module in superheroes-material-design. module.ts. See Listing 10-2.

Listing 10-2. Import MatMomentDateModule Instead of MatNativeDateModule

```
import { MatDatepickerModule } from '@angular/material/datepicker';

// Leaving the commented import to spot the difference
// import { MatNativeDateModule } from '@angular/material/core';
import { MatMomentDateModule } from '@angular/material-moment-adapter'

@NgModule({
  declarations: [
        // Removed code for brevity
  ],
  imports: [
    // Removed code for brevity
    MatDatepickerModule,

    // MatNativeDateModule, -- left commented import to sport the
    difference
    MatMomentDateModule,
  ],
  exports: [
  ],
  providers:[HitCounter]
})
export class SuperheroesMaterialDesignModule { }
```

Date Picker Component

Use Angular Material's mat-datepicker component for a date picker. Figure 10-2 shows a typical date picker's look and feel. When using the date picker in a form, we need an input field to show the selected date. The date picker control seen in Figure 10-2 allows you to select a date. The selected date needs a placeholder form field to showcase the date. We use an input field for this purpose.

Listing 10-3 results in a date picker in a form.

Listing 10-3. mat-datepicker as a form Field

```
<div>
  <mat-form-field>
    <mat-label>Date of birth</mat-label>
    <input  matInput formControlName="dob" [matDatepicker]="dateOfBirth" />
    <mat-datepicker #dateOfBirth [opened]="true"></mat-datepicker>
  </mat-form-field>
</div>
```

When creating a new superhero, date of birth is one of the form inputs. mat-datepicker shows the Material Design date control (see Figure 10-2). The input field is used to show the selected date. It also acts as a placeholder to launch the date picker.

The date picker is enclosed in mat-form-field. Similar to a text field in a form, we use a mat-label to show a label for the date-of-birth form field and a matInput (on the input element) to show the selected date.

Note   The "opened" input element on the mat-datepicker component. Since its value is true, date picker is open on page load.

To tie the input field to the date picker, use the template reference variable. Listing 10-3 uses #dateOfBirth in the date picker. Use the matDatePicker input attribute with a value for the dateOfBirth template reference variable to relate the date picker with the input field.

Figure 10-2 showcases three views for the date picker: default, year, and multiyear. To show the date picker in year or multi-year view when it loads, use the input startView on the mat-datepicker component. See Listing 10-4.

Listing 10-4. Show the Date Picker in Year View

```
<mat-datepicker startView="year" #dateOfBirth ></mat-datepicker>
```

Listing 10-5. Show the Date Picker in Multiyear View

```
<mat-datepicker startView="multi-year" #dateOfBirth ></mat-datepicker>
```

When using reactive forms (explained in Chapter 9), formControlName maps date-of-birth to a form control object in a form group. The model object in the Typescript class component shows the selected date of birth.

To initialize with a default value, we may initialize the form control with a date value. See Listing 10-6.

Listing 10-6. initialize formControl with a Date Value

```
this.superheroFormGroup = new FormGroup( {
  name: new FormControl(", Validators.required),
  // Removed remaining form group for brevity
  dob: new FormControl(new Date('05/20/2019'))
});
```

Listing 10-7 prints the value of the date-of-birth form control.

Listing 10-7. Return Selected Date Value from the Form Group

```
console.log("Selected date value ", moment(this.superheroFormGroup.
value.dob).toDate());
```

If we are not using the form control or form group, we use the input value on the directive to provide a value (see Listing 10-8).

Listing 10-8. Using Input Value for Setting a Date Value

```
<!-- HTML template code -->
<input  matInput [value]="dob"  [matDatepicker]="dateOfBirth" />

// Code in TypeScript component file
export class CreateSuperheroFormComponent implements OnInit {

dob: Date = new Date("05/21/2019");

  // Removed code for brevity
}
```

Note In template-driven forms, you may use data-binding features and ngModel on the input field to read the selected date value.

Toggle the Date Picker on Click

To show the date picker after a click, use the mat-datepicker-toggle component. Consider Listing 10-9.

Listing 10-9. Toggle the Date Picker

```
<div>
    <mat-form-field>
      <mat-label>Date of birth</mat-label>
      <input  matInput [value]="dob"  [matDatepicker]="dateOfBirth" />
      <mat-datepicker-toggle matSuffix [for]="dateOfBirth">
      </mat-datepicker-toggle>
      <mat-datepicker #dateOfBirth ></mat-datepicker>
    </mat-form-field>
  </div>
```

Note the input [for]. The template reference variable is now tied to the toggle as well (in addition to the text field).

The mat-datepicker-toggle component shows the calendar icon prefixed or suffixed to the text field. Listing 10-8 uses the matSuffix attribute to show it at the end. We use matPrefix to show it at the start of the text field. See Figure 10-2.

Figure 10-2. *Prefix/suffix calendar icon with date picker toggle*

Clicking the calendar icons opens the date picker.

We may use a custom icon instead of the calendar icon. Use matDatepickerToggleIcon directive on the mat-icon component. Listing 10-10 and Figure 10-3 use the child_care icon for date of birth.

Listing 10-10. Custom Icon for date picker with matDatepickertoggleIcon

```
<div>
  <mat-form-field>
    <mat-label>Date of birth</mat-label>
    <input matInput [matDatepicker]="dateOfBirth" />
    <mat-datepicker-toggle matSuffix [for]="dateOfBirth">
      <mat-icon matDatepickerToggleIcon>child_care</mat-icon>
    </mat-datepicker-toggle>
    <mat-datepicker #dateOfBirth ></mat-datepicker>
  </mat-form-field>
</div>
```

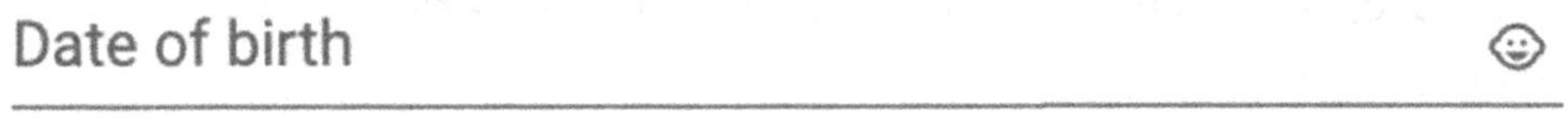

Date of birth   ☺

Figure 10-3. *Custom icon for date picker*

Note   Using Angular Material icons need MatIconModule from @angular/material/icon in SuperheroesMaterialDesignModule. We imported it already. Add it to imports on the @NgModule() decorator, if not already done.

Filter Dates

To ensure the correctness of the date fields in a form, consider the following options to filter unwanted dates on the form.

Min and Max Values

Use min and max inputs on MatDatePicker to disable dates before and after the given dates. To provide a real-world example for a min date value, consider the date of birth. We might need to disable all future dates. As another example, when scheduling an appointment, we might have to disable all past dates.

Listing 10-11 shows max set on matDatePicker (see line 4).

Listing 10-11. Set Max Date

```
1. <div>
2.   <mat-form-field>
3.       <mat-label>Date of birth</mat-label>
4.       <input [max]="dobMaxDate" matInput [matDatepicker]="dateOfBirth" />
5.       <mat-datepicker-toggle matSuffix [for]="dateOfBirth">
6.         <mat-icon matDatepickerToggleIcon>child_care</mat-icon>
7.       </mat-datepicker-toggle>
8.       <mat-datepicker #dateOfBirth ></mat-datepicker>
9.   </mat-form-field>
10.  </div>
```

Note that the variable dobMaxDate is today's date, defined in the TypeScript class component. See Listing 10-12.

Listing 10-12. dobMaxDate is Assigned to a Date Object

```
export class CreateSuperheroReactiveFormComponent implements OnInit {

// new Date() initializes to today's date.
  dobMaxDate = new Date();

// Deleted remaining code for brevity
}
```

Figure 10-4 shows that all future dates are disabled.

Figure 10-4. *Date of birth with future dates disabled*

Setting a min date disables all past dates. See Listing 10-13 and Figure 10-5.

Listing 10-13. Set min date

```
<!-- dobMinDate is today's date -->
    <input [min]="dobMinDate" matInput [matDatepicker]="dateOfBirth" />
```

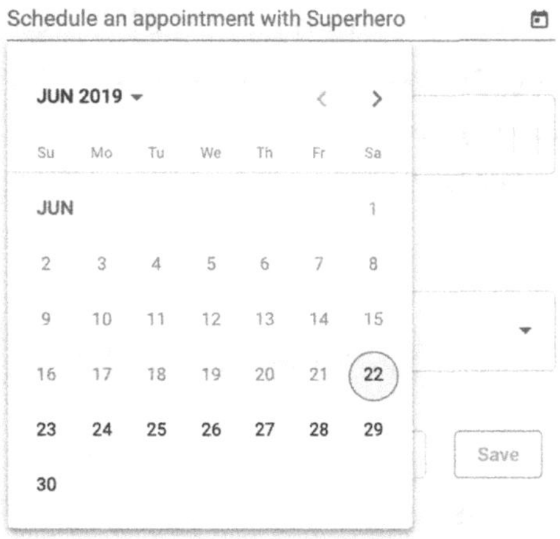

Figure 10-5. *With min date, all dates prior are disabled*

Custom Filter

Consider scenarios to filter dates based on custom logic. For example, do not allow selecting dates over the weekend or holidays. To achieve this, use MatDatepickerFilter on the MatDatepickerInput directive.

Listing 10-14 filters weekends. It is a method on TypeScript class component. Note that the "date" parameter is each date on the date picker. On a date object, the day() function returns a zero-based index. A value of 0 represents the first day of the week—Sunday, and a value of 6 represents the last day of the week—Saturday.

Listing 10-14. Custom Date Filter Function

```
filterWeekends(date: Date){
  // day 0 is Sunday and day 6 is Saturday.
  if(date.day() !== 0 && date.day() !== 6){
    return true;
  }
  return false;
}
```

Use it in the template with MatDatepickerFilter. See Listing 10-15 and Figure 10-6.

Listing 10-15. Using Custom Filter Defined as filterWeekends

```
<input [min]="dobMinDate" [matDatepickerFilter]="filterWeekends"
matInput [matDatepicker]="dateOfBirth" />
```

Schedule an appointment with Superhero

JUL 2019 ▾					‹	›
Su	Mo	Tu	We	Th	Fr	Sa

JUL

	1	2	3	4	5	6
7	8	9	10	11	12	13
14	15	16	17	18	19	20
21	22	23	24	25	26	27
28	29	30	31			

Save

Figure 10-6. *A date picker that filters out weekends with custom logic*

Slider

A slider is a Material Design control for selecting numbers or a value within a range; for example, it is on a scale of 1 to 10. Use Angular Material's matSlider component for the control. Figure 10-7 is a depiction of a slider.

Rate Superhero

Figure 10-7. *Slider for selecting a value in range*

Getting Started

To use Angular Material's matSlider, import the module containing the component. See Listing 10-16. In the Superheroes code sample, all the Material Design components are encompassed in superheroes-material-design.module.ts.

Listing 10-16. Import Modules for Slider

```
import { MatSliderModule } from '@angular/material/slider';

@NgModule({
  declarations: [
        // Removed code for brevity
  ],
  imports: [
        // Removed code for brevity
    MatSliderModule,
  ],
  exports: [
  ],
  providers:[]
})
export class SuperheroesMaterialDesignModule { }
```

Slider in an Input Form

Form fields that need to select a value within a range of numbers, like a feedback rating, may use a slider. In the Create Superhero form, let's add a ratings field (see Listing 10-17).

Listing 10-17. Superhero Ratings with Slider

```
<div>
    <div>
      Rate Superhero
    </div>
    <div>
      <strong> {{ minRating }} </strong>
      <mat-slider [max]="maxRating" [min]="minRating" step="1" thumbLabel >
      </mat-slider>
      <strong> {{ maxRating }} </strong>
    </div>
  </div>
```

The following are the input elements on the slider component.

- min: The start value of the slider range.

- max: The end value of the slider range.

- step: As the user drags the slider, increments whether the rating should increase or decrease.

- thumbLabel: Shows a label for the selected value; especially useful on mobile screens when dragging the slider with your fingers. Note the value of 8, which is the thumb label in Figure 10-7.

Note   You may use data binding on all input values. In Listing 10-17, we bind the minRating and maxRating defined in TypeScript class component. We hard-code this step in the HTML template. If required, we may apply input binding on the step as well.

If we use reactive forms, and the rating is a field on a form group, we may use formControlName. A value is initialized and updated as the user changes it on the screen.

Listing 10-18 line 6 shows the TypeScript file component for a form control named "rating". The form control is mapped in the HTML template with formControlName. See line 4 in Listing 10-19. Note the form group on the form element in line 2.

Listing 10-18. HTML Template with the Form Control Slider

```
1. <!-- formControlName added on the slider -->
2. <form #superheroForm="ngForm" [formGroup]="superheroFormGroup"
   (submit)="submitHanlder()">
3.       <!-- other form fields removed for brevity -->
4.     <mat-slider formControlName="rating" [max]="maxRating"
       [min]="minRating" step="0.5" ></mat-slider>
5. </form>
```

Listing 10-19. TypeScript File Component Using Slider with formGroup and formControl

```
1. // TypeScript component using a form control for rating on FormGroup.
2.  ngOnInit() {
3.    this.superheroFormGroup = new FormGroup( {
4.      name: new FormControl(", Validators.required),
5. // Removed other FormControl objects for brevity
6.      rating: new FormControl(8)
7.  });
8. }
```

If the slider is not part of a reactive form for data binding, we may use the attribute value to set a value on the slider. See Listing 10-20.

Listing 10-20. Using Slider with Value Attribute

```
<mat-slider [value]="rating" [max]="maxRating" [min]="minRating"
step="0.5" ></mat-slider>
```

The variable rating is defined in the TypeScript class component. As the user drags the slider, we may use the event named input to capture the changed value. See Listing 10-21.

Listing 10-21. Capture User Input

```
--- CreateSuperhero.component.html ---
    <mat-slider (input)="onSliderChange($event)" [value]="rating"
    [max]="maxRating" [min]="minRating" step="1" ></mat-slider>

--- CreateSuperhero.component.ts ---
  onSliderChange(event: MatSliderChange){
    console.log(event.value );
  }
```

We pass the event to the onSliderChange function on the TypeScript class component. Use the value object on the event object to retrieve the user-selected value. For defining the data type for the event or the function parameter, import MatSliderChange from the @angular/material/slider module.

Note   In template-driven forms, we may use data-binding features and ngModel on mat-slider to read chosen value or set a new value.

The slider component can be oriented vertically. It is natural to drag up or down with the thumb and useful on mobiles screens. Consider the volume rocker on mobile devices as an example.

Use the vertical input attribute, true ,for vertical orientation.

Toggle Switch and Check Box

We may use toggle switches or check boxes to switch a feature on or off; select from the available options or any similar use case. Both components serve a similar purpose. We may pick one of the two components and use consistently across the application.

Toggle switches provide a relatively modern look and feel, colors, and animation. Figure 10-8 showcases toggle switches.

Use matSlideToggle component in Angular Material for toggle switch implementation.

Check boxes are traditional. We may use the Angular Material component for a Material Design look and feel, including colors and animation (when selecting and unselecting). Figure 10-9 showcases check boxes.

Use the matCheckbox component in Angular Material for check box implementation.

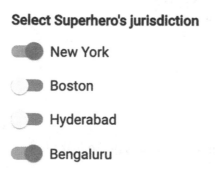

Select Superhero's jurisdiction

New York

Boston

Hyderabad

Bengaluru

Figure 10-8. *Slide toggle to select one or more values from available list*

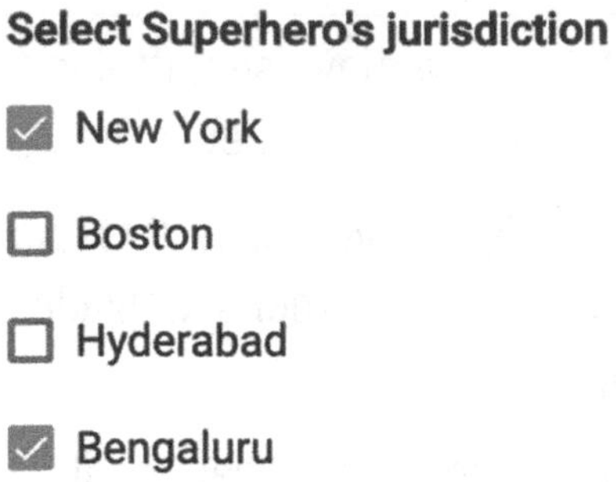

Select Superhero's jurisdiction

☑ New York

☐ Boston

☐ Hyderabad

☑ Bengaluru

Figure 10-9. *Check box to select one or more values from available list*

Getting Started with Toggle Switch

To use Angular Material's matSlideToggle, import the module named MatSlideToggleModule, which contains the component. Consider Listing 10-22. In the Superheroes code sample, all the Material Design components are encompassed in superheroes-material-design.module.ts.

Listing 10-22. Import Modules for Toggle Switch

```
import { MatSlideToggleModule } from '@angular/material/slide-toggle'
@NgModule({
  declarations: [
       // Removed code for brevity
  ],
  imports: [
    // Removed code for brevity
    MatSlideToggleModule,
  ],
  exports: [
  ],
  providers:[]
})
export class SuperheroesMaterialDesignModule { }
```

Getting Started with Check Box

To use Angular Material's matCheckbox, import the module named MatCheckboxModule, which contains the component. See Listing 10-23. In the Superheroes code sample, all the Material Design components are encompassed in superheroes-material-design.module.ts.

Listing 10-23. Import Modules for Check Box

```
import { MatCheckboxModule } from '@angular/material/checkbox';
@NgModule({
  declarations: [
      // Removed code for brevity
  ],
  imports: [
      // Removed code for brevity
    MatCheckboxModule,
  ],
  exports: [
  ],
  providers:[]
})
export class SuperheroesMaterialDesignModule { }
```

Toggle Switch in an Input Form

A toggle switch allows the user to select or unselect a value. The value could be part of a group, like a list of cities, or it could be an isolated value.

Listing 10-24 is for toggling a feature.

Listing 10-24. Show a Toggle, Not Grouped

```
<mat-slide-toggle checked="true" (change)="onToggleChange($event)"
labelPosition="before" disableRipple="true">
        Add a cape to the hero?
</mat-slide-toggle>
```

The following attributes are used on the component.

- checked: If true, shows the toggle selected. We may use this attribute to set a default value.

- labelPosition: By default, it is set to "after". We may use "before" to show the label first and the toggle switch later.

- disableRipple: If true, disables the ripple animation on a Material Design component.

- checked: Emits an event of type MatSlideToggleChange. Listing 10-25 prints the checked property, which indicates if the toggle is selected or not.

Listing 10-25. Change Handler for the Toggle

```
onToggleChange(event: MatSlideToggleChange){
  console.log(event.checked );
}
```

Note   Import the event MatSlideToggleChange from the @angular/material/slide-toggle module. We used it as a parameter on the onToggleChange function. It helps provide data type for the event object in the TypeScript class.

Listing 10-25 is about toggle switches in a form group. It results in showing a list of cities with toggle switch as in Figure 10-10. In the code sample, the component TypeScript file has an array with list of cities. See Listing 10-26. The HTML template iterates through the array with *ngFor to show cities that can be toggled on/off. See Listing 10-27.

Listing 10-26. List of Cities in the TypeScript Class File Component

```
cities = [ {
  name: "New York",
  selectedByDefault: true
},{
  name: "Boston",
  selectedByDefault: false
```

```
    },{
      name: "Hyderabad",
      selectedByDefault: false
    }, {
      name: "Bengaluru",
      selectedByDefault: true
    }];
```

Listing 10-27. Show List of Cities with Toggle Switches in a Form

```
<div formArrayName="jurisdiction" *ngFor="let city of
superheroFormGroup.controls.jurisdiction.controls; let i=index;" >
    <mat-slide-toggle [formControlName]="i" >
      {{cities[i].name}}
    </mat-slide-toggle>
  </div>
```

Note formArrayName in Listing 10-27. In this sample, we are using Reactive Forms and a form group. The toggle switch is part of a form group. See Listing 10-28.

Listing 10-28. Create formArray Based on List of Cities

```
1.  ngOnInit() {

2.    // Create form controls array based on the list of cities

3.    let j = this.cities.map( i => new FormControl(i.selectedByDefault));

4.    this.superheroFormGroup = new FormGroup( {
5.      name: new FormControl(", Validators.required),
6.    // removed other controls for brevity
7.      jurisdiction: new FormArray(j)
8.    });
9.}
```

Note the statements in line 3 and line 7. First, using the list of cities (which we also used to show toggle switches on the HTML template), we create an array of form controls. In the form group, we create a form array named "jurisdiction" that uses the array of form controls.

The form control initializes with selectedByDefault field on the city object. See line 3 in Listing 10-28. The field is defined in each city object in Listing 10-27. The default selected value changes case by case. We arbitrarily set some cities to true and the others to false.

As the user changes the values on the form, including selecting a city as a jurisdiction for the superhero, form controls in the form group are updated. We use this data when we submit the form. Just to demonstrate that the data was updated, Listing 10-29 subscribes to the form group's valueChanges observable. Read Chapter 9 for more information on the observable.

Listing 10-29. Console Log Change Made by the User to the Form

```
this.superheroFormGroup
  .valueChanges
  .subscribe(data => {
    data.jurisdiction.map( (value, it)=> console.log(this.cities[it].
    name, value));
  });
```

With subscribe(), we receive data and a model object representing form controls. In the data, we iterate through a jurisdiction array. Since we have four cities, it returns four true or false values, depending on if the city is selected or not. When printing the debug log, we select the city name and the user-selected value. See Figure 10-10 for the result.

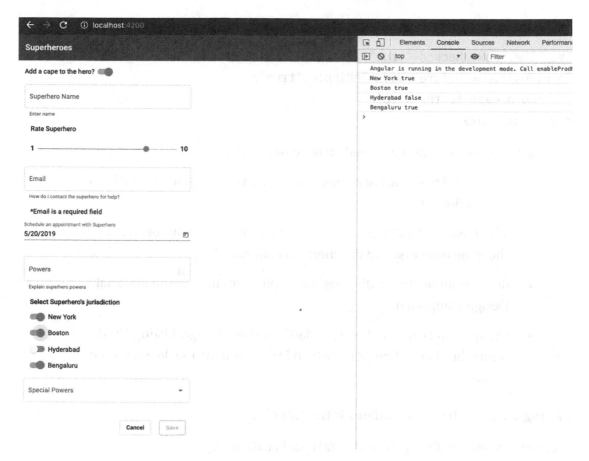

Figure 10-10. *Console log selected cities on the form*

Note   In template-driven forms, we may use data-binding features and ngModel on mat-slide-toggle to read if an option is selected or to toggle true/false.

Check Box in an Input Form

Similar to toggle switches, check boxes could also be part of a group or an isolated value. As mentioned earlier, the matCheckbox component is used for a Material Design look and feel functionality on a check box. See Listing 10-30.

Listing 10-30. Show a Check Box, Not Grouped

```
<mat-checkbox checked="true" (change)=" onToggleCheckboxChange($event)"
labelPosition="before" disableRipple="true">
    Add a cape to the hero?
</mat-checkbox>
```

The following attributes are used on the component.

- checked: If true, the check box is selected. You may use this attribute to set a default value.

- labelPosition: By default, it is set to "after". You may use "before" to show the label first and the check box afterward.

- disableRipple: If true, disables the ripple animation in the Material Design component.

- change: Emits an event of type MatCheckboxChange. Listing 10-31 prints the checked property, which indicates if the toggle is selected or not.

Listing 10-31. Change Handler for the Check Box

```
onToggleCheckboxChange(event: MatCheckboxChange){
  console.log(event.checked );
}
```

Note   Import MatCheckboxChange from the @angular/material/checkbox module. We used it as a parameter on the onToggleCheckboxChange function. It helps provide a data type for the event object in the TypeScript class.

Listing 10-31 is about check boxes in a form group. It results in showing a list of cities with check boxes, as shown in Figure 10-10. In the code sample, the TypeScript file component has an array with a list of cities. See Listing 10-32. The HTML template iterates through the array to show the check boxes.

Listing 10-32. Show List of Cities with Check Boxes in a Form

```
<div formArrayName="jurisdiction" *ngFor="let city of
superheroFormGroup.controls.jurisdiction.controls; let i=index;" >
  <mat-checkbox [formControlName]="i" checked="false">
    {{cities[i].name}}
  </mat-checkbox>
</div>
```

Note formArrayName. In this sample, we are using reactive forms and a form group. The check box is part of a form group. See Listing 10-33.

Listing 10-33. Create formArray Based on List of Cities

```
ngOnInit() {

  // Create form controls array based on the list of cities
  let j = this.cities.map( i => new FormControl(i.selectedByDefault));

  this.superheroFormGroup = new FormGroup( {
    name: new FormControl(", Validators.required),
    // removed other controls for brevity
    jurisdiction: new FormArray(j)
  });
}
```

Note the two statements in Listing 10-33. First, using the list of cities (which we also used to show check boxes in the HTML template), we create an array of form controls. We use these form controls and create a form array. It is named jurisdiction. Notice, the form array, jurisdiction is part of the superhero form group.

The form control initializes with selectedByDefault field on the city object. It is one of the fields on city object (defined in Listing 10-32). We arbitrarily set this value true for some cities and false for the other.

As the user changes values on the form, including selecting a city as a jurisdiction for the superhero, form controls on the form group are updated. We use this data when we submit the form. Just to demonstrate data is updated, consider Listing 10-34, which subscribes to the form group's valueChanges observable. Read Chapter 9 for more information on the observable.

Listing 10-34. Console Log Change Made by the User to the Form

```
this.superheroFormGroup
  .valueChanges
  .subscribe(data => {
    data.jurisdiction.map( (value, it)=> console.log(this.cities[it].
    name, value));
  });
```

On the subscribe, we receive data, a model object representing the form controls. In the data, we iterate through a jurisdiction array. Since we have four cities, it returns four true or false values, depending whether the city is selected. When printing the debug log, we select the city name and the user-selected value. Figure 10-11 shows the result.

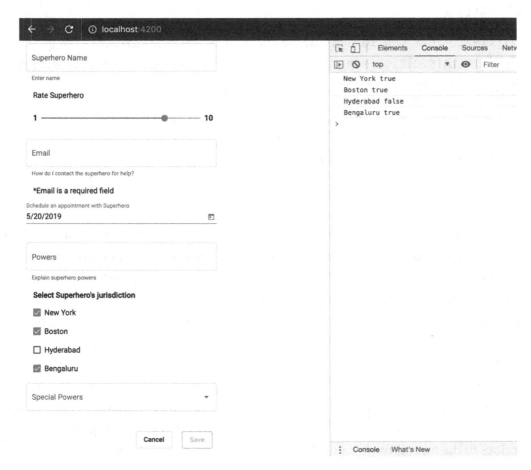

Figure 10-11. *Console log selected cities on the form*

> **Note**   In template-driven forms, we may use data-binding features and ngModel on the mat-checkbox to read if an option is selected or to switch true/false.

Conclusion

This chapter explored the date picker component. We also used the mat-slider component that provides Material Design slider control.

The chapter covered using toggle switches, which are a modern approach to enabling or disabling a feature on a form. Using components with reactive forms was discussed, and traditional ways to select or unselect a feature on a data form using check boxes was covered.

Exercise

In the dinosaurs form, provide options to select the continents that a given dinosaur was found in. Create the form with the following toggle button options. Selecting at least one continent is mandatory.

- North America

- South America

- Greater India

- Europe

- Arabia

- Laurasia

- Gondwanaland

Provide a date-of-discovery option. Do not allow the date to be prior to 1900. The date cannot be later than today (the current system date).

Reference

Angular Material Documentation (https://material.angular.io/)

CHAPTER 11

Angular: Routing

Most Angular applications are SPAs (single-page applications). When transitioning between pages, an SPA does not reload the whole page; only the section of the page with new content refreshes. In general, the header, left navigation, footer, and so forth, reload only if needed.

SPAs are both efficient and better at the user experience. With an SPA, the user does not lose context and the page transition is clean.

This chapter explains routing with Angular. It begins by describing the need for routing, instructions, and route configuration. It also describes linking to various application routes.

Why do we need routing? An Angular application has many views, components, and screens. Users work with and navigate these views. Browsers use URLs and history data for forward/back buttons' functionality. The browser allows bookmarking a page with the help of the URL. Hence, an SPA needs to maintain URLs mapped to each view. Angular routing uses configuration, maps URLs to a component, and renders the view.

Getting Started

When we began with a sample application for superheroes, we used Angular CLI to generate a new application. The --routing option allows us to create a routing module with an empty route configuration. Consider the complete command we used when creating the sample application.

```
ng new superheroes --routing
Snippet-1: Create new Angular application with router.
```

The CLI created a separate routing module and imported it to the main module. Consider Listing 11-1 and Listing 11-2.

© Venkata Keerti Kotaru 2020
V. K. Kotaru, *Angular for Material Design*, https://doi.org/10.1007/978-1-4842-5434-9_11

If you began the project without routing, use the following steps to add it now.

Listing 11-1. Add Routing to the Angular Application

```
yarn add @angular/router
```

or

```
npm install -S @angular/router
```

Now, the routing package is available for the Angular application. Next, import RouterModule and the Routes configuration objects from @angular/router.

Remember, we packaged the Angular Material implementation and code in a separate Angular module. We will do the same for the router implementation as well. If you used Angular CLI, app-routing.module.ts is already created. If you added the router manually, create the TypeScript class file shown in Listing 11-2.

Listing 11-2. Routing Module

```
--- app-routing.module.ts ---
1. import { NgModule } from '@angular/core';
2. import { Routes, RouterModule } from '@angular/router';

3. const routes: Routes = [];

4. @NgModule({
5.   imports: [RouterModule.forRoot(routes)],
6.   exports: [RouterModule]
7. })
8. export class AppRoutingModule { }
```

Note line 3 in Listing 11-2. The routes array is of type Routes. It will contain the route configuration. Later sections in the chapter discuss route configuration. For the moment, remember that the route configuration is entirely in this "routes" variable. We call the static forRoot() function on RouteModule, with the route configuration as a parameter. We import the result in AppRoutingModule.

Next, we import AppRoutingModule to the main module. Angular CLI added the following routing module reference automatically. If you added the router manually, update the main module as shown in Listing 11-2.

Import AppRoutingModule, created in the Listing 11-3, and add to the imports array in the @NgModule decorator.

Listing 11-3. Main Module Importing the Routing Module

```
import { AppRoutingModule } from './app-routing.module';
// Removed code for brevity

@NgModule({
  // Removed code for brevity
  imports: [
    AppRoutingModule,
  ]
})
export class AppModule { }
```

Route Configuration

We use routing to tie a view to a URL. It is also the URL of a page. Route configuration defines the route pattern (or the URL pattern). In the context of the sample application, a page is an Angular component. The component renders the view. Hence, it also ties a component for a given route pattern.

Based on the preceding explanation, two basic fields are required in the configuration.

- **url**: The URL or route pattern

- **component**: References the component to load when the route pattern matches

Listing 11-4 has two routes. Note the lines of code between lines 3 and 12. Each object in the array represents a route tied to a component or a page. Notice the imported components (that were created in previous chapters) referenced in the configuration.

Listing 11-4. Route Configuration Added in app-routing.module.ts

```
1. import { SuperheroListComponent } from './superheroes-material-design/
   superhero-list/superhero-list.component';
2. import { CreateSuperheroReactiveFormComponent } from './superheroes-
   material-design/create-superhero-reactive-form/create-superhero-
   reactive-form.component';

3. const routes: Routes = [
4.   {
5.     path: "heroes",
6.     component: SuperheroListComponent
7.   },
8.   {
9.     path: "create-hero",
10.     component: CreateSuperheroReactiveFormComponent
11.   }
12. ];

13. @NgModule({
14.   imports: [RouterModule.forRoot(routes)],
15.   exports: [RouterModule]
16. })
17. export class AppRoutingModule { }
```

When the URL is heroes, it loads SuperheroListComponent, and when it is create-hero, it loads CreateSuperheroReactiveFormComponent. In Figure 11-1, it loads CreateSuperheroReactiveFormComponent with the create-hero route in the URL.

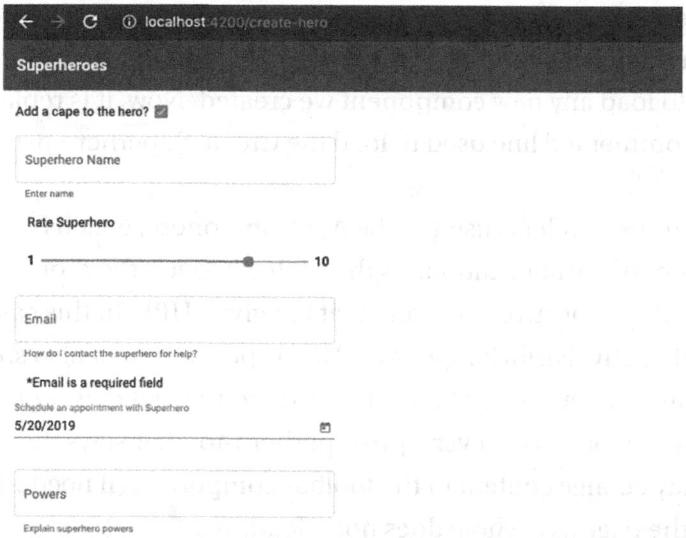

Figure 11-1. *The create-hero route loads the referenced component*

Router Outlet

Now, let's explore where (which location on the page) the
CreateSuperheroReactiveFormComponent loads and how we update only a section of a
page instead of reloading the whole page for each page navigation.

The Angular router uses the router-outlet component as a placeholder. It loads
the component configured for the given route or the URL. In the code sample, to get
the result seen in Figure 11-1, the AppComponent has been updated. It is the root
component of the application. Consider Listing 11-5.

Listing 11-5. App Component with Router Outlet

```
<app-superhero-toolbar>{{title}}</app-superhero-toolbar>
<!--
    <app-create-superhero-reactive-form></app-create-superhero-reactive-
    form> -->
<router-outlet></router-outlet>
```

The app-superhero-toolbar component is in the first line. In an earlier chapter, we used this component to show a toolbar for the application. We temporarily updated the AppComponent to load any new component we created. Now, it is replaced with router-outlet. Note the commented line used to load the Create Superhero page in the previous chapter.

In summary, router-outlet is used in the AppComponent, which is the root component of the application. As the route changes, the root component loads the respective component at the given URL. In this case, it is CreateSuperheroReactiveFormComponent. The AppComponent also shows a toolbar in addition to router-outlet. As we change the URL, router-outlet is replaced with the component at the route. However, app-superhero-toolbar stays the same. It does not reload. We may change content in the toolbar component (if needed), but the component and the page as a whole does not reload.

In Figure 11-2, /heroes loads a different component at the given route.

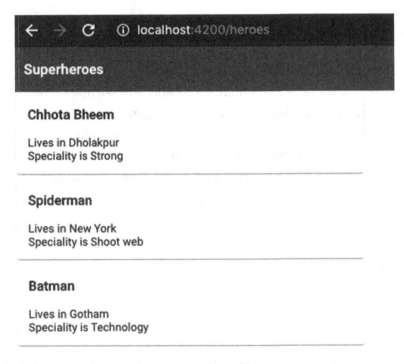

Figure 11-2. *The route heroes load superherolist component*

Figure 11-2 shows only one toolbar, which is common; it does not reload between page loads. In other scenarios, it could be more than a single toolbar component. We may create an application skeleton that includes a toolbar, left navigation, right navigation, and footer that do not reload between page transitions.

Linking to a Route

So far, we created routes in the application. This section covers linking to a route so that users have a way to navigate to it. In the code sample, let's create a button or a link in the toolbar that links to create-hero route.

Traditional hyperlinks attempt to reload the whole page. They may attempt to load the link server-side. Use the routerLink directive, which allows linking to a route in the Angular application in the browser.

In Listing 11-6, we update the toolbar in app.component.ts.

Listing 11-6. Router Link Directive to Link a Route

```
<app-superhero-toolbar>
    {{title}}
    <a routerLink="/create-hero">
        Create Hero
    </a>
</app-superhero-toolbar>
```

As the user clicks the Create Hero link, the router link updates the router outlet with the component at the route. It does not refresh the whole page.

Navigate for Actions

Listing 11-7 manages navigation with a link in the HTML template. Sometimes, navigation might be a consequence of an action. In general, we code actions as buttons. We may use a TypeScript function invoked on the click of a button or a link to navigate. It is useful when there is custom logic in the navigation.

For simplicity, we navigate to /create-hero with a TypeScript method invoked on a click. In Listing 11-7, the (click) event invokes the navigateToCreate() function in the TypeScript file component.

Listing 11-7. router.navigate to Link to a Route

```
--- app.component.html ---
    <a (click)="navigateToCreate()">
        Create
    </a>
--- app.component.ts ---
1. import { Router } from '@angular/router';

2. @Component({
3.        // Removed code for brevity
4. })
5. export class AppComponent {
6.  title: string = "Superheroes";
7.   constructor(private router: Router){
8.  }

9.  navigateToCreate(){
10.    this.router.navigate(['/create-hero']);
11.  }
12. }
```

In line 10, the router is an object of the router service imported from @angular/ Router (line 7 in the constructor). It is injected as a private field on the component class. The navigate() API on the router service instance redirects to the specified route.

Route Parameters

In the preceding sample, the routes are static. Consider an example where we show the profile of a superhero. The component that shows the profile uses a *superhero name* input in the URL. The name can change on the fly.

We can configure this route with a parameter for the name. Consider the route configuration in Listing 11-8. :superheroName is a route segment. It is the variable for which we provide a value on the fly in the URL. We do so while navigating to this route. Remember, in the sample application we created, the route configuration is in app-routing.module.ts.

Listing 11-8. Route Configuration with Parameters

```
import { SuperheroComponent } from './superheroes-material-design/
superhero/superhero.component';
const routes: Routes = [
  // Removed other routes for brevity
  {
    path: "hero/:superheroName ",
    component: SuperheroComponent
  }
];
```

As an example, `http://localhost:4200/hero/spiderman` is a route matching the pattern. For the superheroName variable, Spiderman is the value. Note the way that SuperheroComponent is configured. The router loads this component when the route matches.

In the Superheroes sample application, we built SuperheroProfileComponent, which showcases the data of a particular superhero. It cannot select a superhero. It shows the data for any superhero supplied as input.

Let's build SuperheroComponent in Listing 11-9 to read the route parameter, select the given superhero from the available collection, and pass it as input to SuperheroProfileComponent.

Use the following Angular CLI command to create a new component (see Listing 11-9).

Listing 11-9. Create New Component for Using Route Params

```
ng g component superheroes-material-design/superhero
```

Next, modify the component to import the ActivatedRoute service from the Angular router package. The service has the API to read the route params. Inject the ActivatedRoute service in the component. See line 8 in Listing 11-10.

Listing 11-10. Use Activated Route Service with Superhero Component

```
1. // imports
import { Superhero } from '../models/superhero';
import { ActivatedRoute } from '@angular/router';
2. // Removed code for brevity
```

```
3. @Component({
4.  // Removed code for brevity
5. })
6. export class SuperheroComponent implements OnInit {
7.  hero: Superhero;
8.  constructor(private route: ActivatedRoute) {
9.  }

10.  ngOnInit() {
11.  }
12. }
```

Using Snapshot to Read Route Param

There are two approaches to accessing the value in a route or a URL. Let's first go through an easier approach with the snapshot, which provides instant access to the route parameter. We read the value in the URL at that point in time. Consider Listing 11-11.

Listing 11-11. Read Route Param heroName

```
1.  ngOnInit() {
2.    const heroNameParam = this.route.snapshot.params.heroName;
3.  }
```

Let's decode the second line in Listing 11-11, especially this.route.snapshot.params. heroName. The route variable is an object of type ActivatedRoute. As mentioned, it is injected into the component class (refer to the constructor in Listing 11-11).

All the dynamic route params are available as key/values pairs. As the component initializes, in the ngOnInit() lifecycle method, we access the snapshot of the route with the snapshot field. In its child property params, access the key/value pairs.

Remember, we named the token "heroName" in the route configuration. Hence, the value in the URL is accessible with the heroName variable name.

Next, search for the given hero name among the available hero names. In a typical application, we may retrieve this data from a server-side API. For simplicity, in this sample, the data is in an array. Listing 11-12 finds the hero in an array named "heroes".

Note   The find API in the array object accepts a predicate with each object in the array as a parameter. In the list of heroes, each hero object is represented by the input parameter "i". To ignore case, we may use toLowerCase() function.

Listing 11-12. Find the Hero Input Through Route Param

```
// hero is an object of type superhero, a data model class.
hero: Superhero;

ngOnInit() {

    const heroNameParam = this.route.snapshot.params.heroName || "";

    // find hero in a list of heroes.
    this.hero = this.heroes.find( hero => hero.name.toLowerCase() ===
    heroNameParam.toLowerCase());
  }

private heroes: Array<Superhero> = [
    {
      name: "Chhotta Bheem",
      email: "ChhottaBheem@angularsample.com",
      details: "A hero in Dholakpur village",
      country: "India",
      specialPowers: ["Strong"],
      favFood: ["Laddu"]
    },
    {
      name: "Spiderman",
      email: "spiderman@angularsample.com",
      details: "A hero in New York city",
      country: "United States",
      specialPowers: ["Shoots web"],
      favFood: ["Cheese burger"]
    },
```

```
  {
    name: "Batman",
    email: "batman@angularsample.com",
    details: "A hero in Gotham city",
    country: "United Kingdom",
    specialPowers: ["Martial Arts"],
    favFood: ["Spaghetti"]
  }
];
```

The find() method will return a single object from the list. Use this object in the HTML template to show profile of a superhero. Remember, SuperheroProfileComponent (with the app-superhero-profile selector) is used to show the profile of a superhero using the data provided in the input attributes. Listing 11-13 is the HTML template that uses the app-superhero-profile component.

Listing 11-13. Template That Renders Superhero Profile

```
<app-superhero-profile
    [name]="hero.name"
    [lives-in]="hero.country"
    [superpowers]="hero.specialPowers"
>
</app-superhero-profile>
```

Figure 11-3 shows the result.

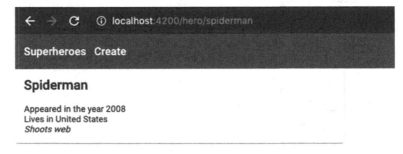

Figure 11-3. *Show superhero profile based on route param*

Using an Observable to Read Route Param

There is a downside to the preceding approach. A snapshot is the value at a point in time. If the component rerenders, we need to write code to identify if there is a change in the route param, and then read the value again. It does not automatically retrieve the new value.

On the other hand, an observable looks for changes to the route param and updates the values.

Listing 11-14 is modified to use an observable instead of a snapshot.

Listing 11-14. Use Observable Instead of Snapshot to Read Route Params

```
this.route
  .params
  .subscribe ( r => {
    this.hero = this.heroes.find( i => i.name.toLowerCase() ===
    r.heroName);
  });
```

params is an observable. Listing 11-14 subscribes to value changes on the observable. The predicate accepts an input variable, r. As the value changes on the route params, the predicate is run. We find the hero object that matches the route param found in the r variable.

The resultant value is stored in the same object as Listing 11-14. This object is used in the HTML template to render the superhero profile.

Note   We may use paramsMap instead of params. It is useful when making a server-side API call, which returns another observable with results. We pipe the results to the switchMap operator, which can flatten the results.

Link a Route with Parameters

The "Linking to a Route" section describes linking a static route. Let's expand the sample to include dynamic parameters when linking. Figure 11-4 shows a list of superheroes. Let's link each card in the list to an information screen. As the user clicks the card, it navigates to the information screen and updates the workspace (router-outlet) with an information card.

In Listing 11-15, routerLink has an array of values. The first item in the array is the static part of the route. The remaining is a list of parameters. In this example, we just have one parameter: superhero name.

Listing 11-15. Router Link with Dynamic Values Are Parameters

```
<div *ngFor="let hero of heroes">
  <a [routerLink]="['/hero', hero.name]">
  <mat-card>
      <!-- removed code for brevity -->
  </a>
</div>
```

hero is one object in the heroes array. The ngFor directive is iterating through the array. We pass the name of the current object as the route param. Figure 11-4 shows the result. The route params results in the href value for the <a /> element.

Figure 11-4. Dynamic route params

Navigate with Route Params for Actions

As you saw in Listing 11-16, we may link to a route in a TypeScript function. We use the router service object injected into the component. It is very similar to the explanation in the "Navigate for Actions" section. However, it supplies dynamic route params.

Listing 11-16 line 1 invokes a navigateToHeroDetails() method in the TypeScript class component instead of linking directly.

Listing 11-16. Invoke a Method to Link to Details Screen

```
--- superhero-list.component.html ---
1.  <a (click)="navigateToHeroDetails(hero.name)">
2.  <mat-card >
3.      <h3>{{hero.name}}</h3>
4.      <div>Lives in {{hero.livesIn}}</div>
5.      <div>Speciality is {{hero.power}}</div>
6.  </mat-card>
  </a>
```

Listing 11-17 passes parameters when linking to a route with the navigate() API on the router service. The navigate() function parameter is an array. The first parameter is the URL. Supply all the route params next. In the code sample, we supply the heroName route param (see line 2).

Listing 11-17. Use Router Service Instance to Navigate

```
navigateToHeroDetails(heroName: string){
  this.router.navigate(["/hero", heroName]);
}
```

Optional Route Params

The router configuration in Listing 11-17 makes the route param mandatory. As an example, /hero/ without the hero's name does not match the pattern. Hence, the route and the component are not invoked.

There are scenarios in which the route parameters are optional. As an example, consider the sort order on the list screen. We may use a default ascending (by name) sort order. If the URL explicitly specifies a descending order, show the list in a descending order. The order field may or may not be present in the URL.

Traditionally in a URL, optional parameters are specified as a query string. Decide the sort order (see http://localhost:4200/heroes?sortOrder=descending).

To access the optional query string params, we continue to use the ActivatedRoute object. On the object, use the queryParams observable instead of the params observable. Listing 11-18 retrieves the optional sort order from the query string.

Listing 11-18. Access queryParams Observable

```
1.   ngOnInit() {
2.      this.route
3.         .queryParams
4.         .subscribe( (p) => {
5.         // Is sort order defined and ht value is descending.
6.           if (p.sortOrder && p.sortOrder === "descending"){
7.           // the reverse() function orders items in the array descending.
8.             this.heroes = _.sortBy(this.heroes, 'name').reverse();
9.           } else {
10.          // The array is sort ascnding
11.            this.heroes = _.sortBy(this.heroes, 'name');
12.          }
13.        });
14.  }
```

Consider the lines between 4 and 13 in Listing 11-18. The conditional logic that checks if the sortOrder field is defined and if the value is descending (line 6). Since it is an optional parameter, if not defined (or explicitly specified as ascending), we show the superhero list in ascending order.

Note   We use _ function sortBy. It is a lodash utility API. To import and use such utilities from lodash, use the following import on top of the file.

```
import * as _ from 'lodash';
```

We may also use queryParams on the snapshot. Again, a snapshot is a value at a point in time. Observable subscribes to changes in the URL, and hence, it is the preferred option. A snapshot does not update unless we explicitly invoke the code to update the value when the URL changes. In Listing 11-19, we simplify Listing 11-18 to use a snapshot. It is useful if we do not have to worry about changing URLs and params with the given route configuration.

Listing 11-19. Using Snapshot Instead of Observable to Retrieve Optional Query Params

```
ngOnInit() {
    const sortOrder = this.route.snapshot.queryParams.sortOrder;
    if (sortOrder && sortOrder === "descending"){
      this.heroes= _.sortBy(this.heroes, 'name').reverse()
    } else {
      this.heroes= _.sortBy(this.heroes, 'name');
    }
  }
}
```

Figure 11-5 shows the result. The descending alphabetical order is by name: Spiderman, Chhota Bheem, and Batman.

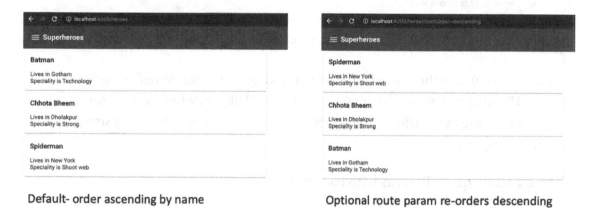

Default- order ascending by name   Optional route param re-orders descending

Figure 11-5. *Superhero sort descending with an optional query string*

Linking with Optional Route Params

To demonstrate linking with optional route params, let's update the code sample. Create two buttons in the header that order the list in ascending order and descending order. In Figure 11-6, the List (Descending) button links to /heroes?sortOrder=descending, and the List (Ascending) button links to /heroes?sortOrder=ascending.

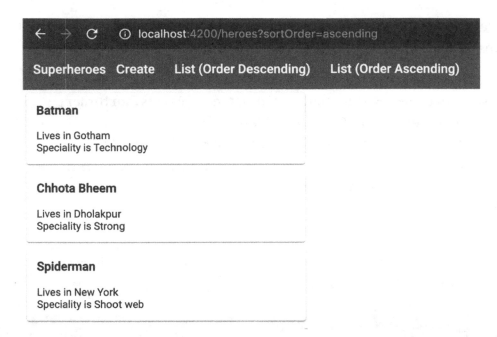

Figure 11-6. *Reorder superhero list by linking with optional route params*

Listing 11-20 uses the routerLink directive and queryParams to define optional params. The optional params are passed in as a JSON object, which will be translated into a query string in the URL by the directive. Figure 11-7 shows the query string generated by queryParams.

Listing 11-20. queryParams with routerLink

```
<a routerLink="/heroes" [queryParams]="{sortOrder: 'descending'}">
    List (Order Descending)
</a>
<a routerLink="/heroes" [queryParams]="{sortOrder: 'ascending'}">
    List (Order Ascending)
</a>
```

```
      href="/create-hero"> Create </a>
...   <a _ngcontent-c0 routerlink="/heroes" ng-reflect-query-params="[object Object]" ng-
      reflect-router-link="/heroes" href="/heroes?sortOrder=descending"> List (Order
      Descending) </a> == $0
      <a _ngcontent-c0 routerlink="/heroes" ng-reflect-query-params="[object Object]" ng-
      reflect-router-link="/heroes" href="/heroes?sortOrder=ascending"> List (Order
      Ascending) </a>
      </mat-toolbar>
```

Figure 11-7. *Optional query string params generated by Router Link directive*

As you saw in Listing 11-19 and Listing 11-20, we may use the router service instance and the invoke API. It can be used on the click of a button in the TypeScript file component. Listing 11-21 uses a method in the TypeScript file component that is handling the click event. We pass an additional queryParams object to the navigate method in the router service.

Listing 11-21. queryParams with Router Service Instance and Navigate API

```
getHeroListDescending(){
    this.router.navigate(['/heroes'], {queryParams:{sortOrder:
    'descending'}});
}
```

In, Listing 11-22, getHeroListDescending is invoked on the click of a button.

Listing 11-22. List (Descending) Link with Handler in TypeScript File Component

```
<a (click)="heroListDescending()">
    List (Order Descending)
</a>
```

Default Route

Consider the route configurations in Listing 11-22 and Listing 11-23. If no path is mentioned by the user, the application will need a default. Imagine that we decided to make the list screen the default. We may define a new route as follows. If we try to access the application at `http://localhost:4200/`, it automatically redirects to `http://localhost:4200/heroes`.

Listing 11-23. Default Route Configured

```
const routes: Routes = [
  // Removed other routes for brevity
  {
    path: "",
    redirectTo: "/heroes",
```

```
      pathMatch: "full"
  }
];

@NgModule({
  imports: [RouterModule.forRoot(routes)],
  exports: [RouterModule]
})
export class AppRoutingModule { }
```

Note pathMatch. The full value qualifies that the path needs to match completely. In this case, it is an empty string. It could be any value but not an empty string.

Multiple Routes to a Component or a Page

Imagine a scenario in which we need to use multiple paths to a single page. Consider the /heroes route. We show a list of superheroes with the help of SuperheroListComponent. Imagine that we need to get to the same route with /list route as well. Use the route configuration in Listing 11-24. Use redirectTo field with a new path: list. It redirects http://localhost:4200/list to http://localhost:4200/heroes.

Listing 11-24. Additional Route to a Component or a Page

```
{
    path: "list",
    redirectTo: "/destinations",
}
```

We may use an additional field: pathMatch. The value prefix in Listing 11-25 updates the configuration to redirect any path that includes a list at the beginning of the URL to redirect to a hero's page.

Listing 11-25. Using pathMatch

```
{
    path: "list",
    redirectTo: "/heroes",
    pathMatch: "prefix"
}
```

The new configuration redirects `http://localhost:4200/list/test` or `http://localhost:4200/list/heroes` to `http://localhost:4200/heroes`. However, it fails if the list is not at the beginning. For example, `http://localhost:4200/test/list/heroes` fails to redirect.

Undefined Route

If the user attempts to load a route that is not defined by the application and the route configuration, the application can decide to redirect to a default route or an error page. Consider the route configuration in Listing 11-26 to handle an undefined route. Notice the final route configuration object in the lines from 12 and 15. The path is configured with a wildcard character (**). If an undefined route (for example, localhost:4200/dummy) is attempted, it redirects to /heroes.

Listing 11-26. Redirect to Default route /heroes if an Undefined Route Attempted

```
1. const routes: Routes = [
2.  {
3.    path: "heroes",
4.    component: SuperheroListComponent
5.  },
6.  // Removed routes for brevity
7.  {
8.    path: "",
9.    redirectTo: "/heroes",
10.    pathMatch: "full"
11.  },
12.  {
13.    path: "**",
14.    redirectTo: "/heroes"
15.  }
16. ];
```

We may also show an error page indicating that a non-existent route was attempted by the user. Consider Listing 11-27 and Figure 11-8. Listing 11-27 uses a component instead of redirectTo (unlike Listing 11-26 with the wildcard route path). Note the last route configuration object (lines 13 to 16) with the wildcard for a route path.

Listing 11-27. Error Page for an Undefined Route

```
1. import { ErrorPageComponent } from './superheroes-material-design/error-
   page/error-page.component';

2. const routes: Routes = [
3.   // removed routes for brevity
4.   {
5.     path: "list",
6.     redirectTo: "/heroes"
7.   },
8.   {
9.     path: "",
10.     redirectTo: "/heroes",
11.     pathMatch: "full"
12.   },
13.   {
14.     path: "**",
15.     component: ErrorPageComponent
16.   }
17. ];
```

Attempted route does not exist

Figure 11-8. *Error component for an undefined route*

Note   The wildcard route needs to be the last route in the configuration. The order of this object in the entire route configuration is important. The wildcard configuration matches all routes (**). If it is at the beginning, it always loads the error page or redirects to the default route. This will block the entire application if placed at the beginning of the route configuration.

Conclusion

Routing is a required feature for building SPAs. Angular provides routing out of the box. The chapter began with instructions to import and make use of routing package, services, directives, components, and so forth.

The chapter described route configuration and explained additional route configurations, including creating a default route, managing single view for multiple routes (or URLs), and handling an undefined route.

The chapter also described the RouterOutlet component, which is a placeholder for loading the view for a given route, route parameters (params), and linking to a particular route. Route params can be read in one of the two ways, either with an observable or with a snapshot at a point in time.

Exercise

Add routing to the dinosaur application. Create a new component that shows a dinosaur list. Use a Material Design card to show each dinosaur on the list. Use a route named /dino-list tied to the list view and the component.

Create another component at the /dinosaur/:dinosaurName route that shows information about a particular dinosaur.

Link dino-list with the /dinosaur/:dinosaurName route. When the user clicks a dinosaur in the list screen, it passes the selected dinosaur name or ID. The name or ID queries and shows all the information about the dinosaur.

Make the dinosaur list screen the default route. If an undefined route is attempted by the user, redirect to the dinosaur list page.

References

Angular documentation (`https://angular.io/`)

Building Single Page Applications with Angular Router (`www.dotnetcurry.com/angularjs/1467/angular-routing-spa`)

Angular Router-Query Parameters (`https://alligator.io/angular/query-parameters/`)

CHAPTER 12

Material Design: Navigation

The previous chapter described implementing SPAs (single-page applications) and routing techniques that navigate between pages. This chapter covers Material Design components for navigation.

The chapter discusses two Angular Material components: toolbar and sidenav. The most common use of the component is application-level navigation between pages. These components are easy to implement and provide a great user experience with the tried and tested Material Design patterns.

Toolbar

Toolbars are typically placed on top of a web page. It provides a title and list of actions that the user may perform on the page. A toolbar encompasses the top navigation of the page.

Getting Started

To use Angular Material's toolbar, import the module containing the component. In Listing 12-1, all the Material Design components are encompassed in superheroes-material-design.module.ts.

Import the MatToolbarModule from the Angular Material repository. Import it into the NgModule (Angular module) encompassing all the Material Design code in the sample application.

© Venkata Keerti Kotaru 2020
V. K. Kotaru, *Angular for Material Design*, https://doi.org/10.1007/978-1-4842-5434-9_12

Listing 12-1. Import Toolbar Module

```
import { MatToolbarModule } from '@angular/material/toolbar';

@NgModule({
  declarations: [
      // Removed code for brevity
  ],
  imports: [

    MatToolbarModule,

  ],
  exports: [

  ],
  providers:[HitCounter]
})
export class SuperheroesMaterialDesignModule { }
```

The <mat-toolbar> component is now available for the application to use. Typically, a toolbar contains the top navigation of a page.

In the sample application, we organize the toolbar as follows. We place the toolbar at the same level as <router-outlet>. The router outlet updates the content and the components based on the route or the URL. Refer to Chapter 11 for more information on <router-outlet>.

In Figure 12-1, the router updates the bottom section of the page. The toolbar does not change because it is outside the scope of the Angular router.

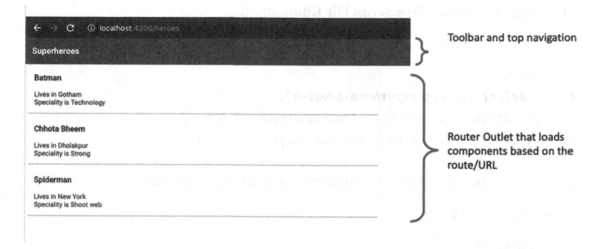

Figure 12-1. *Organization of a page with toolbar*

In the sample application's Superheroes Material Design module, let's create a component that wraps the Angular Material toolbar. We use this component when we need to reference the toolbar. Creating a separate component allows us to customize our application's toolbar. We will reuse the component throughout the application.

To create a new component, run the Angular CLI command shown in Listing 12-2.

Listing 12-2. Create a Component for the Toolbar

```
ng g component superheroes-material-design/superhero-toolbar
```

In the newly created component, add an Angular Material toolbar. Use the <mat-toolbar> component. Listing 12-3 shows basic usage of the component, with just a title on the toolbar.

Listing 12-3. Toolbar with a Welcome Title

```
<mat-toolbar color="primary">
  <h2>Welcome to Superheroes application</h2>
</mat-toolbar>
```

Consider the TypeScript code component in Listing 12-4. Notice line 3. To reference the component in the rest of the application, use the app-superhero-toolbar selector. See Chapter 4 for information on working with components.

Listing 12-4. Toolbar TypeScript File Component

```
1. import { Component, OnInit } from '@angular/core';

2. @Component({
3.    selector: 'app-superhero-toolbar',
4.    templateUrl: './superhero-toolbar.component.html',
5.    styleUrls: ['./superhero-toolbar.component.css']
6. })
7. export class SuperheroToolbarComponent implements OnInit {

8.   constructor() { }

9.   ngOnInit() {
10.   }

11. }
```

We created the component as part of the Superhero Material Design module. In addition to creating new files, Angular CLI updates the Angular module file (see line 2 and line 6). Listing 12-5 is the superheroes-material-design.module.ts file. Angular CLI imports the new component, SuperheroToolbarComponent, and includes it in the declaration array.

Figure 12-2 depicts the toolbar next to <router-outlet>, which is in <app-component>. It is outside SuperheroesMaterialDesignModule. Hence, to use it in AppModule (containing <app-component>), we need to export the component. In Listing 12-5, see line 12. It exports the component from the module.

Note   Consider using --export option with Angular CLI, while generating the component. It generates the code that declares and exports the component from SuperheroesMaterialDesignModule. See Listing 12-6 for the export option included. If we did not use this option while creating the component, we may edit superhero-material-design.module.ts to add the component to exports.

Listing 12-5. Create a Component for Toolbar with --export Option

```
ng g component superheroes-material-design/superhero-toolbar --export
```

Listing 12-6. Export Toolbar Component from SuperheroMaterialDesignModule

```
1. import { MatToolbarModule } from '@angular/material/toolbar';
2. import { SuperheroToolbarComponent } from './superhero-toolbar/
   superhero-toolbar.component';
3. // Removed code for brevity
4. @NgModule({
5.  declarations: [
6.     SuperheroToolbarComponent,
7.  ],
8.  imports: [
9.      // Removed code for brevity
10.  ],
11.  exports: [
12.     SuperheroToolbarComponent,
13.  ],
14.  providers:[]
15. })
16. export class SuperheroesMaterialDesignModule { }
```

Next, we use SuperheroToolbarComponent in AppComponent, the root component of the application. In the sample application, AppModule already imports SuperheroesMaterialDesignModule. See line 9 in Listing 12-7.

Listing 12-7. App Module that imports SuperheroesMaterialDesignModule

```
1. import {SuperheroesMaterialDesignModule} from './superheroes-material-
   design/superheroes-material-design.module';

2. // Removed code for brevity

3. @NgModule({
4.  declarations: [
5.  AppComponent
6.  ],
```

```
7. imports: [
8.   AppRoutingModule,
9.   SuperheroesMaterialDesignModule
10. ],
11. bootstrap: [AppComponent]
12. })
13. export class AppModule { }
```

The <app-superhero-toolbar> component is used in AppComponent, the root component, along with <router-outlet>. See Listing 12-8.

Listing 12-8. App Component Using Superhero Toolbar and router-outlet

```
--- app.component.html ---
<app-superhero-toolbar></app-superhero-toolbar>
<router-outlet></router-outlet>
```

This achieves the structure and organization for the application specified in Figure 12-2.

Actions on the Toolbar

We already created a basic toolbar with just a title. It can contain additional elements. The toolbar is a natural location to place page-level actions. An action could be an operation, like save content, or a trigger for navigation. The toolbar typically contains high-level navigation actions that take the user to a new module or a functionality.

Considering that a page title is already on the toolbar and aligned to the left, let's place the actions aligned to the right.

The Angular Material toolbar does not control the position of the elements. The style sheet manages the position and alignment. In Listing 12-9, we use CSS Flexbox to position the controls. We place two arbitrary actions—View and Create—(indicating view superheroes and create superheroes)in the right corner.

Listing 12-9. Place Actions on Toolbar

```
1. <mat-toolbar color="primary">
2.   Welcome to Superheroes application
3.   <span class="central-stretchable-space"></span>
```

```
4.  <a class="action">View</a>
5.  <a class="action">Create</a>
6. </mat-toolbar>
```

The "central-stretchable-space" CSS class is on line 3. It is applied on the central span between the title and the actions. Because of the CSS class, it stretches based on the toolbar's width (which depends on the browser window's width). Listing 12-10 is for the CSS that collapses or stretches the available space.

Listing 12-10. Flex the Element to Take up Remaining Space

```
--- superhero-toolbar.component.css ---

.central-stretchable-space {
    flex: 1 1 auto;
}
```

In Listing 12-10, flex is a shorthand property for the following.

- **flex-grow**: The first value in Listing 12-10 represents flex-grow. The value is a number indicating how much the given element should grow (or stretch) in relation to the other flex elements around it. With a value of 1, it grows in the available space.

- **flex-shrink**: The second value in Listing 12-10 represents flex-shrink. The value is a number indicating how much the given element should shrink (or collapse) in relation to the other flex elements around it.

- **flex-basis**: The third value in Listing 12-10 represents flex-basis. It is the length of the item. Possible values are auto, inherit, or percentage, or a pixel value.

Figure 12-2 shows the result.

Figure 12-2. *Actions on right top of the page*

Multiple Rows in the Toolbar

A toolbar can have multiple rows. Use mat-toolbar-row to create a toolbar row. Listing 12-11 shows a subheader in the additional row. As an example, we may use the top row as an application title and the second row as the screen-level title.

To create a new row in the toolbar, use the <mat-toolbar-row> component.

Listing 12-11. Multiple Rows in Toolbar

```
<mat-toolbar color="primary" >
  <mat-toolbar-row>
    Welcome to Superheroes application
  </mat-toolbar-row>

  <mat-toolbar-row>
    List of Superheroes
    <span class="central-stretchable-space"></span>
    <a class="action">View</a>
    <a class="action">Create</a>
  </mat-toolbar-row>
</mat-toolbar>
```

We moved actions to the second toolbar row. The result is shown in Figure 12-3.

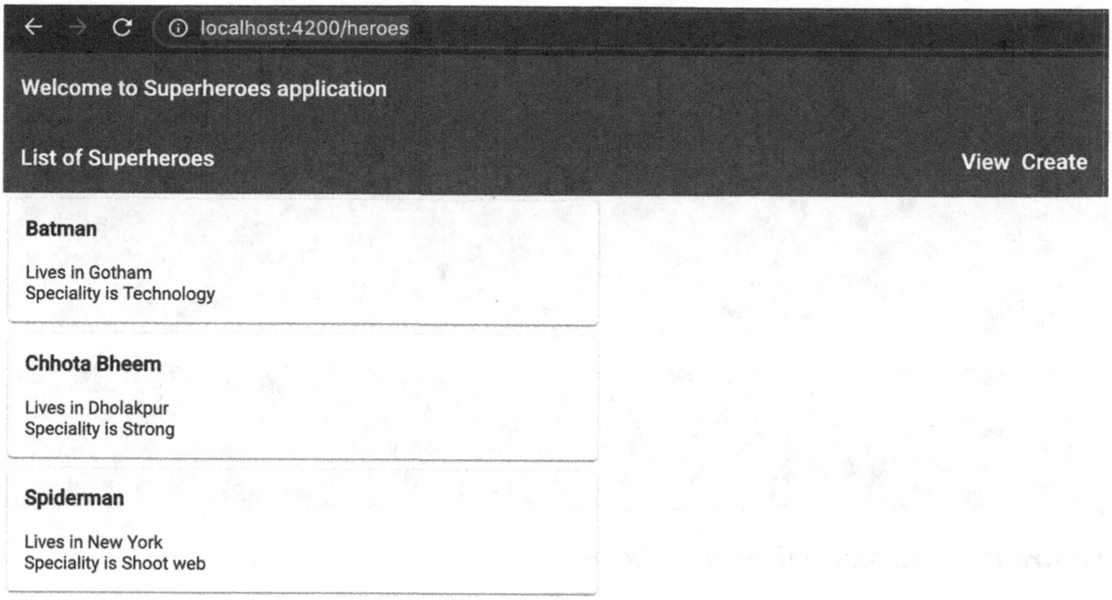

Figure 12-3. *Using rows in toolbar*

Toolbar Theme

Angular Material components support the following color themes.

- **Primary**: The most used primary color on the page.

- **Accent**: The secondary, optional color on a page. Usage of the color helps distinguish the application.

- **Warn**: The color used when a component needs attention; for example, a delete action, an unsaved cancel action, and so forth.

Use the color attribute on mat-toolbar to specify the color on the toolbar (see Listing 12-12).

Listing 12-12. Color on the Toolbar

```
<mat-toolbar color="primary" >
</mat-toolbar>
```

The colors are dependent on the Material Design theme in use. Figure 12-4 shows the colors with the default theme.

Figure 12-4. *Colors with default theme*

Integration with Angular Router

So far, we have created a toolbar, and added and positioned links (or buttons) on it. We created a view link and a create link on the toolbar. The links integrate with the router to navigate to various routes in the application.

In the sample application, imagine we go to /create-hero route on clicking the create link and navigate to /heroes on clicking the view link. We may use the routerLink directive, which helps redirections in an Angular application, without attempting to reload the whole page. Chapter 11 discusses more on routing and the routerLink directive. Listing 12-13 is for the superhero toolbar template. Lines 7 to 12 add the routerLink attribute.

Listing 12-13. Router Integration with the Toolbar

```
1. <mat-toolbar color="primary">
2.  <mat-toolbar-row>
3.    Welcome to Superheroes application
4.  </mat-toolbar-row>

5.  <mat-toolbar-row >
6.    <span class="central-stretchable-space"></span>
```

```
7.    <a class="action" routerLink="/create-hero" >
8.       Create
9.    </a>

10.    <a class="action" routerLink="/heroes" >
11.       View
12.    </a>

13.   </mat-toolbar-row>
14. </mat-toolbar>
```

Remember, we encapsulate routing logic to a module of its own, named AppRoutingModule. This module imports RouterModule from @angular/router, which has the routerLink directive. Hence, we need to import AppRoutingModule into SuperheroesMaterialDesignModule for the routerLink directive to work. Consider Listing 12-14.

Listing 12-14. Import Router Module to Superheroes Material Design Module

```
import { AppRoutingModule } from '../app-routing.module';
@NgModule({
  declarations: [
        // removed code for brevity
],
  imports: [
    AppRoutingModule,
],
  exports: [
        // removed code for brevity.
  ],
  providers:[  ],
  entryComponents: [   ]
})
export class SuperheroesMaterialDesignModule { }
```

There is an alternative approach if we wish to exclude routerLink and the routing logic out of the superheroes Material Design module. Considering the module is aimed to purely provide a Material Design look and feel and behavior to the application, we may move out the routerLink directive implementation from the module and the component.

However, we still have the toolbar for top navigation. It needs the route changes as the user attempts to navigate. We may use content projection with ng-content. Supply the navigation links, including the routerLink integration to the toolbar component. The parent component to the toolbar (AppComponent) may supply the links.

Note   Refer to Chapter 4 to read more about ng-content.

To switch to this approach, modify SuperheroToolbarComponent to show the dynamic content provided by AppComponent. Use ng-content to show dynamic content in the second toolbar row. See line 7 in Listing 12-15.

Listing 12-15. Use ng-content to Show Dynamic Content from AppComponent

```
1. <mat-toolbar color="primary">
2.   <mat-toolbar-row>
3.     Superhero - Warn Color
4.   </mat-toolbar-row>

5.   <mat-toolbar-row>
6.   <span class="central-stretchable-space"></span>
7.    <ng-content></ng-content>
8.   </mat-toolbar-row>
9. </mat-toolbar>
```

We no longer have the links view and create in the toolbar component. Listing 12-16 is for app.component.html, which provides the links to the toolbar as child elements. These links show up in place of ng-content in line 7.

Listing 12-16. Router Links Provided in AppComponent

```
<app-superhero-toolbar>
    <a routerLink="/create-hero">
        Create
    </a>
    <a routerLink="/heroes" >
        View
    </a>
</app-superhero-toolbar>
```

With this approach, we separated the routing logic and the modules from the Angular Material components' implementation.

Sidenav

Sidenav is often used as a navigation control. It can pull from the right or left of a page. It may have application-level or contextual page-level actions. The actions could take the user to a different route or page. We may also use them as actions on data on the page.

Note   Sidenav is often used for navigation elements; however, it is not necessary. It can be used as a container with a form or content that shows and hides as needed.

Figure 12-5 is a sample implementation of the sidenav.

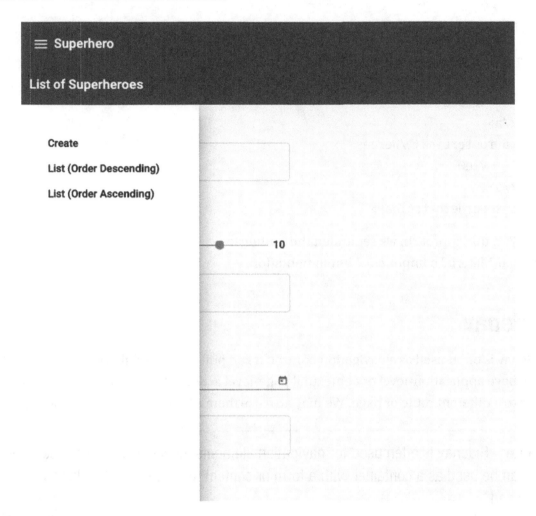

Figure 12-5. *A sample sidenav*

Getting Started

To use Angular Material's sidenav, import the module containing the components and the directives. In Listing 12-17, all the Material Design components are encompassed in superheroes-material-design.module.ts.

Import MatSidenavModule from the Angular Material repository. Import it into the NgModule (Angular Module) encompassing all the Material Design code in the sample application.

Listing 12-17. Import Sidenav Module

```
import { MatSidenavModule } from '@angular/material/sidenav';

@NgModule({
  declarations: [
        // Removed code for brevity
  ],
  imports: [
    MatSidenavModule,
  ],
  exports: [
  ],
  providers:[]
})
export class SuperheroesMaterialDesignModule { }
```

Now that the modules needed for the sidenav are imported, we may create a component in SuperheroesMaterialDesignModule to use the sidenav. Run the Angular CLI command in Listing 12-18.

Listing 12-18. Create sidenav Component for Superheroes Application

```
ng g component superheroes-material-design/superhero-sidenav
```

The command creates SuperheroSidenavComponent. It also imports the component into SuperheroMaterialDesignModule and adds to the declarations. This component is intended to be used outside SuperheroMaterialDesignModule (the Angular Module). Hence, add the component to the exports array list as well. Consider Listing 12-19.

Listing 12-19. Export the sidenav Component from SuperheroesMaterialDesignModule

```
import { MatSidenavModule } from '@angular/material/sidenav';
import { SuperheroSidenavComponent } from './superhero-sidenav/superhero-
sidenav.component';
```

```
@NgModule({
  declarations: [
    SuperheroSidenavComponent,
    // Removed code for brevity
  ],
  imports: [
    MatSidenavModule,
  ],
  exports: [
    SuperheroSidenavComponent
  ],
  providers:[]
})
export class SuperheroesMaterialDesignModule { }
```

Note   Consider using --export option with Angular CLI while generating the component. It generates the code that declares and exports the component from SuperheroesMaterialDesignModule. See Listing 12-20 for the included export option. If we did not use this option while creating the component, we may edit superhero-material-design.module.ts to add the component to the exports.

Listing 12-20. Create and Export sidenav Component for Superheroes Application

```
ng g component superheroes-material-design/superhero-sidenav --export
```

As seen in Figure 12-5, we will show navigation links in sidenav. In the newly created SuperheroSidenavComponent, we will import and use the mat-sidenav component. Listing 12-21 encapsulates links within a mat-sidenav component. The links and div elements are the contents of the sidenav.

Listing 12-21. Sidenav Content

```
<mat-sidenav #sidenav>
 <!-- Sidenav content -->

 <div class="container">
   <div>
     <a href="#">
       Create
     </a>
   </div>

   <!-- more links go here. Deleted code for brevity -->
 </div>
</mat-sidenav>
```

With the sidenav, we can use the configurations in Listing 12-21 as input attributes on the <mat-sidenav> component.

- **Position:** The possible values are "start" and "end". The default value is "start", which refers to the left side of the page. We may change it to "end" for the right side of the page. Figure 12-5 shows the sidenav on right (end).

- **Mode**: The possible values are "over", "push", and "side". We see it with the "over" value in Figure 12-x. Figure 12-x shows the "side" sidenav mode .

- **Opened**: We may set the value to be true/false. If true, the application loads with the sidenav open.

- **Open**(): A function call on the component to open or hide the sidenav.

- **Close**(): A function call on the component to close or hide the sidenav.

Listing 12-22. Sidenav with Additional Configurations

```
<mat-sidenav mode="side" opened position="end" #sidenav>
<!-- deleted code for brevity -->
<mat-sidenav>
```

Figure 12-6 shows the result. We are not done yet. Just adding the code in Listing 12-22 does not show the component. We need to integrate the newly created superhero sidenav component with the application.

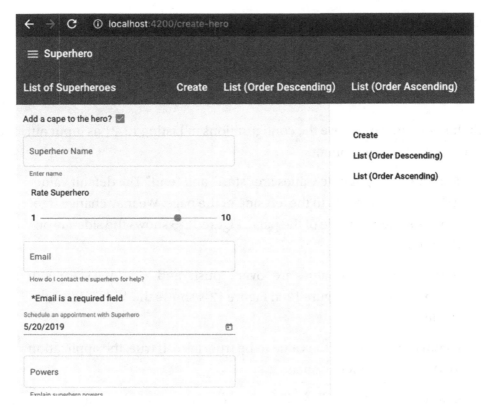

Figure 12-6. *Sidenav on the right*

Organizing the Sample Application for Sidenav

So far, we have created a component (SuperheroSidenavComponent) in SuperheroesMaterialDesignModule and used the mat-sidenav component. We have not yet used the newly created component in the application. Remember, we exported the SuperheroSidenavComponent in Listing 12-22. It is now available for module referencing SuperheroesMaterialDesignModule, which is the main module(AppModule) in the sample application.

mat-sidenav, an Angular Material component, is required to be a child component of mat-sidenav-container. The container may have two child components: the sidenav (mat-sidenav) and the content (mat-sidenav-content). Figure 12-7 is the layout at the application level in the root component.

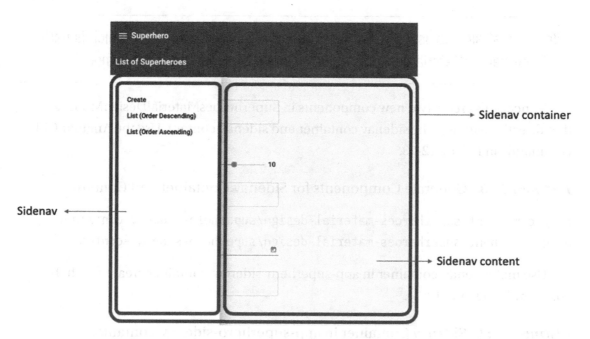

Figure 12-7. *Organizing a sidenav container, content, and sidenav*

The sidenav container is the parent component of everything that the sidenav implements. The component selector for usage in HTML template is mat-sidenav-container. For the sidenav content component, the selector is mat-sidenav-content. For a sidenav component, the selector is mat-sidenav.

Note   There can only be one sidenav in an application.

The *sidenav content* is the workspace of the application. Chapter 11 describes the <router-outlet> loads content of the application at a given route. For most applications, it is the workspace. If the application is using a sidenav, one implementation is to encapsulate <router-outlet> within the sidenav content.

Remember, <router-outlet> is on AppComponent. We may use mat-sidenav-container (the parent component) and mat-sidenav-content in AppComponent. However, so far, we have packaged all Angular Material implementation in SuperheroesMaterialDesignModule. Continuing with this approach, we may want to stay away from using the Angular Material components (mat-sidenav-container and mat-sidenav-component) directly in AppComponent, which belongs to AppModule.

Note   mat-sidenav is referenced in SuperheroSidenavComponent, which is part of SuperheroesMaterialDesignModule. It is already part of the desired module.

Hence, let's create two new components in SuperheroesMaterialDesignModule that directly reference the sidenav container and sidenav content. Use the Angular CLI commands in Listing 12-23.

Listing 12-23. Generate Components for Sidenav Container and Content

```
ng g component superheroes-material-design/superhero-sidenav-container
ng g component superheroes-material-design/superhero-sidenav-content
```

Use mat-sidenav-container in app-superhero-sidenav-container created with the command in Listing 12-24.

Listing 12-24. Sidenav Container in app-superhero-sidenav-container

```
<mat-sidenav-container>
  <ng-content></ng-content>
</mat-sidenav-container>
```

ng-content includes child components and app-superhero-sidenav-container content. All the contents of app-superhero-sidenav-container are transcluded under mat-sidenav-container.

This follows a similar approach in app-superhero-sidenav-content. Consider Listing 12-25.

Listing 12-25. Sidenav Content in app-superhero-sidenav-content

```
<mat-sidenav-container>
  <mat-sidenav-content>
    <ng-content></ng-content>
  </mat-sidenav-content>
</mat-sidenav-container>
```

The mat-sidenav-content component needs the container to be its immediate parent. Hence, we added another mat-sidenav-container. Child components and contents of app-superhero-content are transcluded to the ng-content in Listing 12-26.

Now, we have all the components ready to create the layout demonstrated in Figure 12-7. See the code in app.component.html. See Listing 12-26.

Listing 12-26. AppComponent Code Resulting in Sidenav Layout

```
<app-superhero-sidenav-container>
    <app-superhero-sidenav #sidenav></app-superhero-sidenav>
    <app-superhero-sidenav-content>
        <router-outlet></router-outlet>
    </app-superhero-sidenav-content>
</app-superhero-sidenav-container>
```

Figure 12-8 is a representation of the components in the layout.

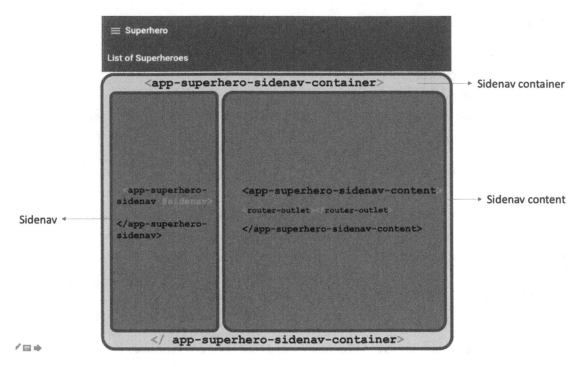

Figure 12-8.   *Organizing sidenav container, content, and the sidenav*

Using a Menu Button to Toggle sidenav

It is typical to toggle a sidenav: show or hide as needed. We may use the menu button next to the superhero title in the toolbar. As the user clicks the menu button, an event is raised. The event will be acted upon by the sidenav component. Consider a solution on how an event created by the menu button is received by sidenav (see Figure 12-9).

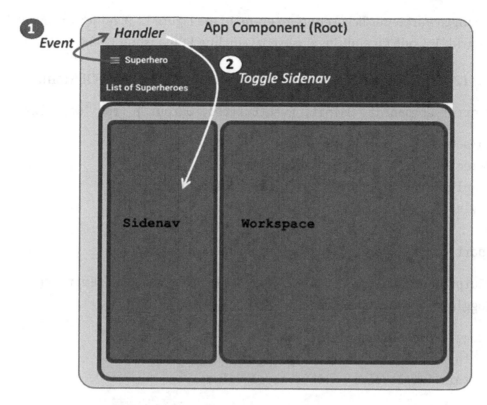

Figure 12-9. *Menu click toggling sidenav*

First, let's look at the implementation in the toolbar. Listing 12-27 adds a menu to the toolbar (superhero-toolbar-component.html). Notice the highlighted section, line 3, for the menu.

Listing 12-27. Toolbar with Menu Icon

```
1. <mat-toolbar color="primary">
2.  <mat-toolbar-row>
3.     <mat-icon (click)="toggleForMenuClick()" class="menu">menu
       </mat-icon>
4.     Superhero
5.  </mat-toolbar-row>

6.  <mat-toolbar-row>
7.    List of Superheroes
8.  </mat-toolbar-row>
9. </mat-toolbar>
```

The toggleForMenuClick() emits an event. In the Figure 12-9, notice the event marked with 1. Code for emitting the event is on line 11 in Listing 12-28.

Listing 12-28. Toolbar Component Raising the Event on Click Of Menu

```
1. import { Component, OnInit, EventEmitter, Output } from '@angular/core';

2. @Component({
3.   selector: 'app-superhero-toolbar',
4.   templateUrl: './superhero-toolbar.component.html',
5.   styleUrls: ['./superhero-toolbar.component.css']
6. })
7. export class SuperheroToolbarComponent implements OnInit {

8.   @Output() menuClick: EventEmitter<boolean> = new EventEmitter();
9.   toggleValue: boolean=true;

10.  toggleForMenuClick(){
11.    this.menuClick.emit(this.toggleValue);
12.    this.toggleValue = !this.toggleValue;
13.  }
14. }
```

The menuClick output event is of type EventEmitter. The generic type on EventEmitter is boolean. The toolbar component toggles a boolean variable each time the user clicks the menu. The event is emitted.

Next, AppComponent, the parent component to Superhero Toolbar, receives the event. In Listing 12-29, App.component.html ties the menuClick output event to a handler function. The handler function is named toggleSidenav().

Listing 12-29. AppComponent Handling the Event Raised by Toolbar

```
<app-superhero-toolbar (menuClick)="toggleSidenav($event)">
  <!-- Removed code for brevity -->
</app-superhero-toolbar>
<app-superhero-sidenav-container>
    <app-superhero-sidenav #sidenav></app-superhero-sidenav>
```

```
<app-superhero-sidenav-content>
    <router-outlet></router-outlet>
</app-superhero-sidenav-content>
</app-superhero-sidenav-container>
```

Note the #sidenav template reference variable representing the sidenav. Listing 12-30 shows the TypeScript code component (app.component.ts) handling the event raised by the toolbar.

Listing 12-30. AppComponent TypeScript Code Handling Event

```
@ViewChild("sidenav") sidenav: SuperheroSidenavComponent;

toggleSidenav(evt: EventEmitter<boolean>){
  evt ? this.sidenav.open() : this.sidenav.close();
}
```

The sidenav instance calls open() or close() functions toggling the sidenav. Notice the view child sidenav representing the template reference variable sidenav. The call open() or close() is #2 in Figure 12-9.

Finally, the superhero sidenav component implements opening and closing the sidenav. Listing 12-30 and Listing 12-31 show the open() and close() implementations in SuperheroSidenavComponent. Look at the template code in Listing 12-31.

Listing 12-31. SuperheroSidenavComponent Template

```
<mat-sidenav mode="side" opened [position]="position" #sidenav>
    <!-- Removed code for brevity -->
</mat-sidenav>
```

Note the template reference variable #sidenav representing mat-sidenav in Listing 12-32 that toggles the mat-sidenav component. The view child sidenav referenced in the TypeScript file component.

Listing 12-32. SuperheroSidenavComponent with Code to Toggle sidenav

```
1. @Component({
2.  // Removed code for brevity
3. })
4. export class SuperheroSidenavComponent implements OnInit {

5.  @ViewChild("sidenav") sidenav: MatSidenav;
6.  @Input("position") position: string = "start";

7.  open() {
8.    this.sidenav.open();
9.  }

10.  close() {
11.    this.sidenav.close();
12.  }
13. }
```

The open() and close() functions called from app.component.ts toggle mat-sidenav. They call the API on the mat-sidenav instance. Lines 7 to 9 in Listing 12-32 show the open() function implementation. Lines 10 to 12 show the close() function implementation.

Conclusion

The Angular Material components described in this chapter help you build navigation patterns for an Angular application. They use Material Design concepts and provide a greater user experience. The Angular Material component provides a title for the application and is a great location for actions and links to other pages in the application.

The chapter described placing actions and links on the toolbar. It covered using Angular Material themes and colors with the component. It explained sidenav, sample layouts, implementing the layout with Angular Material components, and handling events across components between the toolbar and the sidenav.

Exercise

In the Angular routing exercise, we added routing to the dinosaur application. We created two routes: /dino-list and /dinosaur/:dinosaurName.

Provide links to navigate to these pages in a sidenav position on the right.

Add a toolbar that shows a title: Dinosaur App. On the right corner of the toolbar, add a toggle sidenav link. Clicking the link should toggle the sidenav.

Reference

Material Design documentation (`https://material.angular.io/`)

CHAPTER 13

Material Design: Layout

Angular Material provides components and directives that help position and layout the content. The components adhere to Material Design specifications and provide functionality out of the box.

This chapter describes three often-used components that encapsulate content, cards, tabs, and an accordion with an expandable panel. A card provides view for a single entity. The entity could be an order or customer. Tabs allow switching between entities for each tab. The accordion with an expansion panel displays a list of items.

Material Design: Card

A card is a Material Design construct that visually puts together the content and actions of an entity in the system.

In the sample application, we have used cards, and a superhero is an entity. We show information about a superhero in a card. The form that creates a superhero could be on a card. Figure 13-1 shows a card that creates a superhero.

A card can have the following sections.

- **Card Title**: A header or title for the card. Figure 13-1 shows the title *Create a new superhero form.*

- **Card Subtitle**: A subtitle provides brief descriptive information about the purpose of the card. Figure 13-1 describes the form and purpose of the page in the web application.

- **Content**: The functionality of the view or the card.

- **Actions**: Possible operations of the card content. This section is placed at the bottom of the card. In the sample, the actions are to create a superhero or reset the form.

© Venkata Keerti Kotaru 2020

V. K. Kotaru, *Angular for Material Design*, https://doi.org/10.1007/978-1-4842-5434-9_13

- **Footer**: Descriptive text, information, or warning messages can be placed in the footer. The footer is the last section at the bottom of the card.

- **Card Image**: Images and video; provides information about the contents of the card.

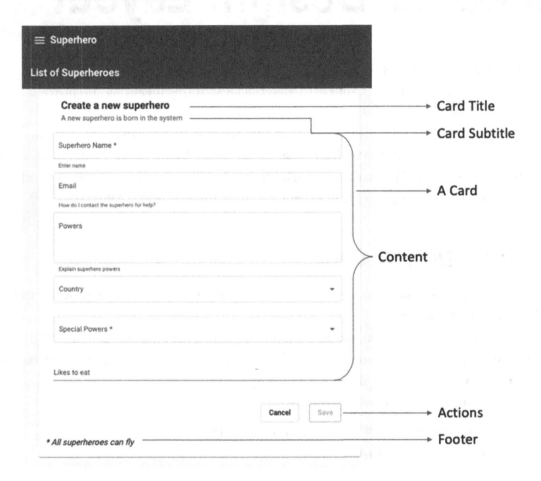

Figure 13-1. *Create superhero form on a card*

Getting Started

To use Angular Material's card, import the module containing the component. In Listing 13-1, all the Material Design components are encompassed in superheroes-material-design.module.ts.

Import the MatCardModule from the Angular Material repository. Import it into the NgModule (Angular module) encompassing all the Material Design code in the sample application.

Listing 13-1. Import Angular Material Card Module

```
import { MatCardModule } from '@angular/material/card';

// Removed code for brevity
@NgModule({
  declarations: [
    // Removed code for brevity
  ],
  imports: [
    MatCardModule,
  ],
  exports: [
  ],
  providers:[]
})
export class SuperheroesMaterialDesignModule { }
```

Using Angular Material Card

Now that we have imported the Angular Material card module, the components that provide the card, card titles, content, and footer are available.

In the sample application, we have already created a component with the form to create a new superhero. We may encapsulate the form in a card. Consider Listing 13-2.

Listing 13-2. Create Superhero Form in a Card

```
1. <mat-card>

2.  <mat-card-header>
3.    <mat-card-title>
4.      Create a new superhero
5.    </mat-card-title>
6.    <mat-card-subtitle>
```

```
7.      A new superhero is born in the system
8.    </mat-card-subtitle>
9.  </mat-card-header>

10.  <mat-card-content>
11.    <form #superheroForm="ngForm">

12.      <!-- Create superhero form goes here.
            Removed code for brevity -->
13.    </form>
14.  </mat-card-content>

15.  <mat-card-actions class="pull-right">
16.    <button mat-stroked-button> Cancel </button>
17.    <button mat-stroked-button [disabled]="!superheroForm.valid"> Save
          </button>
18.  </mat-card-actions>

19.  <mat-card-footer align="end">
20.    * All superheroes can fly
21.  </mat-card-footer>
22. </mat-card>
```

The following are the components and directives for creating a card.

- **<mat-card>** is the root component for all the card content. It includes the child components.

- **<mat-card-header>** is the top section of the card. It may include the following two components: title and subtitle.

- **<mat-card-title>** is the title of the card or the superhero form.

- **<mat-card-subtitle>** is the subtitle/description of the card or the superhero form.

- **<mat-card-content>** is the card content or the superhero form elements.

- **<mat-card-actions>** are the buttons that allow the user to create a superhero or reset the form.

- **<mat-card-footer>** is the footer text at the bottom of the card.

The mat-card-footer has an *align* attribute. The value is set to "end". See line 19 in Listing 13-2. The actions are on the right side of the card. The default value is "start" at which point it is left aligned. Figure 13-2 shows the result.

Angular Material Card with Images

Images on a card are an impressive way to present content to the user. In Figure 13-2, the superhero's profile is presented in a visually impactful manner. We modify superhero-profile.component.html in the code sample to present data in a card. Similar to Listing 13-3, we add mat-card, the header, and title to the profile component.

Use the following directives to show an avatar and an image on the card.

- **mat-card-avatar:** The directive positions the avatar in the header. Add an image to the mat-card-header and the directive mat-card-avatar.

  In Figure 13-2 and Listing 13-3, we use the mat-card-avatar directive on the image element. It is added in <mat-card-header> to show the avatar in the card header, along with the card title and subtitle.

  Consider lines 2 to 6 in the card header. See line 3 for usage of the mat-card-avatar directive.

  mat-card-image: The directive positions a large image on the card to provide a visual depiction of the content.

  Consider Listing 13-3 (line 7) and Figure 13-2. We use the mat-card-image directive on <img> element between the card header and card content. The directives position and size the images accordingly. It fits into the card content perfectly.

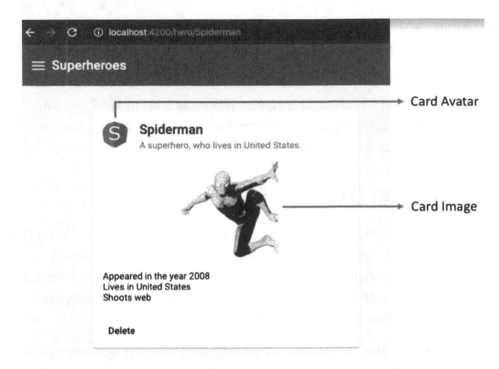

Figure 13-2. *Spiderman profile on a card*

Listing 13-3. Use Material Design Card Components and Directives on Superhero Profile

```
1.  <mat-card class="half">
2.    <mat-card-header>
3.      <img mat-card-avatar src="/assets/Superhero-logo.png" >
4.      <mat-card-title>{{ name }}</mat-card-title>
5.      <mat-card-subtitle>A superhero, who lives in {{ livesIn }}.
        </mat-card-subtitle>
6.    </mat-card-header>
7.    <img mat-card-image src="/assets/spiderman.jpg" >
8.    <mat-card-content>
9.      <div>Appeared in the year {{ firstAppearance }}</div>
10.     <div>Lives in {{ livesIn }}</div>
11.     <div *ngFor="let power of superpowers">
12.       {{ power }}
13.     </div>
```

```
14.    <div *ngIf="address">
15.       Meet the superhero at
16.       <div>
17.          {{ address.firstLine }}
18.       </div>
19.       <div>
20.          {{ address.city }}
21.       </div>
22.    </div>
23.  </mat-card-content>
24. </mat-card>
```

Note   Image URLs are hard-coded for simplicity. They can be obtained from the model object on the superhero-profile.component.ts file.

Material Design: Tabs

Tabs are often used to organize multiple views on a page. The tab title could be text, or an icon, or both. Tabs show one active view at a time (see Figure 13-3).

The Angular Material component for tabs is confined to the control's Material Design specifications. It highlights the active tab with an ink bar. The *superheroes list* in Figure 13-3 animates as we switch between tabs.

Note   Remember, BrowserAnimationsModule was imported into SuperheroesMaterialDesignModule. We can limit animations by switching to NoopAnimationModule instead.

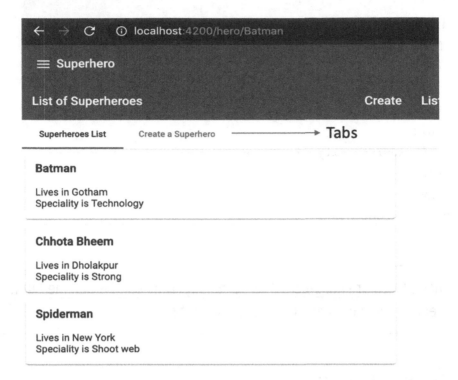

Figure 13-3. *Material Design tabs*

Getting Started

To use Angular Material's tabs, import the module containing the component. In Listing 13-4, all the Material Design components are encompassed in superheroes-material-design.module.ts.

Import MatTabsModule from the Angular Material repository into the NgModule (Angular module) encompassing all the Material Design code in the sample application.

Listing 13-4. Import Tabs Module

```
import { MatTabsModule } from '@angular/material/tabs';

// Removed code for brevity
@NgModule({
  declarations: [
  ],
```

```
  imports: [
    // removed code for brevity
    MatTabsModule,
  ],
  exports: [],
  providers: [HitCounter]
})
export class SuperheroesMaterialDesignModule { }
```

To add tabs to the sample application, consider creating a new component. Run the Angular CLI command in Listing 13-5 to create a component in the Superheroes-material-design module.

Listing 13-5. Create a New Component for Tabs

```
ng g component superheroes-material-design/tab-sample
```

The Angular CLI command in Listing 13-5 updates the declarations array in the superheroes-material-design module. The component is available to use within SuperheroesMaterialDesignModule. We have taken advantage of the scaffolded import (automatically) with many components created using Angular CLI.

Sometimes, however, we want to use the component outside SuperheroesMaterialDesignModule. In the tabs' scenario, we reference it in the root AppComponent, which is in a different module—AppModule; hence, we export it from the SuperheroesMaterialDesign module, which allows us to use the component outside the current module. Lines 12 to 14 in Listing 13-6 export one or more components from the module. Line 2 and lines 5 to 7 are updated by Angular CLI when the component is created.

Listing 13-6. Import Tabs Module

```
1. import { MatTabsModule } from '@angular/material/tabs';
2.    import { TabSampleComponent } from './tab-sample/tab-sample.
      component';
3. // Removed code for brevity

4. @NgModule({
5.   declarations: [
6.           TabSampleComponent,
7.   ],
```

```
8.  imports: [
9.    // removed code for brevity
10.    MatTabsModule,
11.  ],
12. exports: [
13.    // removed code for brevity
14.          ,TabSampleComponent
  ],
  providers:[]
})
export class SuperheroesMaterialDesignModule { }
```

Using Angular Material Tabs

So far, we have imported the required module to use the tabs and created a new component (TabSampleComponent), in which the tabs code can be written.

Let's create the tabs. In tab-sample.component.html (the template file for TabSampleComponent), use the <mat-tab-group> and <mat-tab> components. The <mat-tab-group> component encapsulates multiple tabs. It is the parent component for all tabs. Each tab is represented by <mat-tab>.

The code in Listing 13-7 is for tab-sample.component.html. We create two tabs with <mat-tab> components and the child elements under <mat-tab-group>.

Listing 13-7. Using Tabs

```
<div>
  <mat-tab-group>
    <mat-tab label="Superheroes List">
      <app-superhero-list></app-superhero-list>
    </mat-tab>
    <mat-tab label="Create a Superhero">
        <app-create-superhero></app-create-superhero>
    </mat-tab>
  </mat-tab-group>
</div>
```

Components that list superheroes and create a superhero are child elements within each <mat-tab>. The first tab shows the superhero list, and the second tab shows the create superhero component.

Note the *label* attribute on <mat-tab>. The text input into the label is the tab title (see Figure 13-3).

So far in the sample application, we have created a new component for the tab sample and created two tabs under it. The component was exported from the superhero-material-design module. It has not been used anywhere. Consider using it in app. component.html, the root component (see Listing 13-8).

Listing 13-8. AppComponent at Root, Referencing Tabs

```
<app-superhero-toolbar (menuClick)="toggleSidenav($event)">
  <!-- removed toolbar code for brevity -->
</app-superhero-toolbar>
<app-tab-sample>
</app-tab-sample>
```

Note   For this sample, we use tabs instead of left navigation and workspace. app-tab-sample is the selector for TabSampleComponent; hence, it is used in the HTML template.

While we used the label attribute for a text label (see Listing 13-9), for rich text that includes an icon in the tab label, consider using the mat-tab-label directive. Listing 13-9 uses an <ng-template> with <mat-icon>. See lines 3 to 6 and 9 to 11.

Listing 13-9. Tab Labels with Rich Text

```
1.  <mat-tab-group>
2.    <mat-tab >
3.      <ng-template mat-tab-label>
4.          <mat-icon>list</mat-icon> Superheroes
5.      </ng-template>
6.    <app-superhero-list></app-superhero-list>
7.    </mat-tab>
8.    <mat-tab >
```

```
9.           <ng-template mat-tab-label>
10.                        <mat-icon>create</mat-icon> Add Superhero
11.                </ng-template>
12.       <app-create-superhero></app-create-superhero>
13.    </mat-tab>
14.  </mat-tab-group>
```

Figure 13-4 shows the result.

Figure 13-4. *Rich text for the tab title*

Router Integration with Tabs

We have created two tabs. They load two different components or views without updating the route. The URL does not change as the users switch tabs. However, we might need router integration to let users bookmark a tab. Moreover, if there are a large number of tabs, it is good practice to map a route to each tab.

For Angular router integration, consider Listing 13-10, in which we modify the TabSampleComponent template to use the following directives.

- **mat-tab-nav-bar:** Creates a tab group with router links. Use on a parent component that encapsulates tabs that are router links.

- **mat-tab-link:** A router link with the view of a tab. Use mat-tab-link along with routerLink.

Listing 13-10. Router Integration with Tabs

```
<nav mat-tab-nav-bar>
  <a routerLink="/create-hero" mat-tab-link>
    Create
  </a>
```

```
<a routerLink="/heroes" [queryParams]="{sortOrder: 'descending'}"
mat-tab-link >
    List (Order Descending)
</a>
<a routerLink="/heroes" [queryParams]="{sortOrder: 'ascending'}"
mat-tab-link>
    List (Order Ascending)
</a>
</nav>
```

Note the routerLink directive on the anchor elements. As the user switches tabs, it updates <router-outlet> in AppComponent. Figure 13-5 shows the results. Note the URL reflects the selected tab.

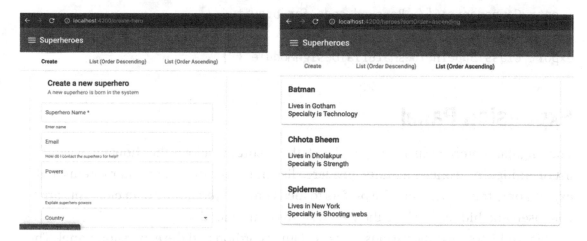

Figure 13-5. *Tabs integrated with router*

For the router to work, RouterModule from @angular/router needs to be imported. Remember, in Chapter 11 we used app-routing.module for the routing logic.

Listing 13-11 uses the router. Import AppRoutingModule from app-routing.module.ts. On SuperheroesMaterialDesignModule, to the imports list, add AppRoutingModule.

Listing 13-11. App Routing Module Import for Router Integration with Tabs

```
import { AppRoutingModule } from '../app-routing.module';
// Removed code for brevity

@NgModule({
  declarations: [
    // Removed code for brevity
  ],
  imports: [
    AppRoutingModule,
  ],
  exports: [/* Removed code for brevity */ ],
  providers:[ /* Removed code for brevity */],
  entryComponents: [/* Removed code for brevity */]
})
export class SuperheroesMaterialDesignModule { }
```

Expansion Panel

The Angular Material expansion panel with the accordion allows the showing of a long list of entities in a concise manner. In a large list, the user can collapse many items and expand only the entities that she prefers to focus on. The remaining data elements are collapsed and hidden, making the view easy to comprehend.

Figure 13-6 shows the various aspects of an accordion and the expansion panel. The accordion holds a list of expansion panels.

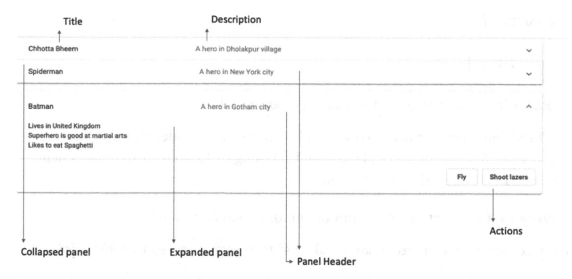

Figure 13-6. *Expansion panel*

Getting Started

To use Angular Material's expansion panel, import the module containing the component. In Listing 13-12, all the Material Design components are encompassed in superheroes-material-design.module.ts.

Import MatCardModule from the Angular Material repository into the NgModule (Angular module) encompassing all the Material Design code in the sample application.

Listing 13-12. Import Angular Material Expansion Panel

```
import { MatExpansionModule } from '@angular/material/expansion';
// Removed code for brevity
@NgModule({
  declarations: [
    // Removed code for brevity
  ],
  imports: [
    MatExpansionModule,
  ],
```

```
  exports: [
  ],
  providers:[]
})
export class SuperheroesMaterialDesignModule { }
```

To add an expansion panel to the sample application, consider creating a new component. Run the Angular CLI command in Listing 13-13 to create a component in the Superheroes-material-design module.

Listing 13-13. Create a New Component for Expansion Panel

```
ng g component superheroes-material-design/superheroes-expandable-list
```

Angular CLI updates the declarations array in the superheroes-material-design module. We require it to reference the router module (app-routing.module.ts). We anticipate using the component outside SuperheroesMaterialDesignModule, in which it was created and declared, so export it from the module (see Listing 13-14).

Listing 13-14. Import Angular Material Expansion Panel

```
import { MatExpansionModule } from '@angular/material/expansion';
import { SuperheroesExpandableListComponent } from './superheroes-
expandable-list/superheroes-expandable-list.component';
// Removed code for brevity
@NgModule({
  declarations: [
      SuperheroesExpandableListComponent
    // Removed code for brevity
  ],
  imports: [
    MatExpansionModule,
  ],
  exports: [
      SuperheroesExpandableListComponent
  ],
```

```
  providers:[]
})
export class SuperheroesMaterialDesignModule { }
```

To show the component at a route, update the router configuration. In Listing 13-15, it is in app-routing.module.ts.

Listing 13-15. Router Configuration For Expansion Panel

```
import { SuperheroesExpandableListComponent } from './superheroes-material-
design/superheroes-expandable-list/superheroes-expandable-list.component';

const routes: Routes = [
  {
    path: "heroes-accordion",
    component: SuperheroesExpandableListComponent
  },
  // Removed code for brevity
];

@NgModule({
  imports: [RouterModule.forRoot(routes)],
  exports: [RouterModule]
})
export class AppRoutingModule { }
```

To see the component in action, navigate to the newly configured url /heroes-accordion.

Using the Expansion Panel

Now that the required modules are imported and the sample application is setup, to use expansion panel, consider the following directives.

- **mat-accordion:** Uses the accordion as the root component for the list of expansion panels.

- **mat-expansion-panel:** Each expandable area under the accordion is an expansion panel. It is the child component of the accordion. A panel can be in one of the two states: expanded or collapsed.

- **mat-expansion-panel-header**: The header is the title section of the expansion panel. This section always shows minimal information about the panel, even in a collapsed state. Typically, clicking the header section expands to show more information about the panel. It is a child component of mat-expansion-panel (see Figure 13-6).

- **mat-panel-title:** The title text or section of the panel. It is a child component of mat-expansion-panel-header. See Figure 13-6.

- **mat-panel-description:** Provides descriptive information about the panel. It is a child component of mat-expansion-panel-header (see Figure 13-6).

- **mat-action-row:** Actions are typically buttons or links that perform operations on the panel or the entity in the panel. The buttons show in an expanded state and hide with the collapsed panel. It is a child component of mat-expansion-panel.

- **MatExpansionPanelContent**: Typically, the whole list of panels under the accordion load upfront. To delay loading the panel only on *Click to expand*, use the MatExpansionPanelContent directive.

Listing 13-16 is the template used in the newly created superheroes-expandable-list. component.

Listing 13-16. Using Material Design Expansion Panel

```
1. <mat-accordion>
2.  <mat-expansion-panel *ngFor="let hero of heroes">
3.    <mat-expansion-panel-header>
4.      <mat-panel-title>
5.        {{ hero.name }}
6.      </mat-panel-title>
7.      <mat-panel-description>
8.        {{ hero.details }}
9.      </mat-panel-description>
10.   </mat-expansion-panel-header>
11.   <div>Lives in {{hero.country}}</div>
```

```
12.    <div>
13.       Superhero
14.       <span *ngFor="let power of hero.specialPowers">
15.          {{ power }} 
16.       </span>
17.    </div>

18.    <div>
19.       Likes to eat
20.       <span *ngFor="let food of hero.favFood">
21.          {{ food }}
22.       </span>
23.    </div>
24.    <mat-action-row>
25.       <button mat-stroked-button> Fly </button>
26.       <button mat-stroked-button> Shoot lazers </button>
27.    </mat-action-row>
28.  </mat-expansion-panel>
29. </mat-accordion>
```

Note *ngFor in the expansion panel in line 2. We iterate through list of superheroes. Listing 13-17 is the TypeScript file component with a list of mock hero objects.

Listing 13-17. TypeScript File Component with Heroes Objects Defined

```
import { Superhero } from '../models/superhero';

@Component({ /* removed code for brevity */ })
export class SuperheroesExpandableListComponent implements OnInit {

  private heroes: Array<Superhero> = [
    {
      name: "Chhotta Bheem",
      email: "ChhottaBheem@angularsample.com",
      details: "A hero in Dholakpur village",
      country: "India",
      cardImage: "spiderman.jpg",
      specialPowers: ["is strong"],
```

```
      favFood: ["Laddu"],
      isExpanded: true,
    },
    // removed code for brevity
  ];

  constructor() { }
  ngOnInit() {}
}
```

Each superhero is shown in a single mat-expansion-panel element. It is similar to the list screen in earlier samples except that the expansion panel allows the user to focus on one of the rows for more information (by expanding just one item).

Typically, the user clicks a panel to expand. To show one of the panels expanded by default, use the expanded input attribute and set the value to true (see line 2 in Listing 13-18).

Listing 13-18. Expand Panel by Default

```
1. <mat-accordion>
2.    <mat-expansion-panel *ngFor="let hero of heroes" [expanded]="hero.
      isExpanded">
3.      <mat-expansion-panel-header>
4.        <!-- removed code for brevity -->
5.      </mat-expansion-panel-header>
6.        <!-- removed code for brevity -->
7.        <mat-action-row>
8.        <!-- removed code for brevity -->
9.        </mat-action-row>
10. </mat-expansion-panel>
```

We used data binding to expand a panel on load. The accordion allows only one of them to open. As another panel is expanded, the open item collapses.

In Listing 13-19, just one item's isExpanded is expected to be true. It is part of the hero object, which is an item in the heroes array. If more than one objects' isExpanded is true, the last value takes effect.

To let more than one item expand at a time, use the *multi* input attribute on mat-accordion. Listing 13-19 shows all the panels open on load. See the highlighted code in line 1 and line 2.

Listing 13-19. All Panels Expanded

```
1. <mat-accordion multi="true">
2.    <mat-expansion-panel *ngFor="let hero of heroes" expanded="true">
3.      <mat-expansion-panel-header>
4.        <!-- removed code for brevity -->
5.      </mat-expansion-panel-header>
6.        <!-- removed code for brevity -->
7.        <mat-action-row>
8.        <!-- removed code for brevity -->
9.        </mat-action-row>
10. </mat-expansion-panel>
```

Conclusion

The chapter discussed three Angular Material components: cards, tabs, and the accordion with an expansion panel. The Angular Material card showcases an entity, categorized with a title (within the header), content, footer, and actions.

The chapter also covered importing the Angular Material tabs module. We created a separate component using Angular CLI that showed tabs for a create component and a list of superheroes. The expansion panel and accordion were explained. The component shows a list of superheroes that is expandable or collapsible as the user clicks a section.

Exercise

In the dinosaur application, create a new component to show a list of dinosaurs. Use expansion panels for the list. Expand the first item in the list on load.

Create a new tabbed component. Add the newly created dinosaur list as the first tab. Create additional tabs that show the add dinosaur and the dinosaur details components.

References

Angular Material documentation (`https://material.angular.io/`)

Material Design Specification for Cards (`https://material.io/design/components/cards.html`)

Spiderman image by Naumovski on Pixabay (`https://pixabay.com/illustrations/spiderman-movie-superhero-spider-4378357/`)

CHAPTER 14

Material Design: Using Lists

Representing a collection of data in a UI screen is a common use case. It could be a list of users, orders, or any other entity in the system. In the sample application that we are building, it is a list of superheroes. This chapter covers using Angular Material lists and grid lists to showcase a collection of data.

The chapter begins with Material Design lists, providing instructions on importing the required module, directive, and components. It discusses using Angular Material components to build the variations.

Next, the chapter goes over Material Design grid lists. It provides a different perspective on a collection of data. It places content in tiles arranged in a two-dimensional list, and it describes how to use Angular Material directives and components to build a grid list.

Similar to the earlier chapters, we enhance the sample application.

Material Design List

We begin with Angular Material list directives and components. A list can show detailed information, or a list could be minimalistic. This section of the chapter explains how to build a list screen, and includes variations in showing holistic information, or only a title that allows navigation to a screen that shows the details.

We begin with getting-started instructions and update to the sample application in preparation to creating a list screen. Next, we build a screen that shows a list of superheroes (see Figure 14-1). Then, we modify the component to use the items in the list as buttons that navigate to a new screen with more of the details. This approach is useful when there is large amount of data to show. At the end of the section, we

© Venkata Keerti Kotaru 2020
V. K. Kotaru, *Angular for Material Design*, https://doi.org/10.1007/978-1-4842-5434-9_14

showcase an example that allows the user to select more than one item in a list. We can perform bulk actions, like edit or delete, on selected items.

Figure 14-1 is a sample list.

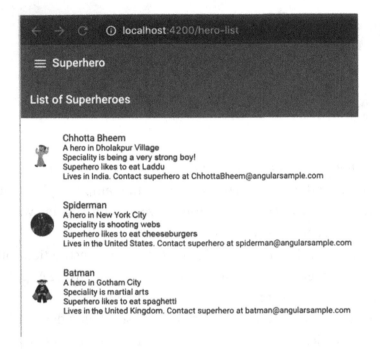

Figure 14-1. *Material Design list*

Getting Started

To use Angular Material's list, import the module containing the components and directives. In Listing 14-1, all the Material Design components are encompassed in superheroes-material-design.module.ts.

Import MatListModule from the Angular Material repository. Import it into NgModule (Angular module), encompassing all the Material Design code in the sample application.

Listing 14-1. Import Angular Material List Module

```
import { MatListModule } from '@angular/material/list';

// Removed code for brevity
@NgModule({
  declarations: [
    // Removed code for brevity
  ],
  imports: [
    MatListModule,
  ],
  exports: [
  ],
  providers:[]
})
export class SuperheroesMaterialDesignModule { }
```

Now that the Material Design list module is imported, we can use the list component. To showcase the list component, create a new sample component that shows the list of superheroes. We created a list component in an earlier chapter. However, we used a list of cards to show the superheroes. To truly use a list, we will create another component. In the sample, we called it superheroes-new-list.

Update the Superhero Sample Application

To create a new component using Angular CLI, run the command in Listing 14-2.

Listing 14-2. Create a Superhero List Component for Angular Material List

```
ng g component superheroes-material-design/superhero-new-list
```

The command updates superheroes-material-design-module. Before the component name, we used the module folder name: superheroes-material-design. The command generates a new component with the given name and adds declaration. We need to use this component outside the Superhero Material Design module. Hence, add it to the export array, as shown in Listing 14-3.

Listing 14-3. Declare and Export New Sample Component for the List

```
import { MatListModule } from '@angular/material/list';
import { SuperheroNewListComponent } from './superhero-
new-list.component';
// Removed code for brevity
@NgModule({
  declarations: [
      SuperheroNewListComponent
    // Removed code for brevity
  ],
  imports: [
    MatListModule,
  ],
  exports: [
      SuperheroNewListComponent,
    // Removed code for brevity

  ],
  providers:[]
})
export class SuperheroesMaterialDesignModule { }
```

Consider using the --export option with Angular CLI when generating the component. It generates the code that declares and exports the component from SuperheroesMaterialDesignModule. Listing 14-3 includes the export option. Both result in Listing 14-4.

Listing 14-4. Create a Superhero List Component That Exports from the Module

```
ng g component superheroes-material-design/superhero-new-list --export
```

To show the newly created component at a particular route, consider creating a new route. The route configurations are in app-routing.module.ts. Update the configuration to use the newly exported component from the Superheroes Material Design module. See Listing 14-5, and consider lines 7 and 8.

Listing 14-5. Route Configuration to Show the New List Component

```
1. import { SuperheroNewListComponent } from './superheroes-material-
   design/superhero-new-list/superhero-new-list.component';

2. const routes: Routes = [
3. {
4.    path: "heroes-accordion",
5.    component: SuperheroesExpandableListComponent
6. },{
7.    path: "hero-list",
8.    component: SuperheroNewListComponent
9.    },// Removed rest of route configuration for brevity
10. ];

11. @NgModule({
12.   imports: [RouterModule.forRoot(routes)],
13.   exports: [RouterModule]
14. })
15. export class AppRoutingModule { }
```

> **Note**   The App-routing module does not directly import the Superhero Material
> Design module. In the sample application, AppModule imports the App-Routing
> module and the Superhero Material Design module. Hence, the exported modules
> are available for route configuration, even though it does not directly import the
> component.

Navigate to the new route to see an empty component (as shown in Figure 14-2). The
path (route) configured is hero-list in Listing 14-5. We will use this component to build a
superhero list with the Material Design list component.

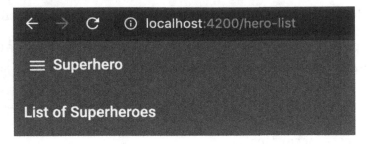

superhero-new-list works!

Figure 14-2. *Empty superhero list component*

Using Material Design List Component

Let's now update the component to create a superhero list. Consider the following list of Angular Material components and directives to create a Material Design list.

- **mat-list:** The component, mat-list, is the container for all the items in the list.

- **mat-list-item:** Use mat-list-item for each list item. In our sample (seen in Figure 14-1), it is one superhero.

- **matLine:** When there are multiple items in the list, use the MatLine directive to split HTML elements into separate line items. If the information in each list item is shown in a single line, we do not need this directive.

- In Figure 14-1, each superhero (a list item) has five lines of information, including the name, the place the hero comes from, favorite food, and so forth. Hence, we use the directive in Listing 14-5.

- **matListAvatar:** Use the directive to show an image as an avatar representing the line item in the list. Typically, the directive is used on an image element. In Listing 14-5, the directive fits the image to the line item and depicts it as an avatar (an image in a circle), as shown in Figure 14-1.

Note   All the components and directives are part of the MatListModule Angular module, which we imported earlier.

In Listing 14-5, the mat-list-item is iterating through the heroes. See fourth line in Listing 14-7. It creates the same number of items as those in the heroes array. The heroes array has mock objects. Note the same in Listing 14-6.

Listing 14-6. Show Hero List with Material Design List Component

```
<!-- mat-list encompass all list items -->
<mat-list>
    <!-- mat-list-item for each line item -->
    <mat-list-item *ngFor="let hero of heroes">
        <img [src]="hero.cardImage" matListAvatar alt="">
        <div matLine>{{ hero.name }}</div>
        <div matLine>{{ hero.details }}</div>
        <div matLine>Speciality is {{ hero.specialPowers[0] }}</div>
        <div matLine> Superhero likes to eat <span *ngFor="let f of hero.
        favFood"> {{ f }}</span></div>
        <div matLine>Lives in {{ hero.country }}. Contact superhero at {{
        hero.email }}</div>
    </mat-list-item>
</mat-list>
```

Listing 14-7 is the TypeScript class component that has mock objects for superheroes. Superhero is a class imported from the models/superhero folder. The "heroes" class property is used in the HTML template in the ngFor iterator.

Listing 14-7. TypeScript Code Component with Mock Objects for Superheroes

```
@Component({
    // Removed code for brevity
})
export class SuperheroNewListComponent implements OnInit {

  public heroes: Array<Superhero> = [
    {
      name: 'Chhotta Bheem',
      email: 'ChhottaBheem@angularsample.com',
      details: 'A hero in Dholakpur village',
      country: 'India',
```

```
    cardImage: '/assets/chhottabheem.png',

    specialPowers: ['Strong'],
    favFood: ['Laddu']
  },
  {
    name: 'Spiderman',
    // Removed code for brevity
  },
  {
    name: 'Batman',
    // Removed code for brevity
  }
];

constructor() { }
ngOnInit() { }
}
```

Navigate to the Details After Clicking a Superhero

One user experience paradigm is to show a list of items in the Material Design list. With a click, the user navigates to an information screen that shows more information about the selected item. Let's modify the list component built in the previous section.

Use the mat-nav-list component, which updates the view of an item as a link. In Figure 14-3, the list item that has a mouse cursor hovering over it is highlighted. Once the user clicks it, the Material Design ripple effect is similar to a Material Design button.

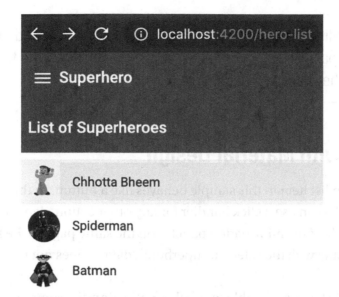

Figure 14-3. *Material Design navigation list*

Listing 14-8 is a list that navigates to an information screen. We can show partial information in each line item. It is best to not show too many lines of data. For this sample, we include only the superhero name.

Listing 14-8. Navigation List

```
<mat-nav-list>
    <mat-list-item *ngFor="let hero of heroes" >
        <img [src]="hero.cardImage" matListAvatar alt="">
        <a mat-list-item [routerLink]="['/hero', hero.name]" >
            {{ hero.name }}
        </a>
    </mat-list-item>
</mat-nav-list>
```

Unlike in Listing 14-7, we use the anchor element instead of div. The <a> element allows you to use routerLink for navigation to the information screen. The URL built for navigation leads to a path: /hero/hero-name. As an example, upon clicking, the user navigates to /hero/spiderman.

Note   The mat-list-item directive on the <a> element was added for better alignment and spacing. It helps with the correct positioning of the two elements: the avatar and the linked text (superhero name).

Action List with Material Design

As described, each list item in this sample behaves like a button. In the sample, we used it for navigation. We can use a click handler for any other action, depending on the use case. As an example, if the information panel is on the same page as the list screen, we can update the panel with the selected superhero's data. It does not need to navigate to a new route.

For an action list, it is preferable to use the mat-action-list component (rather than mat-nav-list). Listing 14-9 uses the click event that calls a function on the TypeScript class component. It provides the selected hero object as an input parameter to the function.

Listing 14-9. List with Click Handler

```
<mat-action-list>
    <mat-list-item *ngFor="let hero of heroes">
        <img [src]="hero.cardImage" matListAvatar alt="">
        <a mat-list-item (click)="listItemSelected(hero)">
            {{ hero.name }}
        </a>
    </mat-list-item>
</mat-action-list>
```

Listing 14-10 logs the selected hero object. We can use the object to update data binding for the information panel, if it exists on the same page.

Listing 14-10. Navigation List Handler Function

```
listItemSelected(hero){
  console.log(hero);
  // Code to update data binding and details view goes here.
}
```

The results are shown in Figure 14-4.

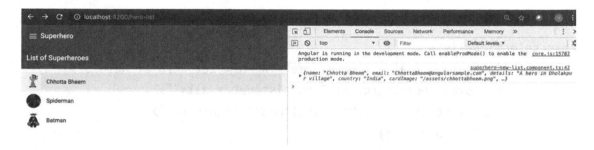

Figure 14-4. *Handler function logs selected hero object to console*

Selection List with Material Design

A selection list allows the user to select one or more elements. It is useful in scenarios that need a bulk action on multiple items. The bulk action could be delete, move to a different category (bulk update), or so on (see Figure 14-5).

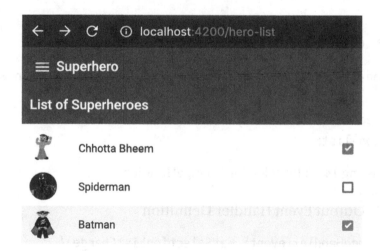

Figure 14-5. *Selection list*

Use the following components to build a selection list.

- **mat-selection-list:** The component, mat-selection-list, is a container for all the list options.

- **mat-list-option:** Use mat-list-option for each list option (a row in the list).

297

Consider Listing 14-11.

Listing 14-11. Selection List with Material Design

```
<mat-selection-list>
    <mat-list-option [value]='hero.name' *ngFor="let hero of heroes">
        <img [src]="hero.cardImage" matListAvatar alt="">
        <a mat-list-item (click)="listItemSelected(hero)">
            {{ hero.name }}
        </a>
    </mat-list-option>
</mat-selection-list>
```

mat-selection-list encompasses all the options (rows). The mat-list-option component renders each list option.

mat-selection-list uses a selectionChange output event handler because selection or deselection occurs in options. It helps track selected and unselected items (see Listing 14-12).

Listing 14-12. Output Event Handler for Change

```
<mat-selection-list #selected (selectionChange)="selectionChangeHandler
($event)">
    <!-- removed code for brevity -->
</mat-selection-list>
```

Consider Listing 14-13 for selectionChangeHandler.

Listing 14-13. Output Event Handler Definition

```
selectionChangeHandler(event: MatSelectionListChange){
  console.log(event.option.value, event.option.selected);
}
```

There is logged data, the value of the selected item, and the selection status (selected or unselected). The result is shown in Figure 14-6. The console log indicates that Chhotta Bheem was selected first and then unselected at the end.

Figure 14-6. *Selection status logged on console*

Grid List

The lists we have seen so far are simplistic representations of collections of data. A grid list takes it to the next level. It lays out tiles in a two-dimensional matrix (see Figure 14-7). Each tile holds content. It could be images, information about an entity in the system, a user or an order, or a superhero. In the sample application, we show a Material Design card with a grid list layout.

We begin the following section with getting-started instructions and by updating the sample application to create a new component that shows superhero cards in a grid list. Next, components and directives to build the grid list are covered.

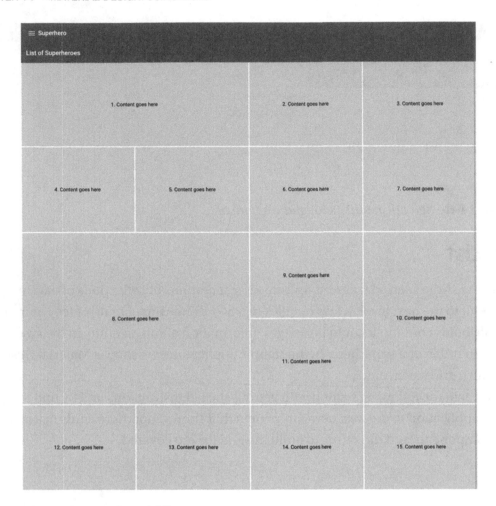

Figure 14-7. *A sample grid list*

Getting Started

To use Angular Material's grid list, import the module containing the components and directives. In Listing 14-14, all the Material Design components are encompassed in superheroes-material-design.module.ts.

Import MatGridListModule from the Angular Material repository. Import it into NgModule (Angular Module), encompassing all the Material Design code in the sample application.

Listing 14-14. Import Angular Material Grid List Module

```
import { MatGridListModule } from '@angular/material/list';

// Removed code for brevity
@NgModule({
  declarations: [
    // Removed code for brevity
  ],
  imports: [
    MatGridListModule,
  ],
  exports: [
  ],
  providers:[]
})
export class SuperheroesMaterialDesignModule { }
```

Now that the Material Design grid list module is imported, we can use the grid list component. To showcase the grid list component, create a new sample component that shows a list of superheroes.

Update the Superhero Sample Application

To create a new component using Angular CLI, run the command in Listing 14-15.

Listing 14-15. Create Superhero Grid List Component

```
ng g component superheroes-material-design/superhero-grid-list
```

The command updates superheroes-material-design-module. Before the component name, we use the module folder name: superheroes-material-design. The command generates a new component with the given name and adds a declaration. We need to use this component outside the superhero Material Design module. Hence, add it to the export array (see Listing 14-16).

Listing 14-16. Declare and Export New Sample Component for the List

```
import { MatGridListModule } from '@angular/material/list';
import { SuperheroGridListComponent } from './superhero-grid-list/
superhero-grid-list.component';
// Removed code for brevity
@NgModule({
  declarations: [
      SuperheroGridListComponent
    // Removed code for brevity
  ],
  imports: [
    MatListModule,
  ],
  exports: [
      SuperheroGridListComponent,
    // Removed code for brevity

  ],
  providers:[]
})
export class SuperheroesMaterialDesignModule { }
```

Consider using the --export option with Angular CLI when generating the component. It generates the code that declares and exports the component from SuperheroesMaterialDesignModule. Listing 14-17 has the export option included.

Listing 14-17. Create and Export Superhero Grid List Component

```
ng g component superheroes-material-design/superhero-grid-list --export
```

To show the newly created component at a particular route, consider creating a new route. The route configurations are in app-routing.module.ts. Update the configuration to use the newly exported component from the superheroes Material Design module (see Listing 14-18).

Note   App-routing module does not directly import Superhero Material Design Module. In the sample application, AppModule imports the App-Routing module and Superhero Material Design Module. Hence, the exported modules are available for route configuration, even though they do not directly import the component.

Listing 14-18. Route Configuration to Show the Grid List Component

```
import { SuperheroGridListComponent } from './superheroes-material-design/
superhero-grid-list/superhero-grid-list.component';
const routes: Routes = [
  {
    path: "heroes-accordion",
    component: SuperheroesExpandableListComponent
  },
  {
    path: "hero-grid-list",
        component: SuperheroGridListComponent
  }, Removed rest of route configuration for brevity
];

@NgModule({
  imports: [RouterModule.forRoot(routes)],
  exports: [RouterModule]
})
export class AppRoutingModule { }
```

Navigate to the new route to see an empty component. The configured path (route) is hero-list in Listing 14-18. The URL is shown in Figure 14-8.

We will use this component to build a superhero grid list with the Material Design grid list.

superhero-grid-list works!

Figure 14-8. *Empty superhero list component*

Using Material Design Grid List Component

Let's create a grid list similar to Figure 14-8. Use the following list of components and directives to create the Material Design grid list.

- **mat-grid-list**: Encapsulates tiles (items in a grid). The component provides a layout based on the parameters provided as input. Consider the following input.

  - **cols**: Sets the number of columns on the grid list.

  - **rowHeight – ratio**: Sets the height of a row. Values can be provided as a ratio (for example, 4:3, 16:9, 4:5).

  - **rowHeight – fixed**: Sets the height with a fixed value in px, em, or rem. By default, pixel units are used.

  - **rowHeight – fit**: Fits the height of the grid to the available space spread across the rows of the grid.

  - **gutterSize**: The gutter is the space between tiles. By default, a 1px value is set between tiles. You can configure a different value.

Note   The columns on a grid list are configured with cols; however, rows depend on the data and the number of items in a list. It is not configured.

- **mat-grid-tile**: Each item in the grid is defined by the component, mat-grid-tile. You can have additional input parameters on a tile.

- **colspan**: A grid is evenly distributed in a matrix of rows and columns. You can choose a tile to spread multiple columns. Use the colspan attribute to set a value. The value should be less than or equal to the total number of columns.

- **rowspan**: You can choose a tile to spread multiple rows. Use the rowspan attribute to set a value. Unlike a column span, there is no restriction on the number of rows that a tile can span.

- **mat-grid-tile-header**: Each grid tile can have optional header text and content encapsulated in mat-grid-tile-header.

- **mat-grid-tile-footer**: Each grid tile can have optional footer text and content encapsulated in mat-grid-tile-footer.

Listing 14-19 shows the superhero profile cards as tiles. Each tile shows a superhero card. The cards are laid out based on the grid list configuration.

Listing 14-19. A Sample Grid List for Superheroes

```
1. <mat-grid-list cols="3" rowHeight="4:3" gutterSize='3px'>
2.  <mat-grid-tile [colspan]="i === 0 ? 2 : 1" [rowspan]="i === 0 ? 2 : 1"
    *ngFor="let hero of heroes; let i=index">
3.     <app-superhero-profile
4.      height="30%"
5.      [name]="hero.name"
6.      [lives-in]="hero.livesIn"
7.      firstAppearance="2008"
8.      [superpowers]="hero.specialPowers"
9.      [card-image]="hero.cardImage">
10.    </app-superhero-profile>
11.  </mat-grid-tile>
12. </mat-grid-list>
```

Listing 14-19 creates a grid with three columns. See line 1; the cols attribute has a value of 3. It creates rows on the fly based on the number of tiles. If there are 12 superheroes, with each row placing three tiles, there will be four rows. Line 2 has *ngFor iterating over an array to render multiple mat-grid-tile components.

We configured a row height of 4 : 3 (see line 1, the rowHeight attribute). Typically, it is decided based on the content in a tile. Figure 14-9 shows the cards in a tile. Hence, the row height ratio is dependent on a card's width and height.

We set an arbitrary value of 3px for the gutter size. As specified earlier, this is an optional value. By default, the value is set to 1px.

The iterator, ngFor, loops through superheroes. It renders as many mat-grid-tiles as that of superheroes. The expression "i === 0 ? 2 : 1" is in line 2 on the row span and col span attributes; it is for demonstration purposes only. For the first tile, we set the row span and the col span to a value of 2. The first tile spreads across two columns and rows.

Within each grid-list-tile, we show a superhero card. The sample uses the app-superhero-profile component, which shows the superhero data in a Material Design card. See lines 3 to 10 in Listing 14-19.

The result is shown in Figure 14-9.

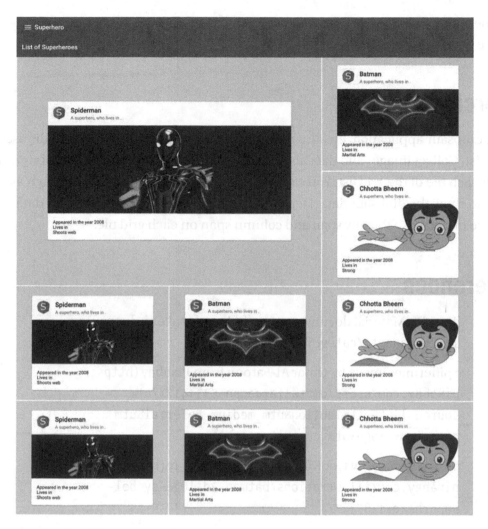

Figure 14-9. *Grid list of superheroes*

Conclusion

The chapter covered representing a collection of items and data in a view. It used two Angular Material concepts: lists and grid lists.

Lists are a simplistic representation of a collection. The chapter updated the Superheroes sample application and built a list with Angular Material components and directives. It showed three variations of lists: a detailed view of a superhero (or any entity in the system) with multiple lines of data, a minimalistic view that allows navigating to a different screen on a click, and a third variation to allow selecting one or more items in the list for bulk actions like edit or delete. The edit or delete actions were not in the scope of this chapter.

The chapter also covered grid lists, updating the Superheroes sample application to use the new component.

Exercise

In the dinosaur application, create a new component to show a collection of dinosaurs in a grid list. Collect images and data about eight dinosaurs. Show the dinosaur information within each tile of the grid list. You can optionally use another component, such as a card to show the dinosaur data. Depending on the dinosaur image size and data, increase or decrease the row span and column span on each grid tile.

References

Angular Material documentation (`https://material.angular.io/components/categories`)

Spiderman image by Omar Al-Farooq from Pixabay (`https://pixabay.com/users/omaralfarooqpn-5334412/?utm_source=link-attribution&utm_medium=referral&utm_campaign=image&utm_content=4112322`)

Batman image by GooKingSword from Pixabay (`https://pixabay.com/illustrations/batman-3d-logo-symbol-superhero-1387347/`)

Chhotta Bheem image by Sonam Prajapati from Pixabay (`https://pixabay.com/illustrations/sketch-character-funny-cute-art-3053682/`)

CHAPTER 15

Material Design: Alerts and Dialogs

Alerts and dialogs have been integral to UI applications. They show messages and information that need the user's attention in UI pop-overs. Most of these UI paradigms are a layer on top of the original interface. Although it is needed for prompting and conveying significant content and messages, do not show multiple alerts or pop-overs at once. Overusing alerts and dialogs can lead to a bad user experience.

The dialogs and alerts described in this chapter follow Material Design specifications. We begin by introducing Material dialog. This chapter provides getting-started instructions, usage in the sample application, and various configurations.

This chapter introduces the bottom sheet. This control is typically used for showing menus, options, and prompts. Integrating bottom sheets with the Angular application and the consistent approach followed while integrating additional Angular Material components are explained.

Finally, this chapter discusses using a snack bar for showing alerts and messages.

Material Dialog

Angular Material provides a dialog implementation that confines to Material Design principles. It provides the same look and feel and animations when opening and closing the dialog . The Material dialog's components and directives are ready-made and easy to use.

A dialog can have detailed text and images. The UI paradigm supports elaborate content and multiple actions. In Figure 15-1, the user agreement is shown in a Material dialog. It allows the user to either agree or cancel.

© Venkata Keerti Kotaru 2020
V. K. Kotaru, *Angular for Material Design*, https://doi.org/10.1007/978-1-4842-5434-9_15

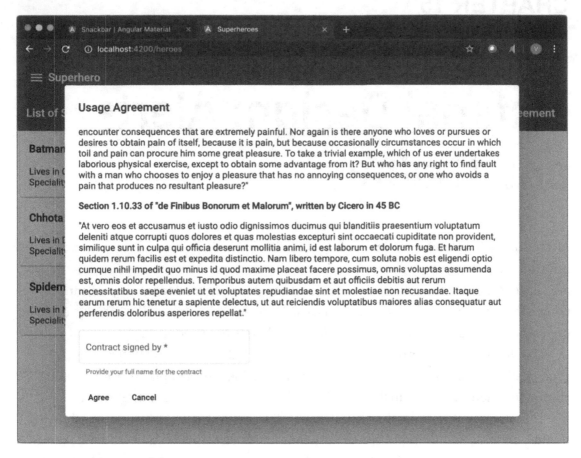

Figure 15-1. *Sample Material dialog component*

Getting Started

To use Angular Material's model dialog, import the module containing the components and directives. In Listing 15-1, all the Material Design components are encompassed in superheroes-material-design.module.ts.

Import the MatDialogModule from the Angular Material repository. Import it into the NgModule (Angular module) encompassing all the Material Design code in the sample application.

Listing 15-1. Import Angular Material Dialog Module

```
import { MatDialogModule } from '@angular/material/dialog';

@NgModule({
  declarations: [
      // Removed code for brevity
  ],
  imports: [
    MatDialogModule,
  ],
  exports: [
      // Removed code for brevity
  ],
  entryComponents: []
})
export class SuperheroesMaterialDesignModule { }
```

Sample: Confirm Cancel

In the sample application, consider a scenario in which we show a confirmation message when creating a new superhero. We do so with a Material dialog. Let's edit the Create Superhero Component to use the model dialog for the confirmation message.

We encapsulate code for the Material Dialog in a new component. Use an Angular CLI command to create a new component. Listing 15-2 creates the component in the superheroes-material-design module. The component is named CancelConfirmDialogComponent.

Listing 15-2. Create a Component for Creating the Model Dialog

```
ng g component superheroes-material-design/cancel-confirm-dialog
```

The newly created component needs to be added as an entry component in the SuperheroMaterialDesignModule. It is required for the Angular compiler. Consider Listing 15-3. Update the entryComponents array to include CancelConfirmDialogComponent. Lines 1 and 5 are added by the Angular CLI. See line 13, where we update the component as an entry component in the module.

Listing 15-3. Declare Cancel Confirm Dialog in the Angular Module

```
1. // imports
   import { MatDialogModule } from '@angular/material/dialog';
   import { CancelConfirmDialogComponent } from './cancel-confirm-dialog/
   cancel-confirm-dialog.component';

2. @NgModule({
3.  declarations: [
4.    // Removed code for brevity
5.      CancelConfirmDialogComponent
6.  ],
7.  imports: [
8.    MatDialogModule,
9.  ],
10.  exports: [
11.    // Removed code for brevity
12.  ],
13.  entryComponents: [CancelConfirmDialogComponent]
14. })
15. export class SuperheroesMaterialDesignModule { }
```

We use the following directives to create a Material dialog. Listing 15-3 builds a Material dialog. It is the HTML template for the component. Figure 15-2 shows the result.

- **mat-dialog-title**: Title for the dialog. Always shows even if the content or body of the dialog scrolls. See lines 1, 2, and 3 in Listing 15-3.

- **mat-dialog-content**: Workspace or the main content of the dialog. Shows a scrollbar when content exceeds predefined height of the dialog. See lines 4, 5, and 6 in Listing 15-3.

- **mat-dialog-actions**: Footer section of the dialog. Always shows, like the title. Typically, encompasses action buttons like Confirm, Cancel, and so forth. See lines 7 to 10 in Listing 15-3.

- **mat-dialog-close**: The directive works on actions or buttons. It closes the dialog on click. In Listing 15-4, see lines 8 and 9. Notice the JSON specified. The field names and values in it are arbitrary.

It returns the JSON result to the parent component. In the sample, we identify the button clicked by providing the title of the OK or Cancel button. The parent component receives this JSON and makes the appropriate decision.

Listing 15-4. Model Dialog HTML Template

```
1.  <h1 mat-dialog-title>
2.   Are you sure?
3.  </h1>
4.  <div mat-dialog-content>
5.   Are you sure to cancel without saving the data?
6.  </div>
7.  <div mat-dialog-actions>
8.    <button mat-button [mat-dialog-close]="{clicked:'Ok'}">Ok</button>
9.    <button mat-button [mat-dialog-close]="{clicked:'Cancel'}">Cancel
     </button>
10. </div>
```

Figure 15-2 shows the result.

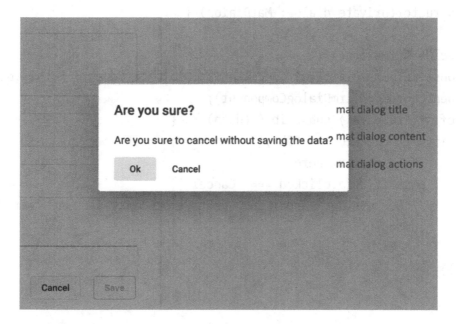

Figure 15-2. *Material Dialog on cancel in Create Superhero*

Launch Material Dialog

So far, we have created a dialog that shows on click of the Cancel button. Next, we will launch the component in Listing 15-4 from the Create Superhero component. It is the parent component for the Material dialog. Remember, the Create Superhero component has an elaborate form to accept superhero information. If the user chooses to abort creating a superhero, she may click the Cancel button. The application shows a dialog to confirm the cancel action.

We use the MatDialog service to launch the dialog. Import and inject the service to CreateSuperheroComponent. In Listing 15-5, note the constructor in line 3, which injects the service.

Listing 15-5. Launch Material Dialog

```
1. // Imports
   import { MatDialog, MatDialogRef } from '@angular/material/dialog';
   import { CancelConfirmDialogComponent } from '../cancel-confirm-dialog/
   cancel-confirm-dialog.component';
2. // Removed code for brevity
3. export class CreateSuperheroComponent implements OnInit {
4.   constructor(private dialog: MatDialog) {
5.   }
6.   cancelHeroCreation() {
7.     const ref: MatDialogRef<CancelConfirmDialogComponent> = this.dialog.
       open(CancelConfirmDialogComponent);
8.     ref.afterClosed().subscribe( (data) => {
9.       if(data.clicked === "Ok"){
10.        // Reset form here
11.      } else if(data.clicked === "Cancel"){
12.        // Do nothing. Cancel any events that navigate away from the
           component.
13.      }
14.    });
15.  }
16.}
```

The cancel action invokes a cancelHeroCreation() function, which is defined in line 6. Next, to launch the dialog component created in Listing 15-5, we call the open() function on the service instance (this.dialog). Use the open() function with an input parameter and the dialog component class reference, which is imported in line 1.

In line 7, the open function returns a reference of the dialog component. It is assigned to a variable ref of type ModelDialogRef. It also uses a generic type to which we specify the component name created in Listing 15-5.

We have launched the model dialog. Next, we need to code the logic that acts on user choice. She may confirm aborting a superhero creation or continue with the create form. In either case, as the user chooses, the Model Dialog closes.

To do this, we call afterClosed(), which returns an observable. Subscribe to it (see lines 8 to 14). The success callback is invoked as the user finishes with the model dialog. The user can click the OK button or the Cancel button. Depending on the selection, the parent component makes a decision to reset the form or do nothing.

The JSON object returned from the Material dialog in Listing 15-5 (lines 8 and 9) is received on the success handler of subscribe in the parent component (see line 8 in Listing 15-5).

Send Data to the Material Dialog

We can provide additional parameters when opening the Material dialog. Data is one of the pieces of information that the parent component can provide to the Material dialog. In Listing 15-6, the parent component provides a message to be shown in the Material dialog. See lines 3 to 5.

Listing 15-6. Provide Data to the Material Dialog

```
--- create-superhero.component.ts ---
1.    let ref: MatDialogRef<CancelConfirmDialogComponent>
2.        = this.dialog.open(CancelConfirmDialogComponent, {
3.        data: {
4.            message: "Create Superhero action attempted to be cancelled"
5.        }
6.    });
```

To access the data, the object is injected into the constructor of the model dialog component. Use the MAT_DIALOG_DATA token to identify the dialog data. Consider Listing 15-7.

Listing 15-7. Access Data Provided by the Parent

```
--- cancel-confirm-dialog.component.ts ---
1. import { MatDialogRef, MAT_DIALOG_DATA } from '@angular/material/
   dialog';

2. @Component({
3.     // Removed code for brevity
4. })
5. export class CancelConfirmDialogComponent implements OnInit {
6.   message: string;

7.   constructor(public dialogRef: MatDialogRef<CancelConfirmDialogComponent>,
8.     @Inject(MAT_DIALOG_DATA) data: { message: string}) {
9.        this.message = data.message;
10.  }
11. }
```

Note   In line 8, we are using an anonymous type for simplicity. We can use a predefined class instead.

The data object and the message field are the data provided by the parent component in line 9. We set the message in the class property, which is used in the HTML template. It shows the message in the dialog.

We can set the following parameters (or configurations) when launching a dialog. Listing 15-8 is a sample that sets the height, width, and backdrop, in addition to providing text (or data). Figure 15-3 shows the result. Compare it to Figure 15-2, to which we did not provide any configuration.

- **id**: Overrides the default auto-generated ID for the dialog

- **width**: A predefined width for the dialog, including units, pixels (px), points (pt), and so forth.

- **minWidth**: A predefined minimum width for the dialog, including units , pixels (px), points (pt), and so forth. The dialog grows if the content does not fit in the provided width. It would at least be set at this width, even if the content is smaller.

- **height**: A predefined height for the dialog, including units, pixels (px), points (pt), and so forth.

- **minHeight**: A predefined minimum height for the dialog, including, pixels (px), points (pt), and so forth. The dialog grows if the content does not fit in the provided height. It would at least be set at this width, even if the content is smaller.

- **panelClass**: A CSS class for the panel. Overrides the default.

- **position**: Set a value—top, bottom, left, or right—for the dialog position.

- **autoFocus**: Automatically focuses on the first element in the dialog.

- **disableClose**: If true, the dialog will not close on keyboard escape or from clicking outside the dialog area.

- **hasBackdrop**: If false, the dialog does not add a layer dimming the backdrop parent component.

Listing 15-8. Launch Material Dialog with a Configuration

```
let ref: MatDialogRef<CancelConfirmDialogComponent>
    = this.dialog.open(CancelConfirmDialogComponent, {
      width: "800px",
      height: "200px",
      data: {
        message: "Create Superhero action attempted to be cancelled"
      },
      hasBackdrop: true
    });
```

The results are shown in Figure 15-3.

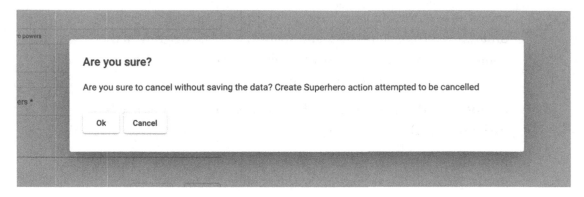

Figure 15-3. *Material dialog launched with a configuration, by the parent component*

Provide Default Configuration for Material Dialog

We can provide a default configuration at the module level. It is used by all instances of the Material dialog. It is useful if we do not wish to customize each instance of a model dialog. Rather, use the parameters (or configuration) throughout the entire module. It helps provide consistency in the look and feel and behavior.

Listing 15-9 uses the MAT_DIALOG_DEFAULT_OPTIONS provider key. It is of type InjectionToken<MatDialogConfig<any>>. This configuration for the Material dialog is supplied by module-level providers. Hence, it is applied on all relevant components of the module

Listing 15-9. Material Dialog Default Configuration

```
import { MatDialogModule, MAT_DIALOG_DEFAULT_OPTIONS } from '@angular/
material/dialog';
@NgModule({
  declarations: [
      // Removed code for brevity
  ],
  imports: [
      // Removed code for brevity
  ],
  exports: [
      // Removed code for brevity
  ],
```

```
providers:[
  {
    provide: MAT_DIALOG_DEFAULT_OPTIONS,
    useValue: {
      minWidth: "1020px",
      minHeight: "800px",
      hasBackdrop: true,
      disableClose:false
    }
  }
],
entryComponents: [CancelConfirmDialogComponent]
})
export class SuperheroesMaterialDesignModule { }
```

Send Data to the Parent Component

Consider the Material dialog that we created earlier. The two lines of code in Listing 15-10 show the Confirm and Cancel buttons.

Listing 15-10. (Partial Snippet from Listing 15-9) OK and Cancel Buttons in Material Dialog

```
<button mat-button [mat-dialog-close]="{clicked:'Ok'}">Ok</button>
<button mat-button [mat-dialog-close]="{clicked:'Cancel'}">Cancel</button>
```

We sent data to the parent component using the mat-dialog-close directive. The data identified the button selected by the user in the Material dialog. Based on the selection, the parent component decides to either clear the form or do nothing.

Alternatively, we may use a Material dialog reference to communicate from the dialog component to the parent component. Consider Figure 15-4. We briefly mentioned the use case at the beginning of the chapter. Imagine that the user agreement dialog is launched from the toolbar. In Figure 15-4, the Material dialog component shows the content of the user agreement. As the user types his name in the text field and submits the form, the toolbar receives the data. Figure 15-4 shows the name of the user.

To access the dialog reference, inject the ModelDialogRef service into the Material dialog component (the component that shows the user agreement). See Listing 15-10. We did the same in Listing 15-11 for CancelConfirmDialog.

Listing 15-11. Inject Material Dialog Reference

```
export class SoftwareAgreementComponent implements OnInit {
  constructor(public dialogRef: MatDialogRef<SoftwareAgreementComponent>) {
  }
}
```

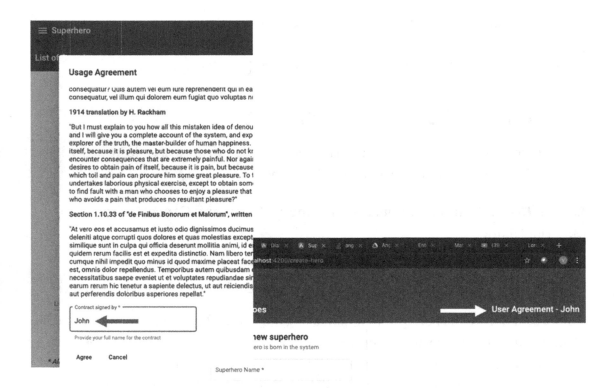

Figure 15-4. *Pass data from Material dialog to parent component*

Consider the function on clicking the Agree button in Listing 15-12. We use a dialog reference variable and close the model dialog. Pass the two fields of information: the title of the selected button (agree/cancel) and the full name entered by the user.

Listing 15-12. Close the Dialog and Send Data to Parent Component

```
onAgree(){
  this.dialogRef.close({
    clicked: "agree",
    fullName: this.fullName
  });
}
```

This accomplishes functionality similar to that of mat-dialog-close. However, mat-dialog-close is a directive used in the HTML template. It closes the model dialog. It provides limited but commonly used, ready-made functionality.

MatDialogRef provides finer control. We may choose to conditionally close the dialog, perform additional actions, and so on. We may send elaborate content or JSON objects back to the parent component, which is difficult to achieve with a directive in the HTML template.

The parent component accesses the dialog state as before. Listing 15-12 (the user agreement example) is similar to Listing 15-13's lines 8 to 13. We show the name field accessed from the model dialog on the component.

Listing 15-13. Access Data Obtained from the Dialog

```
dialogRef.afterClosed()
.subscribe(
  (data) => this.fullName = data.fullName
);
```

Bottom Sheet

Bottom sheet provides supplementary content and alerts. We may use it to show a list of the available options, menu items, and so forth.

As the name suggests, it is positioned at the bottom of the page. Consider an example in the context of Superheroes application. For a selected record, a list of available actions can be shown in a bottom sheet. Figure 15-5 shows options to share, print, message, or delete a selected superhero.

Similar to Material dialog, a bottom sheet supports selecting from multiple available actions. It may not use as much screen space as that of a dialog. The UI paradigm is useful for targeted actions that do not need to showcase elaborate information.

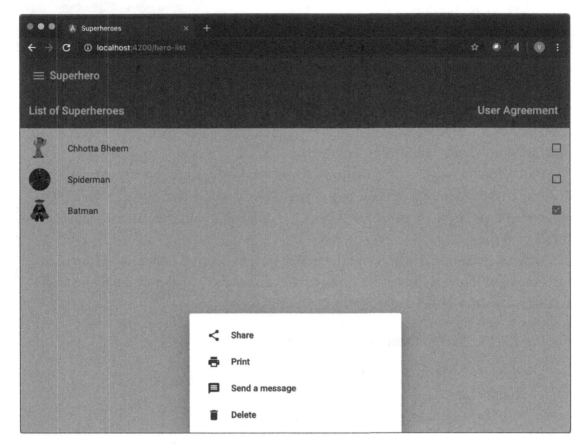

Figure 15-5. *Material Design bottom sheet*

Getting Started

To use Angular Material's bottom sheet, import MatBottomSheetModule, which contains the components and directives. In Listing 15-14, all the Material Design components are encompassed in superheroes-material-design.module.ts.

Import MatBottomSheetModule from the Angular Material repository into the NgModule (Angular module) encompassing all the Material Design code in the sample application.

Listing 15-14. Import Angular Material Bottom Sheet Module

```
import { MatBottomSheetModule } from '@angular/material/bottom-sheet';

@NgModule({
  declarations: [
        // Removed code for brevity
  ],
  imports: [
    MatBottomSheetModule,
  ],
  exports: [
        // Removed code for brevity
  ],
  entryComponents: []
})
export class SuperheroesMaterialDesignModule { }
```

Let's continue with the use case discussed with the Material dialog. On aborting to create a new superhero, we show a confirmation message (on click of the Cancel button). We may do so with a bottom sheet (instead of a Material dialog). Let's edit Create Superhero Component to use the bottom sheet for the confirmation message (see Figure 15-6).

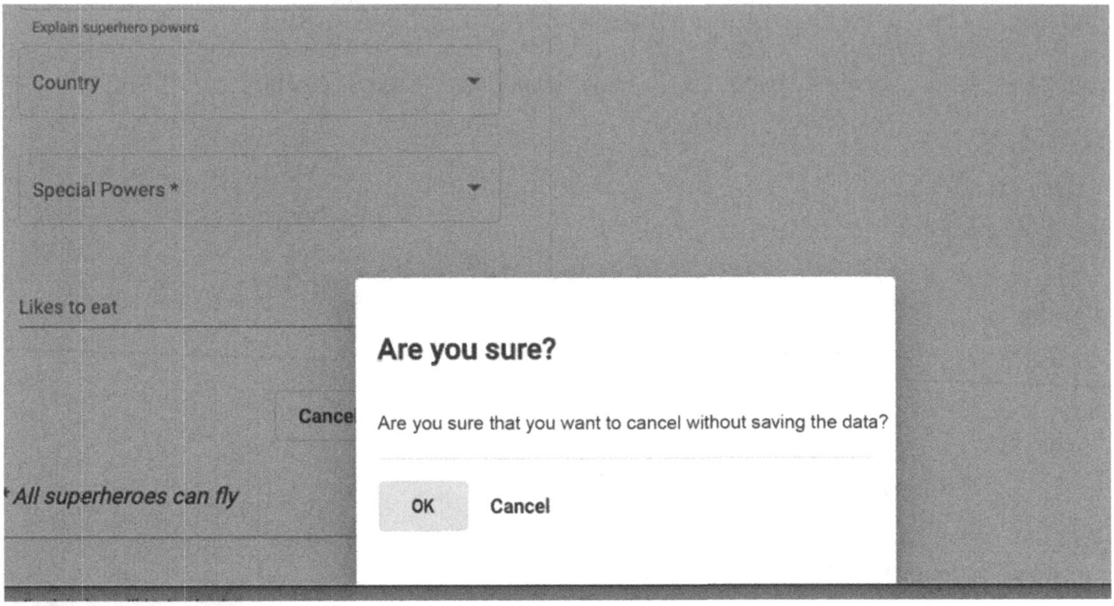

Figure 15-6. *Cancel confirmation with bottom sheet*

We encapsulate the code for the bottom sheet in a new component. Use the Angular CLI command to create a new component. Listing 15-15 creates the component in the superheroes-material-design module. The component is named CancelConfirmBottomSheetComponent.

Listing 15-15. Create a Component for Creating the Model Dialog

```
ng g component superheroes-material-design/cancel-confirm-bottomsheet
```

Like Material dialog, the bottom sheet needs to be registered as an entry component in the superhero-material-design module. This is required for the Angular compiler. Listing 15-16 line 1 imports the newly created component. Line 12 adds the component to the entry components array in the Angular module.

Listing 15-16. Import Angular Material Dialog Module

```
1. import { CancelConfirmBottomSheetComponent } from './cancel-confirm-
   bottomsheet/cancel-confirm-bottomsheet.component';
2. @NgModule({
3.   declarations: [
4.     // Removed code for brevity
5.   ],
```

```
6.  imports: [
7.    MatBottomSheetModule,
8.  ],
9.  exports: [
10.   // Removed code for brevity
11.   ],
12.   entryComponents: [CancelConfirmBottomSheetComponent]
13.})
export class SuperheroesMaterialDesignModule { }
```

Next, edit the HTML template of the newly created bottom sheet component. We show the confirmation message here (see Listing 15-17).

Listing 15-17. Form Cancel Confirmation Message in Bottom Sheet

```
1. <div>
2.   <h2>
3.     Are you sure?
4.   </h2>
5.   <div>
6.     Are you sure to cancel without saving the data?
7.     {{ message }}
8.   </div>
9.   <mat-divider></mat-divider>
10.   <div>
11.     <button mat-button (click)="onOkClick()">Ok</button>
12.     <button mat-button (click)="onCancelClick()">Cancel</button>
13.   </div>
14. </div>
```

Note   The mat-divider component is in line 9. It is a horizontal ruler or a separator between the message and the action buttons.

The click events data binding with TypeScript component functions is shown in lines 11 and 12 (onOkClick() and onCancelClick()). Consider code for the same in Listing 15-17. The bottom sheet component communicates with the parent component and passes the state of the bottom sheet. It passes the information whether the user clicked the OK button or the Cancel button. See the complete code in Listing 15-18.

Listing 15-18. Bottom Sheet TypeScript File Component

```
1. import { MatBottomSheetRef } from '@angular/material/bottom-sheet';

2. @Component({
3.  // removed code snippet for brevity
4. })
5. export class CancelConfirmBottomSheetComponent implements OnInit {
6.  constructor(private bottomSheetRef: MatBottomSheetRef) { }

7.  ngOnInit() {
8. }

9.  onOkClick(){
10.    this.bottomSheetRef.dismiss({ clicked: "Ok"});
11.  }

12.  onCancelClick(){
13.    this.bottomSheetRef.dismiss({ clicked: "Cancel"});
14.  }
15.}
```

In the constructor in line 6, we inject the MatBottomSheetRef variable, referencing the bottom sheet. We use this reference variable to dismiss the bottom sheet in the click event handler function and cancel the event handler function.

When we create and show the bottom sheet (in the parent component), the reference is also returned to the parent component. The parent component can subscribe to observables in BottomSheetRef. The subscription helps receive data from the child component (the bottom sheet is the child component) and perform actions like "close". This time, the close action can be performed from the parent component.

In lines 10 and 13, the dismiss API accepts the JSON object as an input parameter. In this sample, we pass the information, whether or not the OK or Cancel buttons have been clicked.

In Listing 15-19, the parent component subscribes to the observable that receives data from the bottom sheet. The observable is returned by the afterDismissed() function, which streams an event only after dismissing the bottom sheet (see line 3).

Listing 15-19. Parent Component Subscribes to Observable from Bottom Sheet

```
1.  cancelCreate(){
2.      let ref = this.bottomSheet.open(CancelConfirmBottomSheetComponent);
3.      ref.afterDismissed().subscribe( data => {
4.       if(data.clicked === "Ok"){
5.         // Reset form here
6.       }else if(data.clicked === "Cancel"){
7.         // Do nothing. Cancel any events that navigate away from the
           component.
8.       }
9.     });
10. )
```

Send Data to the Bottom Sheet

We can provide additional parameters (or configuration) when opening the bottom sheet. Data is one of the pieces of information that the parent component can provide to the bottom sheet. Listing 15-20 provides a message to be shown in the Material dialog (see lines 3 to 5).

Listing 15-20. Provide Data to the Bottom Sheet

```
1.      let ref = this.bottomSheet.open(CancelConfirmBottomSheetComponent,
2.        {
3.          data: {
4.          message: "Create Superhero action attempted to be cancelled"
5.        }
6.      });
```

To access the data, the object is injected into the constructor of the cancel confirmation bottom sheet component. Use the MAT_BOTTOM_SHEET_DATA token to identify the bottom sheet data (see Listing 15-21).

Listing 15-21. Access Data Provided by the Parent

```
1. import { MatBottomSheetRef, MAT_BOTTOM_SHEET_DATA } from '@angular/
   material/bottom-sheet';
2. export class CancelConfirmBottomSheetComponent implements OnInit {
3.   message: string;
4.   constructor(private bottomSheetRef: MatBottomSheetRef,
5.       @Inject(MAT_BOTTOM_SHEET_DATA) bottomsheetData:{ message:string}) {
6.           this.message = bottomsheetData.message;
7. }
```

Note   In line 5, we are using an anonymous type for simplicity. We can use a predefined class instead.

The bottomsheetData object and the message field are the values provided by the parent component. In line 6, we set a message on the class variable, which is used in the HTML template. It shows the message on the bottom sheet. Consider Listing 15-22.

Listing 15-22. HTML Template Shows the Message, if Available

```
<div>
    Are you sure to cancel without saving the data?
    <div *ngIf="message">
      <strong>{{message}}</strong>
    </div>
</div>
```

The following are additional configurations that we can set on the bottom sheet.

- **panelClass**: A CSS class for the panel. Overrides the default.

- **autoFocus**: Automatically focuses on the first element in the bottom sheet.

- **disableClose**: If true, will not close the bottom sheet on keyboard escape or by clicking outside the bottom sheet area.

- **hasBackdrop**: If false, the bottom sheet does not add a layer dimming the backdrop parent component.

Provide Default Configuration for Bottom Sheet

We can provide default configuration at the module level. It is used by all instances of the bottom sheet. It helps provide consistency in the look and feel and behavior.

Listing 15-23 uses the MAT_BOTTOM_SHEET_DEFAULT_OPTIONS provider key. It is of type InjectionToken<MatBottomSheetConfig<any>>.

Listing 15-23. Bottom Sheet Default Configuration

```
import { MatBottomSheetModule, MAT_BOTTOM_SHEET_DEFAULT_OPTIONS } from
'@angular/material/bottom-sheet';
@NgModule({
  declarations: [
      // Removed code for brevity
  ],
  imports: [
    MatBottomSheetModule,
      // Removed code for brevity
  ],
  exports: [
      // Removed code for brevity
  ],
  providers:[
    {
      provide: MAT_BOTTOM_SHEET_DEFAULT_OPTIONS,
      useValue: {
        hasBackdrop: false,
        disableClose: true
      }
    }
  ],
  entryComponents: [CancelConfirmBottomSheetComponent]
})
export class SuperheroesMaterialDesignModule { }
```

Snack-bar

The snack-bar is useful for showing alerts and messages. The messages do not interrupt the user. Based on the configuration, fewer import messages are dismissed automatically after a stipulated number of milliseconds. This helps the user to not become distracted by all the messages and notifications.

A typical snack-bar message is shown at the bottom center of the page. However, it can be repositioned to display in any corner of the page. A snack-bar may have an action to discuss the alert. Alternatively, it may not have any action, and it is dismissed automatically after a few seconds.

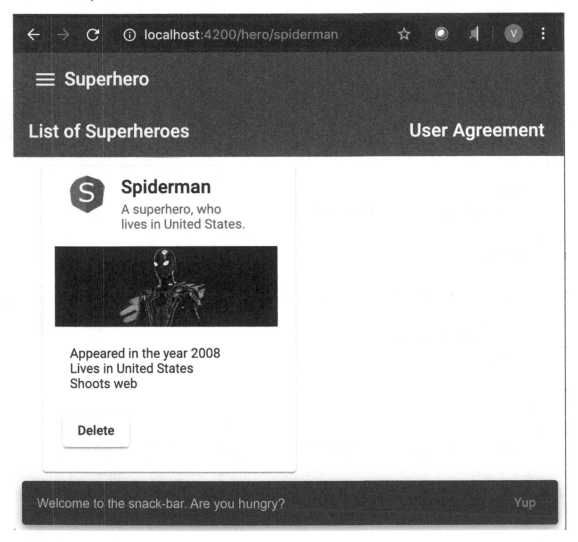

Figure 15-7. *Material Design snack-bar*

Getting Started

To use Angular Material's snack-bar, import MatSnackBarModule, which contains the components and directives. In Listing 15-24, all the Material Design components are encompassed in superheroes-material-design.module.ts.

Import MatSnackBarModule from the Angular Material repository into the NgModule (Angular module) encompassing all Material Design code in the sample application.

Listing 15-24. Import Angular Material Snack-bar Module

```
import { MatSnackBarModule } from '@angular/material/snack-bar';

@NgModule({
  declarations: [
        // Removed code for brevity
  ],
  imports: [
    MatSnackBarModule,
  ],
  exports: [
        // Removed code for brevity
  ],
  entryComponents: []
})
export class SuperheroesMaterialDesignModule { }
```

To demonstrate showing an alert with snack-bar, imagine that an error occurred when deleting a record. For the simplicity of the code sample, we show the snack-bar alert as the user clicks the Delete button in the Superhero Details screen.

Now that the required Angular module for the snack-bar has been imported, inject the MatSnackBar service to the Superhero Profile Component. We use this instance to show a snack-bar alert. Consider Listing 15-25.

Listing 15-25. Import and Inject MatSnackBar Service to the Component

```
1. import { MatSnackBar } from '@angular/material/snack-bar';
2. @Component({
3.  // Removed code for brevity
4. })
5. export class SuperheroProfileComponent implements OnInit, OnChanges {
6.  constructor(private matSnackBar: MatSnackBar) {
8.  }
9. }
```

Make use of the snack-bar service injected to show the alert as needed. Listing 15-26 shows an error message. The first parameter of the open() function is the message shown in the snack-bar. The second parameter is the title of the action button in the snack-bar. Figure 15-8 shows the results.

Listing 15-26. Show the Snack-bar Alert

```
showDeleteError(){ // invoked when delete action errors out.
  this.matSnackBar.open("Error attempting to delete", "Okay!");
}
```

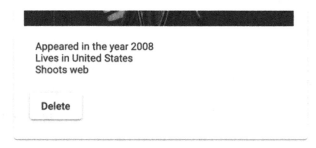

Figure 15-8. *Snack-bar alert after delete action fails*

The following are additional configurations that we can use when showing a snack-bar.

- **duration**: Shows the snack-bar for a specified number of milliseconds. After the timeout, it automatically closes if a value is specified.

- **horizontalPosition**: Position the snack-bar on the left, center, or right of the screen. Possible values are "start" or "left", "center", "end" or "right".

- **verticalPosition**: Position the snack-bar on the top or bottom.

- **panelClass**: A list of CSS classes that can be applied in a snack-bar.

- **direction**: Specify the direction of the content within the snack-bar" left to right or right to left. Use the values ltr or rtl.

Listing 15-27 shows the message in the top right; it automatically closes after five seconds. It is aligned to show content from right to left. Figure 15-9 shows the result.

Listing 15-27. Snack-bar Additional Configuration

```
this.matSnackBar.open("I am positioned different", "Okay!", {
    duration: 5000,
    horizontalPosition: "right",
    verticalPosition: "top",
    direction: "rtl"
});
```

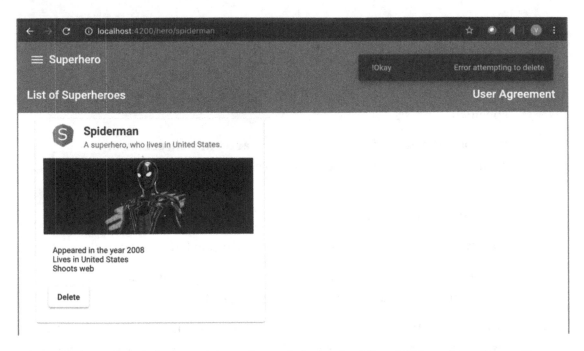

Figure 15-9. *Snack-bar positioned top right and with additional configuration*

Conclusion

The chapter explains the purpose and usage of dialogs, pop-overs, and alerts. We began by introducing Material dialog.

Next, we covered importing and using a bottom sheet. The chapter explained sharing information between components as the user selects from available options in the bottom sheet.

Finally, the chapter introduced using a snack-bar to show alerts, including snack-bar configurations and positioning on the page.

Exercise

Modify the dinosaur information screen to be a Material dialog component. Show the dinosaur name and the complete details on the dialog. Provide options to delete, edit, and share. Show these options on a bottom sheet. Show success and failure messages using a snack-bar.

References

Angular Material documentation
(`https://material.angular.io/components/`)

Material Design specifications for components
(`https://material.io/design/components/`)

CHAPTER 16

Angular: HTTP Client

An Angular application running in a browser uses remote services to retrieve and update data. The communication occurs over HTTP. Browsers widely support XMLHttpRequest (XHR) over HTTP. Out of the box, Angular provides services that ease making XHR calls in an Angular application. JSON (JavaScript Object Notation) is a good format for exchanging data between the server and a browser application. It is lightweight and efficient, considering JSON objects are simple text. Also, browsers readily interpret JSON data without needing additional libraries.

This chapter goes over getting started with an HttpClient service. We enhance the sample application to import the module and the service. Building remote services is beyond the scope of this book. To demonstrate interfacing with a typical RESTful remote service, we mock a sample service that provides and updates superhero data.

The GET, POST, PUT, and DELETE HTTP methods are largely used. The chapter explains implementing these methods for retrieve, create, update, and delete actions.

Getting Started

This chapter covers using the HttpClient Angular service that helps make XHR calls (XML HTTP Request) from an Angular application. It is part of the Angular module, HttpClientModule. We import it to make use of the HttpClient Angular service.

In the sample application, we have created three modules.

- superheroes-material-design, which contains all the Material Design components and functionality

- app-routing, which contains the routing logic for the single-page application

- app, the main module for the application

© Venkata Keerti Kotaru 2020
V. K. Kotaru, *Angular for Material Design*, https://doi.org/10.1007/978-1-4842-5434-9_16

Let's create a new module encapsulating functionality for making remote HTTP calls. To create a new module using Angular CLI, run the command in Listing 16-1. We named the module app-http-calls.

Listing 16-1. Generate a Module for Remote HTTP Calls

```
ng g module app-http-calls
```

Next, create a service that makes HTTP calls. To generate a service using Angular CLI, run the command in Listing 16-2. The data service is created under the newly created app-http-calls module.

Listing 16-2. Generate a Service for Service Calls

```
ng g service app-http-calls/superhero-data
```

Note   Chapter 7 discusses building, injecting, and using Angular services. The service is a reusable TypeScript class in Angular, which can be instantiated and injected into components and other services. Unlike components and directives, services are without a user interface.

Primarily, we use a service HttpClient for making HTTP calls. HttpClientModule encapsulates the functionality for making HTTP calls. We import it into the newly created app-http-calls module. Consider Listing 16-3.

Listing 16-3. Import HTTP Client Module

```
import { NgModule } from '@angular/core';
import { CommonModule } from '@angular/common';
import { HttpClientModule } from '@angular/common/http';

@NgModule({
  declarations: [],
  imports: [
    CommonModule,
    HttpClientModule
  ]
})
export class AppHttpCallsModule { }
```

Now, a new module named AppHttpClassModule is created, and it imports HttpClientModule. To use it in the rest of the application, import it into App.Module (see Listing 16-4).

Listing 16-4. The Primary App Module Imports the New AppHttpCallsModule

```
import {SuperheroesMaterialDesignModule} from './superheroes-material-
design/superheroes-material-design.module';
import { AppHttpCallsModule } from './app-http-calls/app-http-calls.
module';

@NgModule({
  declarations: [
    AppComponent
  ],
  imports: [
    SuperheroesMaterialDesignModule,
    AppHttpCallsModule
  ],
  bootstrap: [AppComponent]
})
export class AppModule { }
```

We imported HttpClientModule to be able to make API calls. We created a new module, AppHttpCallsModule, and added a new service to it. This service is expected to contain the code to make HTTP calls.

AppHttpCallsModule is imported in the primary app module along with SuperheroMaterialDesignModule. The new service, Hero Data Service, can be used in all modules referenced by the app module. The service is for making HTTP calls for hero data.

A typical RESTful (REpresentational State Transfer) API allows the following HTTP methods.

- GET: Retrieves data about one or more entities in the system. The entity could be an order, student, customer, or so forth. In the sample application, superheroes are the entities.

- POST: Creates an entity.

- PUT: Updates the complete entity.

- PATCH: Updates partial data in an entity.

- DELETE: Removes an entity from the system.

Mock Data

For the purpose of the sample application, let's run a Node.js-based service that returns data from a mock JSON file. Consider creating a JSON file with superhero data.

JSON Server is an npm package that creates an ExpressJS-based web server from a mock JSON file. A typical service may have business logic and data access logic for saving and retrieving data from a database or a data source.

To set up JSON Server, install it using Yarn or npm. Consider the command in Listing 16-5. It is installed globally on the machine. Most dependencies install at the project level. Considering JSON Server is a developer tool used across projects, we install it at globally at the machine level.

The command might need elevated permissions on the machine. You can install it without the global flags. Remember to run the library from the installed directory.

Listing 16-5. Install JSON Server for Mock Data

```
yarn global add json-server
Or
npm install json-server –global
```

In the sample application, place a mock JSON file with superhero data in the src folder. Run the command in Listing 16-6 to start a web server that returns data from this file. Run the newly installed JSON Server.

Listing 16-6. Run JSON Server

```
json-server data.json
```

Now, access the mock response by attempting the following URL in a browser: http://localhost:3000/. In Figure 16-1, /heroes is an array object based on the structure defined in the mock JSON file.

Note   To access a mock JSON response mimicking a real server-side API, we chose JSON Server. You may use any tool for this purpose, as long as it supports RESTful services.

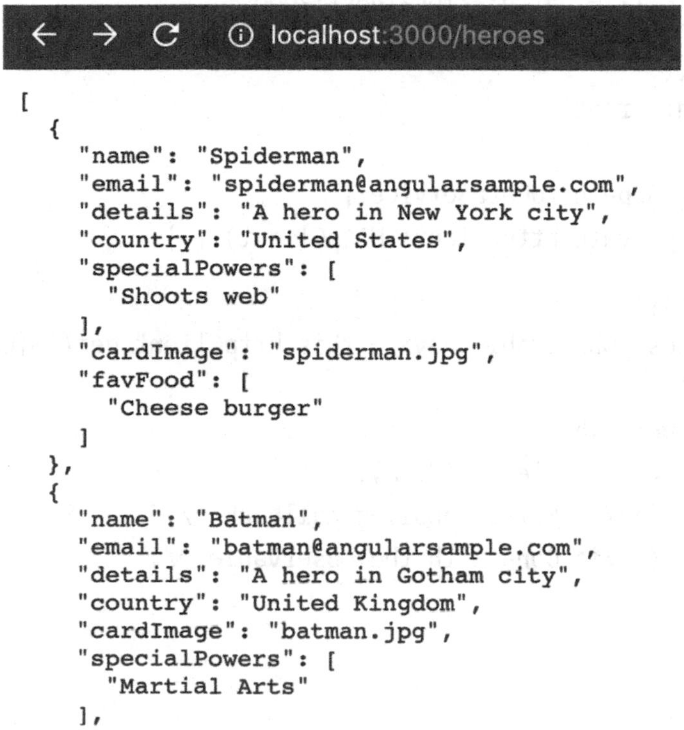

Figure 16-1. *Access mock response using JSON Server*

Use HttpClient to Make HTTP Calls

The superhero data service imports HttpClient from @angular/common/http. The Angular module was imported in the preceding section.

In Listing 16-7, the service is decorated with an injectable and provided at the root. It also injects the HttpClient service. The HttpClient object is used to make an HTTP GET call (see line 11).

Listing 16-7. HTTP Call Using HttpClient

```
1. import { Injectable } from '@angular/core';
2. import { HttpClient } from '@angular/common/http';
3. import { Observable } from 'rxjs';

4. const URL_PREFIX = "http://localhost:3000";

5. @Injectable({
6.   providedIn: 'root'
7. })
8. export class SuperheroDataService {
9. constructor(private httpClient: HttpClient) { }

10.  getHeroes(){
11.    let heroes: Observable<any> = this.httpClient.get(`${URL_PREFIX}/
       heroes`);
12.    heroes.subscribe (
13.      (data) => console.log(data),
14.      () => ({})/** Error handling callback */,
15.      () => ({})/** Done with the observable */,
16.      );;
17.  }
18. }
```

getHeroes uses the httpClient instance and makes a GET call, which makes a remote HTTP call. It returns an observable, which is assigned to a variable named *heroes* (see line 11).

The subscribe function is on heroes (observable). A success handler (callback function) on the subscribe function receives and logs the JSON response from a server-side API. See line 13 in Listing 16-7 for the success callback. Figure 16-2 shows the console output and the HTTP call (in a Google Chrome Network tab). The get() function call results in the HTTP call seen in the Network tab.

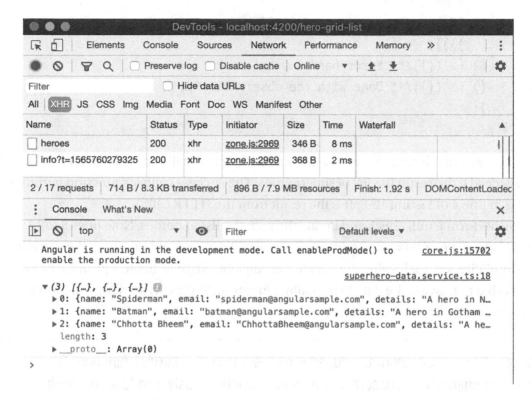

Figure 16-2. Console log of API response

Listing 16-8 showcases code to parse the HTTP response and create the desired object for use in the Angular application.

Listing 16-8. Iterate to Create Hero Objects from Service Response

```
1  getHeroes(){
2    let heroes: Observable<any> = this.httpClient.get(`${URL_PREFIX}/
     heroes`);
3    heroes.subscribe (
4      (data) => {
5        console.log(data && data.forEach( (hero) => ({
6          "name":hero.name || "",
7          "email":hero.email || "",
8          "details":hero.details || "",
9         "country":hero.country || "",
10         "specialPowers":hero.specialPowers || [],
11         "cardImage":hero.cardImage || "/defaultImage.jpg",
```

```
12            "favFood":hero.favFood || []
13          }))))},
14        () => ({})/** Error handling callback */,
15        () => ({})/** Done with the observable */,
16        );
17    }
```

The subscribe function is invoked as the get function call succeeds or fails. If the GET call succeeds, the result is a list of superheroes. The success callback function parameter data is in line 4 of Listing 16-8. It is the result from the HTTP call.

We perform a null check and iterate through the list of heroes. Note lines 5 to 13. Fields from the response are assigned to a new JSON object and logged to the console. For simplicity, we are logging the data to the console. We may create a promise or an observable to provide the data to the calling function. Typically, a calling function is part of a component or another service.

Note   We cannot return the superhero object from the service function. The success callback on subscribe is invoked asynchronously. The function control returns the component class (or any other calling function) after invoking the get function on line 2. The function was already returned before executing lines 4 to 13. We create a promise or an observable to return data from this function.

Explicitly Type Response Object

An advantage of using TypeScript is that we can define a class or a type for the response structure. It helps simplify the code, and it is a good practice.

In Listing 16-9, the httpClient get function is in line 2. It uses a template of type Array of the Superhero object. The Superhero class is structured to match the API response.

Subsequently, the success handler in line 4 uses the same data type as that of the get function. Hence, we can iterate through the objects to process the data further.

Listing 16-9. Remote Service Response Typed to a Class in Angular

```
1.  getHeroes(){
2.    this.httpClient.get<Array<Superhero>>(`${URL_PREFIX}/heroes`)
3.      .subscribe(
4.        (data: Array<Superhero>) => data.map( i => console.log(i.name,
          i.country, i.email)),
5.        () => ({/** Error handling code goes here */}),
6.        () => ({/** Observable complete */})
7.      );
8.  }
```

Note   Unlike the prior sample, we have not created a separate object for a returned value from the get function. It returns an observable. We chained the function call with a subscribe(). It is useful, considering the heroes observable is not used in other places in the function. Creating a separate variable is redundant.

Typed objects help IDEs like Visual Studio Code provide better IntelliSense. Figure 16-3 shows a list of fields on the superhero object.

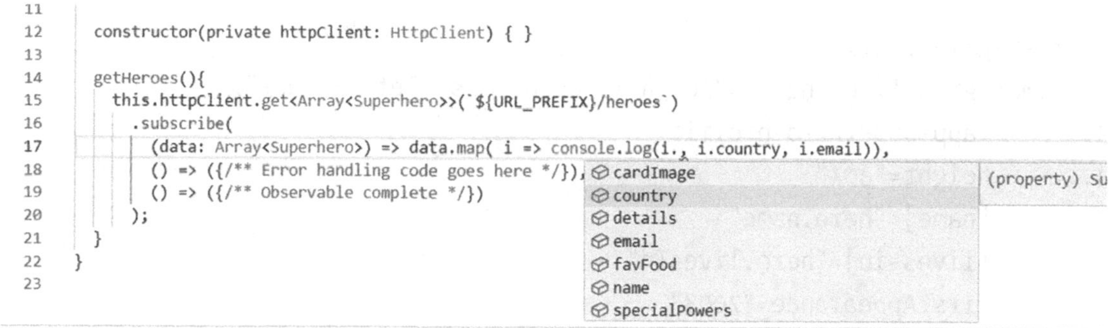

Figure 16-3. *Visual Studio Code IntelliSense on TypeScript object*

Return Data to the Calling Function

In the preceding code samples, the Angular service logged data obtained from the remote service to the console. The sample obtains a superhero list from the remote service (mocked with JSON Server). If we used the subscribe() function in the Angular service (similar to line 3 in Listing 16-9), results from the remote service are obtained. If the results can be used as-is in the component (or any other calling function), we may avoid subscribing in the Angular service function. Listing 16-10 returns the observable returned by the get function call as-is to the calling function.

Listing 16-10. Return Observable from HTTP Client to the Calling Function

```
getHeroes(): Observable<Array<Superhero>> {
    return this.httpClient.get<Array<Superhero>>(`${URL_PREFIX}/heroes`);
}
```

The calling function may subscribe and use the data. In Listing 16-11, a component sets the return value on a class variable. The data is shown in the component by the template. Listing 16-12 is the HTML template for the component. Line 2 iterates through the heroes array reference.

Listing 16-11. Results from the Angular Service Assigned to a Class Variable

```
this.heroService
  .getHeroes()
  .subscribe(data => this.heroes = data);
```

Listing 16-12. Results from the Angular Service Assigned to a Class Variable

```
1. <mat-grid-list>
2.  <mat-grid-tile *ngFor="let hero of heroes; let i=index">
3.      <app-superhero-profile
4.      height="30%"
5.      [name]="hero.name"
6.      [lives-in]="hero.livesIn"
7.      firstAppearance="2008"
8.      [superpowers]="hero.specialPowers"
9.      [card-image]="hero.cardImage">
10.     </app-superhero-profile>
11.  </mat-grid-tile>
12.</mat-grid-list>
```

Alternatively, we may return assign the observable directly to a variable used in the template. In Listing 16-13, the datatype of the variable heroes is Observable.

Listing 16-13. Assign Hero Service Result to An Observable

```
export class SuperheroGridListComponent implements OnInit {
  heroes: Observable<Array<Superhero>>;
  constructor(private heroService: SuperheroDataService) { }
  ngOnInit() {
    this.heroes = this.heroService
      .getHeroes();
  }
}
```

Use an Async pipe in the template with the observable. Note the highlighted area on line 2 in Listing 16-14.

Listing 16-14. Async Pipe on Observable

```
1. <mat-grid-list>
2.   <mat-grid-tile *ngFor="let hero of heroes | async; let i=index">
3.       <app-superhero-profile
4.       height="30%"
5.       [name]="hero.name"
6.       [lives-in]="hero.livesIn"
7.       firstAppearance="2008"
8.       [superpowers]="hero.specialPowers"
9.       [card-image]="hero.cardImage">
10.     </app-superhero-profile>
11.   </mat-grid-tile>
12. </mat-grid-list>
```

In some cases, we need to change the object structure, and process the response data with additional logic. In this scenario, the Angular service subscribes to the observable returned by the HttpClient get() function. It processes the data and returns the results to the calling function.

The function cannot directly return the results. Considering the subscribe callback function is invoked asynchronously, control from the Angular service getHeroes() function already returns to the calling function. In this scenario, we can create and return another observable or promise from the Angular service getHeroes() function.

Listing 16-15 returns an observable.

Listing 16-15. Angular Service getHeroes() Function Returning Observable

```
1.  getHeroes(): Observable<Array<Superhero>> {
2.    return Observable.create((observer) => {
3.      let results: Array<Superhero> = [];
4.      this.httpClient.get<Array<Superhero>>(`${URL_PREFIX}/heroes`)
5.        .subscribe(
6.          (data: Array<Superhero>) => {
7.            data.map( i => {
8.              // perform additional processing and transformation of data
                 obtained from the service.
9.              results.push(i)
10.            });
11.           observer.next(results);
12             observer.complete();
13.          },
14.          () => ({/** Error handling code goes here */}),
15.          () => ({/** Observable complete */})
16.        );
17.    });
18.  }
```

Line 2 creates and returns an observable. The calling function has reference to the observable. In the calling function, the subscribe function is called on the new observable created by getHeroes().

The static create() function on the Observable class acts as a factory to create an observable. It expects a callback function with an input parameter for the observer. Results can be accessed by the subscriber (a calling function or the component), with the next() function call on the observer (see line 11).

The observable returned by the HttpClient get() function is subscribed in line 5. We iterate through the results from the remote service. Perform additional processing or transformation of the object structure. In line 8, a placeholder is used for this purpose. Afterward, we iterate through all the results, and use the next() function on the observer to send data to the subscriber in the calling function (see line 11).

Note   Follow the links in the references section at the end of chapter to learn more about RxJS and observables.

We may also return a promise (see Listing 16-16).

Listing 16-16. Angular Service getHeroes() Function Returning Promise

```
1.  getHeroes(): Promise<Array<Superhero>>{
2.    return new Promise<Array<Superhero>>( (resolve /*, reject */)=> {
3.      let results: Array<Superhero> = [];
4.      this.httpClient.get<Array<Superhero>>(`${URL_PREFIX}/heroes`)
5.        .subscribe(
6.          (data: Array<Superhero>) => {
7.            data.map( i => {
8.              // perform additional processing and transformation of data
                 obtained from the service.
9.              results.push(i)
10.           });
11.           resolve(results);
12.         },
13.         () => ({/** Error handling code goes here */}),
14.         () => ({/** Observable complete */})
15.       );
16.   });
17. }
```

The getHeroes() function creates and returns a promise (see line 2). The observable returned by the HttpClient get() function is subscribed in line 5. We iterate through the results from the remote service. Perform additional processing or transformation of the object structure. In line 8, a placeholder is used for this purpose.

Afterward, we iterate through all the results, and use the resolve() function, which is the first parameter in the constructor to the promise. With resolve, send data to the calling function. In this sample, the calling function is in a component. Listing 16-17 is the component making use of the data obtained from the component.

Listing 16-17. Angular Component Using the Promise

```
this.heroService.getHeroes().then( data => this.heroes = data);
```

The results from the Angular service are set on an object in the component class; namely, heroes (this.heroes). The HTML template uses this component variable to show the results on the screen. See Listing 16-18.

Listing 16-18. Angular HTML Template Component Showing the Results

```
1. <mat-grid-list >
2.  <mat-grid-tile *ngFor="let hero of heroes; let i=index">
3.      <app-superhero-profile
4.      height="30%"
5.      [name]="hero.name"
6.      [lives-in]="hero.livesIn"
7.      firstAppearance="2008"
8.      [superpowers]="hero.specialPowers"
9.      [card-image]="hero.cardImage">
10.     </app-superhero-profile>
11.  </mat-grid-tile>
12.</mat-grid-list>
```

Note   Most HTTP services, especially the services that adhere to REST standards, return data about a single entity with the ID specified in the URL. Consider a sample URL with JSON Server, `http://localhost:3000/heroes/001`. It returns hero with ID 001. We can use the HttpClient instance get() method with the relevant URL to retrieve a single entity or a subset of the list.

Handling Errors with Remote Service Calls

An Angular application needs to handle HTTP errors that occur while using the remote service. The errors need to be handled gracefully, rather than crashing the whole page.

The subscribe function on an observable (from the HTTP calls or otherwise) has three handlers: success, error, and subscription complete (see Listing 16-19).

Listing 16-19. Subscribe on an Observable

```
1.    observableInstance.subscribe(
2.        (data) => ({/** success callback */}),
3.        (error) => ({/** error callback */}),
4.        () => ({/** Done */}),
```

You have seen success callback functions in the code samples. The second callback function is an error handler. We can use it to handle errors that occur while calling the remote services. Listing 16-20 lines 8 and 9 use a logger service to gracefully handle errors.

Listing 16-20. Observable Handling Errors

```
1.  getHeroes(): Observable<Array<Superhero>> {
2.    return Observable.create((observer) => {
3.      let results: Array<Superhero> = [];
4.      this.httpClient.get<Array<Superhero>>(`${URL_PREFIX}/heroes`)
5.        .subscribe(
6.          (data: Array<Superhero>) => ({/** Success handler */}),
7.          (error) => ({
8.            this.errorHandler.log("Error while getting heroes", error);
9.            this.errorHandler.alertFriendlyInfo("Error while getting
             heroes", observer)
10.         }),
11.         () => ({/** Observable complete */})
12.       );
13.   });
14.  }
```

Remember, the error handler is on the subscribe function of the observable. Referring back to Listing 16-20, if the observable was returned directly from the Angular service, without a subscribe(), it loses the option to handle errors. If there are multiple calling functions, the code needs to be integrated in all of those places.

To address this scenario, we may pipe an error handling operator with the observable. See line 7 in Listing 16-20. The Angular service function returns the observable without a subscription. As the error occurs, the Angular service still handles the error gracefully.

In Listing 16-21, we log the error information (see line 9). We also throw an error to the calling function, which subscribes to the observable. We continue to do so as the subscriber needs to know that the error occurred, regardless of whether the Angular service logs it or not.

Listing 16-21. Observable Pipes Error Handler

```
1. import { Observable, Observer, throwError } from 'rxjs';
2. import { catchError } from 'rxjs/operators';

3. // removed code for brevity
4. export class SuperheroDataService {

5.   getHeroes(): Observable<Array<Superhero>> {
6.     return this.httpClient.get<Array<Superhero>>(`${URL_PREFIX}/heroes`)
7.     .pipe(
8.       catchError( (error: HttpErrorResponse) => {
9.         this.errorHandler.log("Error while getting heroes", error);
10.        return throwError("Error while getting heroes");
11.      }));
12. }
```

POST Calls with HttpClient

We have seen using GET calls that retrieve a list of superheroes with HttpClient. As mentioned at the beginning of the chapter, use the HTTP POST method to create an entity—a new superhero. Use the POST method on the HttpClient instance to create a new superhero. Consider Listing 16-22.

Listing 16-22. POST Method with HttpClient

```
createHero(hero: Superhero2){
  return this.httpClient
    .post(`${URL_PREFIX}/heroes`, hero);
    .pipe(
      catchError( (error: HttpErrorResponse) => {
        this.errorHandler.log("Error while creating a hero", error);
        return throwError("Error while creating a hero");
      }));
}
```

The second parameter is the entity being created. In a POST HTTP call, the entity is shared in the body of the HTTP request. Figure 16-4 shows network data for the POST call.

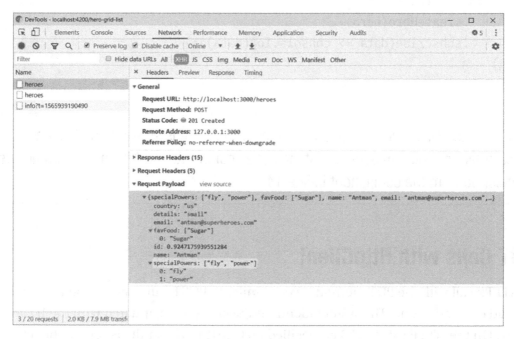

Figure 16-4. *POST call on the network*

In the Superheroes sample application, update the create superhero form component to invoke the new Angular service function. In Listing 16-23, we inject the service to create an instance (see line 7). The new createHero function is called in line 13.

Listing 16-23. Create Superhero Component

```
1. import { SuperheroDataService } from 'src/app/app-http-calls/superhero-
   data.service';

2. @Component({
3. // removed code for brevity
4. })
5. export class CreateSuperheroComponent implements OnInit {
6.  superhero: Superhero;
7.  constructor(private dataService: SuperheroDataService) {
8.    this.superhero = new Superhero();
9.  }
```

```
10.  submitForm(){
11.    let hero = this.superhero
12.    this.dataService
13.      .createHero(hero)
14.      .subscribe(data => console.log(data));
15.  }
16. }
```

Note   The POST call is not made until the observable is subscribed. Just calling createHero on the dataService instance does not invoke the API. In the sample, we subscribe from the component in line 14.

PUT Calls with HttpClient

An HTTP call with the PUT method is very similar to POST, but used to update an entity instead of creating one. The system identifies the entity to be updated with the ID on the entity. On the HTTP call, the ID is specified on the URL. The entity is sent to the remote server in the HTTP request body, similar to POST. In Listing 16-24, we create the URL with the ID of the entity as a parameter (see line 3).

Listing 16-24. Update Entity with HTTP Client

```
1.  updateHero(hero: Superhero, heroId: string){
2.    return this.httpClient
3.    .put(`${URL_PREFIX}/heroes/${heroId}`, hero)
4.    .pipe(
5.      catchError( (error: HttpErrorResponse) => {
6.        this.errorHandler.log("Error while updating a hero", error);
7.        return throwError("Error while updating a hero");
8.      }));
9.  }
```

Figure 16-5 shows network data for the PUT call.

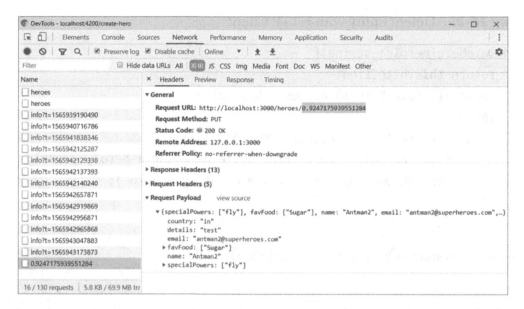

Figure 16-5. *PUT call on the network*

Note   Similar to PUT, PATCH is an HTTP method to update an entity in the system. A RESTful API, while updating an entity, uses PATCH to update a subset of fields without overriding the whole entity, whereas PUT is used to update the entire entity. On the HttpClient instance, we can use the patch function; however, the behavior depends on remote API implementation.

DELETE Calls with HttpClient

Use the HTTP DELETE method to delete an entity from the system. Similar to GET, a DELETE HTTP call does not contain a request body. The system identifies the entity to be deleted with a unique ID. The ID is included in the URL. In Listing 16-25, see line 3. We pass an ID of the hero to be deleted. The service implementation typically selects and marks the entity for deletion in the system.

Listing 16-25. Delete Entity with HTTP Client

```
1.  deleteHero(heroId: string){
2.    return this.httpClient
3.    .delete(`${URL_PREFIX}/heroes/${heroId}`)
4.    .pipe(
5.      catchError( (error: HttpErrorResponse) => {
6.        this.errorHandler.log("Error while deleting a hero", error);
7.        return throwError("Error while deleting a hero");
8.      }));
9.  }
```

Figure 16-6 shows network data for the DELETE call.

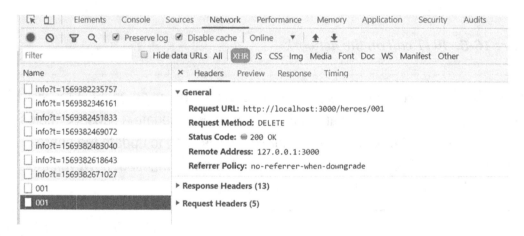

Figure 16-6. *DELETE call on the network*

Conclusion

Angular provides utilities to request XHR (XMLHttpRequests) calls out of the box with the HttpClient service. It is part of the @angular/common/http module. In this chapter, we started with instructions to include needed dependencies. It is a good practice to separate remote service integration to a new module.

The chapter described using a JSON Server npm package to mock API responses. JSON Server is one of many options to mock API responses. We may use any package or library that helps mimic remote services.

The chapter also explained using the get() method on an HttpClient instance to retrieve data. It makes the HTTP call using the GET method. Use the post() method on an HttpClient instance to create an entity. It makes the HTTP call using POST method. Use the put() or the patch() method on an HttpClient instance to update an entity. It makes the HTTP call using PUT or PATCH, respectively. Use the delete() method on HttpClient instance to delete an entity. It makes the HTTP call using the DELETE method.

Exercise

Create dinosaur data in JSON format. Save the file with a .json extension. Use JSON Server (or any other mocking tool) to serve the data as a remote service.

Integrate the dinosaur list screens using the screens created throughout the book with the remote service. Use GET calls to retrieve data.

Integrate the details screen with a GET call that retrieves data by ID. Use the dinosaur ID specified in browser URL and in the XHR call.

Integrate a reactive form for creating a dinosaur with the remote service. Use the POST call to create a dinosaur entity.

References

Angular documentation on HttpClient (`https://angular.io/guide/http`)

JSON Server npm package (`www.npmjs.com/package/json-server`)

Learn RxJS and create an observable (`www.learnrxjs.io/operators/creation/create.html`)

Index

A, B

Angular framework, 5
Asynchronous function calls, 109

C

Change detection, 86
    Ajax calls, 86
    component tree, 87
    default strategy, 89
    JavaScript API, 86
    OnPush strategy, 91
    user interactions, 86
Class binding, 75
    boolean variables, 76
    CSS classes, 76
    ngClass directive, 77
    showBorder, 77
Components, 49
    component tree, 57
    creation, 51
    DOM tree, 49
    elements and child components, 50
    encapsulation, 55
    event handler, 64
    footer component, 58
    HTML template code, 54, 57
    input elements, 62
    ngOnChanges, 63
    providers, 55

    selector value, 53
    setter function, 62
    style attribute, 54
    styleUrls, 54
    templateUrl, 53
    view providers, 56, 59
CSS classes, 77

D

Data binding
    import forms module, 85
    interpolation, 71
    ngModel directive, 85
Date picker control, 187
    default value, 192
    filter unwanted dates, 194
        custom logic, 196
        min and max values, 194
    form field, 191
    import modules, 188
    MatNativeDateModule, 189
    toggle switch, 193
    year and multi-year view, 191
Dependency injection, 116
    component level, 124
    counter implementation, 122
    counter values, templates, 123
    HitCounter component, 123
    incrementCounter function, 124

V. K. Kotaru, *Angular for Material Design*, https://doi.org/10.1007/978-1-4842-5434-9

S

T, U

V, W, X, Y, Z

Printed in the United States
By Bookmasters